Bi...

in his

To

With best wishes

VAL. MOORE.

About the author

Chris Wright is the author of over twenty books. He served as an aerial reconnaissance photographer with Royal Air Force squadrons in Germany and Malta. This was at the height of the cold war, with surveillance being done at high altitude over Middle East countries and along the Soviet border. Leaving the RAF to specialise in industrial photography, Chris has gone on to develop remotely operated cameras and equipment to inspect components deep within nuclear reactors.

The Timpitters' Mine was the first of seven children's adventure titles with Victory Press (now Kingsway), many of which were sold as Sunday School prizes. In the 1980s Chris rewrote seven Christian Classics for young readers published by Bridge in the United States, and later an updated edition of FW Bourne's *The King's Son.* Five of his thrillers have recently been published by Hard Shell (www.hardshell.com) in the USA.

The parents of three grown up children, Jonathan, Simon and Emma - Chris and his wife Liz live in the West Country, where Chris has been a home group leader in his local church for many years.

The website www.billybray.com is maintained by the author.

About Highland Books

You can find out more about our publishing programme from our website www.highlandbks.com. If you see any mistakes, you can e-mail us on errata@highlandbks.com: there's also an error page on our website where we post corrections.

Billy Bray
in his own words

Chris Wright

Highland

Godalming, Surrey

First published in 2004 by Highland Books, Two High
Pines, Knoll Road, Godalming, Surrey GU7 2EP.

Line illustrations © 2004 Simon Wright.

The Journal of Billy Bray is reproduced by courtesy and
permission of the Director and Librarian of the John Rylands
University Library of Manchester and the Methodist Church
of Great Britain.

ISBN: 1-897913-73-7

Cover design by Steve Carroll

Printed in Finland by WS Bookwell

Table of Contents

ACKNOWLEDGMENTS

I would like to thank many people for their great encouragement and assistance in the writing of this book. In particular:

Dr Peter Nockles, Head of Methodist Archives & Research Centre, JRULM, Manchester, UK;

Rev'd Dr Alan Bartlett, Programme Director MA in Theology and Ministry, Tutor in Church History, Cranmer Hall, St John's College, Durham, UK;

Rev'd Luke Walton, Associate Minister, Christ Church Clifton, Bristol, UK;

Colin Edwards, Principal Archivist, Cornwall Record Office, Truro, UK.

In alphabetical order, these Cornishmen good and true, who all gave me more support than they probably realise:

Andrew Besley, John Gillbard, Barrie S May;

and especially Peter Tremewen, Secretary and Treasurer of the Billy Bray Memorial Trust.

Also Janet Oganah for her genuine interest and assistance with audio typing of much of the transcription.

And most importantly, my wife Liz, for patience beyond the call of duty over the past two years!

Although these people have provided help, none of them has read the full manuscript before publication. Therefore all errors and omissions are definitely the author's.

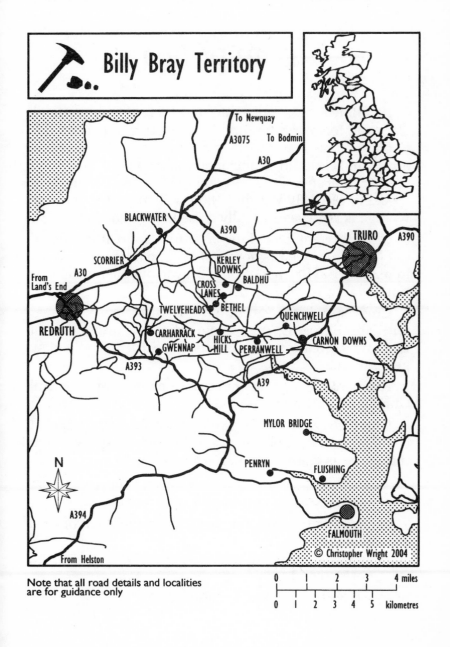

Billy Bray Territory

To Newquay
A3075
To Bodmin
A30

BLACKWATER
A390
TRURO
A390
SCORRIER
From Land's End
A30
KERLEY DOWNS
BALDHU
CROSS LANES
TWELVEHEADS
BETHEL
QUENCHWELL
REDRUTH
CARHARRACK
GWENNAP
HICKS MILL
PERRANWELL
CARNON DOWNS
A393
A39

MYLOR BRIDGE

N

PENRYN
FLUSHING

A394

FALMOUTH

From Helston

© Christopher Wright 2004

Note that all road details and localities
are for guidance only

0   1   2   3   4 miles
0   1   2   3   4   5   kilometres

FOREWORD

In 1864 Billy Bray, a remarkable man of God who impacted Cornwall for half a century, completed his memoirs. He wrote in one continuous sentence, including spelling errors, and excluding punctuation, and spoke of "the good brother that (would) translate this journal"! He was speaking of Chris Wright – little knowing that the task would take 140 years to fully come to fruition.

Chris Wright has done a work of great historical importance, as well as doing all of us an immense favour, in making the Journal of Billy Bray available for the first time.

Chris employs the accuracy of an historian, combined with the empathy of a biographer, to bring one of England's greatest Evangelists alive to a whole new generation.

Read on and be challenged and inspired by a radical Christianity seldom seen today.

Chris Wright's Billy Bray dances off every page! It could well be said of Billy: "By faith he still speaks even though he is dead" – in his own words!

Greg Downes

Former Tutor in Evangelism, London School of Theology
Evangelist-in-Residence, St Andrew's Chorleywood
Chaplain, Pembroke College Oxford

FINDING BILLY BRAY

I HAVE DRIVEN INLAND through a maze of narrow lanes, leaving the fishing villages and tourist beaches of Cornwall far behind. My map tells me I am exactly halfway between Redruth to the west, and the tiny city of Truro four miles (6km) to the east. The lanes and steep hills have earth banks that allow only occasional glimpses of the rugged countryside. Lovers of the outdoor life would call this the real Cornwall. Holidaymakers who venture no further than the sandy bays and rocky coves would call it bleak.

The mines of Devon and Cornwall were once famous for their tin and copper, and this area hummed with activity, providing employment for thousands of men, women and children. Models of tall stone chimneys with ruined engine houses can be bought in any Cornish souvenir shop. The remains that dot the landscape may look romantic now, but these relics of an industrial past represented a hard and dangerous life to every mining family.

I am here today because I have taken up mining. Not tin mining. The last working mine, South Crofty at Pool, closed in 1998. Even if commercial mining resumes, it will never be on the scale of the eighteenth and nineteenth centuries. There are literally hundred of abandoned tin and copper mines on this remote finger of southwest England that reaches out into the Atlantic. On a clear day you can see the Scilly Isles from the cliffs at Land's End. And beyond the Scilly Isles? Next stop – America.

For the past eighteen months I have been mining for words. Words that are a true account of the life of a miner called Billy Bray – a life so amazing that it is widely known in these parts, and is still being told around the world.

Three men knew and worked with Billy, and they were all ordained ministers. FW Bourne was a Bible Christian, Mark Guy Pearse a Methodist, and William Haslam an Anglo Catholic priest. Billy and William Haslam held hugely conflicting views on how Christian worship should be conducted, and initially they were unable to share anything in the way of their faith. This makes their encounter electrifying.

These men provide vivid first-hands accounts of Billy's life. Billy died in June 1868. FW Bourne first published *The King's Son* in May 1871, Mark Guy Pearse wrote *The Story of Billy Bray* as a booklet around the same time, and William Haslam published *From Death Into Life* in 1880.

The road widens slightly and ahead is a small sign saying *Billy Bray's Chapel*. I stop the car in front of a low building that has three windows in a row. I have been here several times over the past eighteen months. This is Three Eyes Chapel, constructed by Billy in the face of mockery and ill feeling. Not only he did raise the funds, he rolled up his sleeves to get it built. The chapel is locked, but a notice tells me it will be opened soon.

The Bible Christian Book-Room brought out Bourne's famous book *The King's Son, a Memoir of Billy Bray*, just three years after Billy's death. The book got its title from something Billy often called himself. In one instance he and a friend were on a money-raising expedition and were coming to the house of a wealthy man. Billy was making for the front door, and his friend said it would be better if they went round the back. "No," said Billy, "I am the son of a King, and I shall go frontways."

Various publishers have reprinted *The King's Son* over the years. Sitting on the grass outside the chapel I thumb through the copy I have brought with me today. *The King's Son*, by FW Bourne. The initials FW stand for Frederick William. The Reverend Frederick William

Bourne, to give him his full title. Born in Kent in 1830, Bourne later moved to the West Country and in 1859 married a Devon woman called Mary Horswell. They had five children.

Bourne got to know Billy well during the nine years their lives overlapped in Cornwall. I'd like to say thank you to Bourne for the hard work he did in compiling *The King's Son*, but he died in 1905. His grave is not far away, at Lake Chapel in Shebbear. Maybe I'll get there one day, but the purpose of this expedition has been to tie up a few loose ends about the dancing preacher. The places around me have names like Twelveheads, Cross Lanes, Kerley Downs, Baldhu. This is Billy Bray territory.

My copy of *The King's Son* is dated 1890, and claims to be *A New and Revised Edition*, but I think it says that in nearly every edition I have at home. I can see plenty of quotation marks showing the words written by Billy Bray and his friends, and plenty of words added by Frederick Bourne. There are enough exclamation marks to fill a bucket. I don't want to knock Bourne's thoughts, but most people nowadays would see his observations as rather heavy sermonizing.

Perhaps Victorian readers expected to read a book full of devout comments. Indeed, the *Bible Christian Book-Room* might not have dreamt of publishing *The King's Son* without them. Maybe their readers not only expected, they even insisted on such additions.

Or maybe not.

In the back of my copy of *The King's Son* is a book review by the Rev Mark Guy Pearse. The review is of the biography of another Cornishman, Miller Manning. Pearse writes that the story is, "Well told in a simple and straightforward style, and is rigorously confined to the man himself, without any moralising or reflections such as often swell the pages and annoy the reader. There is not a page to be skipped or skimmed."

It definitely sounds like my sort of book. I have a feeling Frederick Bourne has somewhat muddied the waters for today's readers. I had a previous encounter with Billy, in 1987. A publisher in the UK asked me to edit The *King's Son* to make it easier for modern readers. I changed sentence and paragraph lengths, and some of Bourne's difficult wording. The result was *I Can't Help Praising The Lord*, published by Bridge. What I am doing now is far more radical than editing. I have discovered major events in Billy's life that have never seen the light of day.

These discoveries come from the richest mine I have explored so far. It is the extensive *Journal* Billy wrote in 1864, at the suggestion of a Quaker woman called Martha Bowden. Billy's handwriting is exceptionally hard to read, and it has taken me several months to decipher its 282 pages. (The last page is numbered 269, but some numbers have been used twice.) Bourne said he did not have the time to transcribe the *Journal* after Billy's death, and it was thanks to efforts of a fellow minister, John Batt, that Bourne was able to use excerpts from it in *The King's Son*.

Surprisingly, Bourne used only a quarter of Billy's *Journal*, preferring to draw on his own memories and those of others. Maybe he thought his readers would be upset or offended by some of Billy's accounts. He could well have been right. But time has healed the local disagreements that took place between nineteenth century Cornish preachers, and we should be able to read the *Journal* with unprejudiced eyes – and be challenged and encouraged by what we read.

The first edition of *The King's Son* was quite slim. In it Bourne writes: "It is hoped that personal friends into whose hands this memoir will come will furnish characteristic facts and incidents not included therein – the Author well knows that there is a great number – so that they may be incorporated therewith if another Edition should be called for."

Not only was a reprint called for within just a few weeks, but *The King's Son* grew in its early editions as characteristic facts and incidents came in. Interestingly, some small details were removed, and I am using a few of these in this book as they sometimes throw more light on some accounts. I continue to leaf through my 1890 copy. Fifty percent of the words are carefully edited incidents, and the other fifty percent are mostly what MG Pearse would call *moralising* and *reflections*. Even though they could be helpful to some readers, these thoughts don't belong here. I have deciphered the whole of Billy's *Journal* and have all the material I need to present the full, uncensored life: *Billy Bray In His Own Words*.

The chapel is now open. I sit on a wooden pew at the back and try to hear in my mind the noise and excitement that frequently filled this building many years ago. The chapel remains silent, but the pages of Billy's *Journal* fairly explode with sound. It is time for the story of Billy Bray to be told in *a simple and straightforward style, and rigorously confined to the man himself* – to use the words of Mark Guy Pearse. I couldn't have put it better myself.

Three Eyes Chapel at Kerley Downs
redrawn from an engraving in *The King's Son*

AUTHOR'S NOTE

MUCH OF THIS BOOK comes directly from Billy Bray's own *Journal*. In Appendix 1 on page 245 I have given details of the *Journal*, reproducing short passages exactly as Billy writes them, with his own spelling from the Cornish dialect and incorrect use of capital letters.

The *Journal* is one long sentence of 49,000 words – with no punctuation. After chopping my transcription into sentences, I found that almost every one started with *and, so, for, then* and *but*. I have removed the majority of these words, corrected the spelling, and inserted simple missing words. An example of this is where Billy writes that someone should: *have been the disciples' side*, when he clearly means: *have been on the disciples' side*. Words like this were probably omitted through writing quickly.

I have very occasionally altered the structure of a sentence to make some accounts easier to read, always using the original words. Where a word must be missing, but its identity is not obvious, I have put my best guess in brackets. A question mark immediately before a word is a likely reading, but the word itself is either not known or I may not have deciphered it correctly. The occasional unexpectedly erudite words are always Billy's. Billy wrote his *Journal* in 1864, and apart from the story of his conversion he seems to tell the various incidents in his life as they occur to him. I have attempted to rearrange them into their most likely time sequence.

When Billy mentions the Lord, he often writes *the dear Lord*, including *bless and praise his holy name,* and then adds words like, *for his goodness to me.* He also makes many references to how he would be down in hell by now if the Lord had not saved him. I realise this is indicative of Billy's deep faith, but when these expressions appear several times on a page they can be distracting. I have therefore tried to strike an editorial balance.

Of the 49,000 original words, I have omitted about one thousand. Apart from the changes mentioned above, most of these words are repetitions or occasional Bible passages given by Billy in full. Absolutely nothing has been left out that could cause embarrassment to readers who are fans of Billy. In other words, nothing has been censored.

For other accounts of Billy's life I am using various editions from the first to the last of *The King's Son* by FW Bourne (1871 to 1906); *The Story of Billy Bray from Short Stories And Other Papers* (early 1870s) and *The Ship Where Christ Was Captain* (1926), both titles by MG Pearse; *Strange Tales Volume 5* by John Ashworth (1879 edition); and *From Death Into Life* by William Haslam (1880). All references to Bourne's writing come from a variety of editions of *The King's Son*, and are not in Billy's *Journal*. I will make clear throughout the book the source of the material. Further details on these books can be found in Appendix 5.

I have attempted to be scrupulously careful to get my facts right. Where I have carried out minor editing on some of the original accounts by Bourne and others it has been done simply to make them more digestible, and never to change the intentions of their authors, or give a different meaning to the words. Anyone wanting to study these authors' accounts of the life of Billy Bray may like to read the originals.

When trying to put a little more flesh on what are sometimes just surnames or initials in *The King's Son*, I have used the word *probably* or *possibly* if I need to indicate that it is not a definite identification.

It is not possible to tell the story of Billy Bray without inserting occasional notes and explanations. These sometimes involve background information that will already be known to some readers, so I am putting them in boxes. In this way they won't interfere with the amazing story of one of Cornwall's most famous sons.

Finally, I must make it clear that I have written this book for a general readership, although I hope it will lead scholars of church history and early Methodism down previously unexplored paths.

Chris Wright
Bristol, 2004

Publisher's note

In order to distinguish between source material and authorial comment, we have set the work as follows: Authorial comment is set (like this paragraph) with a justified right margin and a wider line length.

> All quoted source material (like this paragraph) is set with a shorter line length and with a ragged right margin. All, and only, entries from Billy Bray's Journal are set in this font.

CHAPTER 1

A FORTUNATE ESCAPE

IN HIS OWN WORDS, Billy Bray lived "a bad life", and it nearly ends inside a copper mine when the roof crashes to the ground.

William Trewartha Bray, the man who has the fortunate escape, was born in the summer of 1794 at Twelveheads, a village near Truro in Cornwall. At this time the village consisted of a few thatched cottages inhabited by tin miners, and a small Methodist chapel that Billy's grandfather helped build.

Billy tells the story of his early life in the opening pages of his *Journal*, and no one can tell it better than Billy himself. FW Bourne says Billy spoke with a great sense of humour. I believe he wrote in the same way. Many readers will find Billy's down-to-earth grammar, which I have not corrected, adds to the fascination.

Billy writes:

My grandfather was one of the old Methodists, for he joined them when Mister Wesley first came to Cornwall. He was my father's father. My father died when we was young, and left my mother with five small children. After father died, grandfather took us to rear. He could not read a letter in the book, but I have heard him say, "We must be born again, and I was born again up in our croft among the furze.[1] I was so happy I could tell the bushes to praise God. I thought I was in a new world."

---

1   This is the grandfather's conversion, not Billy's. Furze is the local name for gorse. This was probably an open-air meeting out on the Cornish croft – the rough hill-

My grandfather, and a few more that was converted when he was, built a little chapel in a place called Twelveheads. There was a special little class, and they had a leader called Sando.[2]

I write to honour my God. You will not wonder how I praise him when you read what he has done for me, bless his holy name.

I was born in the parish of Kea in the county of Cornwall in June 1794. My father died when I was about eight years old and, as I have already said, my grandfather reared me. I lived in Cornwall until I was seventeen years old, and then I went up to Devonshire and there I lived a bad life.

I got in with a bad company of drunkards. I remember one time getting drunk in the town of Tavistock. When going to our home we met with a very large horse in the way. It was late in the night and two of us drunk men got up on the horse. We had not rode far before the horse struck his foot against a stone and fell down. It turned right over, and it was very near he had killed us both. But the Lord spared us, bad as we was, thanks be to his holy name.

Another time I got drunk, and while sitting with a man my hat fell off from my head. It fell into the fire and was burnt. I stole a hat to wear home and I was very near to be sent to jail for that, but the man had the hat again.

Another time we were a company of drunkards coming home from the alehouse all drunk, and we unhung all the gates from the fields as we came by. We was near to be sent to jail for that. So you that read this will see that I have great reason to praise the Lord for

side – for Billy's grandfather goes on to say that several people were converted at the same time. Although Twelveheads is not far from Gwennap – a place famous for both John and Charles Wesley's preaching – it is interesting to note that Billy quotes his grandfather as saying *our croft*, implying the meeting was local.

2   Here, and later, this is Billy's spelling. The surnames *Sando* and *Sandoe* are both known in Cornwall.

what he have done for me, bless his holy name. These is but a few of my bad deeds out of many.

Although Billy puts just these three rather mild instances of his "bad life" in his *Journal*, Bourne refers to Billy as, "a drunken and lascivious miner filled with bitter hatred;" adding, "Billy's soul was stained with viler sins than any that have been mentioned."

As we shall see, Billy feels unable to elaborate on his past life. But all this is about to change:

While I was working underground in Wheal Friendship mine in Devonshire I heard a scat[3] over my head. I ran out from where I was working, and I think forty tons fell down where I came out from. I was spared, so did I not ought to praise the Lord?

I was pert[4] to the captain that I worked under in the mine, and got turned away. I went to another part of Devonshire and got work, and went to live at a beer shop. There with another drunkard we were drinking all the night long, but I had a sore head and a sick stomach. And that was not all, for I had horrors of mind. No one knows what I felt. I have been afraid many times – afraid to sleep for fear I should wake in hell. I made many promises to the Lord to be better, and have been as bad or worse again. You see how the Lord beared with me. Well may his people say, "He would not the death of a sinner, but wish all to come to him and be saved." I believed it to be true, praise his holy name.

After being in Devonshire for seven years I came home to Cornwall again, a drunkard.

It is 1818 when Billy returns to Cornwall. On July 16 1821, at the age of twenty-seven, he marries Johanna Bray - a common surname at this time - in Kea Church. His wife Joey (Johanna, although sometimes spelt without the h in

3   A sudden cracking
4   Insolent

official records) is heading for trouble. She is marrying a drunkard, and she has drifted from the Christian faith.

Billy continues:

> I was not only a drunkard but bad in other ways, and it is too bad to put down here. Great was the mercy of God towards me or I should not be here, bless and praise his holy name for what he done for me in delivering my soul from the pit.
>
> Young women, be sure you go not with a drunkard. If you do, and he marry you, he will not care for you nor the children. My dear wife have a great reason to praise the Lord that I was converted.
>
> One time I remember I went for some coal that my wife sent me for. I got the coal, and there was a beer shop in the way, and there I stayed. I got drunk, and my poor wife was forced to come for me and wheel home the coal herself.
>
> So you see that a drunkard is a bad husband. When the Lord bless him with money he will give it for drink to the landlord sooner than to his wife and children. I know at one time the Lord blessed me and gave me two good months' wages at one time. I paid the landlord five pounds for drink,[5] and all I had was a sore head and a sick stomach — and a tormented mind.
>
> The landlords and landladies in general are very greedy. Just after I paid him the five pounds, me and my wife and child came one day when the landlord and his wife was to dinner. They had a leg of mutton, but did not ask us to have one bit. My wife thought much about it and she asked me whether I would do so again.[6]
>
> There is bad houses and they are bad people that keep them. I learnt the greatest past of my wickedness in them houses, for I sinned against light and law. I never got drunk without being

5   This would have been at least half of Billy's "two good months' wages".

6   Presumably: whether he would continue drinking.

Billy Bray's cottage
redrawn from an engraving in *The King's Son*.

condemned for it, and by night I often dreamed wisht[7] dreams. It was my fault. The Lord was willing to make me happy, but I was not. This is the great wonder how he spared me, and I so great a sinner against the Lord.

Billy's account of his conversion is vivid. It is the late autumn of 1823. He has been married for five years, and is now a family man aged twenty-nine. In the cottage Billy finds a copy of John Bunyan's book *Visions of Heaven and Hell*.

---

7 Billy uses the word *'wisht'* several times. It is a catch-all Cornish word meaning something like *pale, unwell, poorly* and *bad*, depending on the context. Thus Billy's *wisht* dream is a bad one. When Billy says later that his comrades are *wisht* to see him praying, he means they are upset. Billy also talks about a miser's table looking *wisht*, meaning it looks a poor one.

Billy writes:

John Bunyan, when he was in the prison writing the Visions of Heaven and Hell, he did not know the Lord would make him instrumental in converting my soul. But he was, and I bless the Lord that ever John Bunyan was put in prison. Bless his holy name that little book called Bunyan's Visions of Heaven and Hell was brought into our house. Who brought it there I do not know. Bless the Lord for sending of it there. I took it in my hand and began to read it.[8]

I read the Visions of Heaven first, and then Visions of Hell. Bunyan said he saw two lost souls down in hell cursing one another for being the author of one another's misery. He said though they love one another here, they will hate one another in hell.

There was a man at that time that I kept company with, and we was fond of one another. We worked at the mine together, for we was miners, and we went to the alehouse and got drunk together. When I read in Bunyan's Visions of Heaven and Hell about the two down in hell, I thought shall S Coad[9] and me be like that, that is that so fond of each other? I felt from that very time to be a better man.

When I was sitting down to the end of the table reading the book, my wife was sitting by the fire. She had been converted when young but she went back before we went together, so she was a backslider. I asked her what it was to be happy.

She said, "No tongue can tell what they enjoy that serve the Lord."

8   Since Billy has already said that his Methodist grandfa-
     ther could not read a word, the Bible and hymnbook
     may have been his father's, who we learn later was also a
     Methodist. Where Bunyan's Visions of Heaven and Hell
     came from is more puzzling. Surely Billy would have
     known if it was his father's, for it is unlikely that a
     miner's home at that time would have many books.
     Maybe it came from Joey's family, for certainly Joey's
     mother was alive, as was Billy's mother.

9   No other name is given for S Coad.

Then I said, "Why don't you begin again? I may begin too."

I thought if she was to begin it would be better for me, for I was ashamed to go to my knees to pray before her that very night. I felt in my mind that I ought to fall on my knees and ask God for mercy, but the devil had such a hold in me that he made me ashamed of my wife.[10]

I went into bed without prayer, and it was about ten o'clock at night. At three in the morning, I think, I awaked and thought about what I read the night before. I thought, if I stay until my wife is converted I may never be saved.

Then I rose out of the bed and went to my knees for the first time. My wife heard me but she could not see me for it was dark. Bless and praise the Lord, I have never been ashamed of my wife since that night, and there is forty years gone since that time.

That very day I made up my mind to serve the Lord by his help, and I began to pray. It was on a Friday, but what day of November it was I do not know. The more I prayed, the more I felt to pray. It was our payday or setting day that day, I hardly know which, for it is a long time ago.

I stayed upstairs all the forenoon asking the Lord to have mercy upon me, and in the afternoon I went to the alehouse to meet with my comrades, the men I work with. We always went, we miners, on setting days and paydays to the alehouse to eat and to drink, and to get drunk and to tell lies. I was the worse liar of the whole, and their chairman among them.[11]

10 When Billy says here and later that he is ashamed of his wife, he must mean he is ashamed to *pray* in front of her, not that he is ashamed *of* her. Billy has already said he was ashamed to go on his knees before Joey, and this and the following statement seem to be badly worded repetitions of his feelings.

11 From later references by Billy, *to tell lies* must mean to tell dirty jokes, as he is now ashamed of telling them to make the men laugh. Billy admits to being the chief teller.

We was eight men that worked together. When I came in among them they looked at me, and they knew that I was not like I was some time before. Yes, they had lost their chairman, and one of them swore.

THE BRYANITES AND BIBLE CHRISTIANS

Cornish-born William O'Bryan (1778-1868) was a dissident Wesleyan Methodist preacher who felt called to evangelism in Cornwall, but was unsupported by the Methodist leaders over the way he wanted to go about it. O'Bryan founded the Bryanites in 1815 at Lake Farm, in the Devonshire village of Shebbear. The Connexion – the religious body – functioned in a way that was similar to the Primitive Methodists. To a certain extent the early Bible Christians and the Methodists were rivals (there were several divisions of Methodists), a cause of ill feeling between some of the members, as we will see from some of Billy's accounts.

Within a year the Bryanites became known as the Bible Christians, although the original name stuck for a long time among the public. Following an internal disagreement, O'Bryan left for America in 1836. FW Bourne was elected president in 1867. Eventually the membership numbered over 30,000. Following Bourne's death in 1905, the Bible Christians merged with the Methodist New Connexion and the United Methodist Free Church in 1907. In 1932 all the Methodist bodies except the Weslyan Reform and Independent Methodists united to become the Methodist Church of today. An impartial reference to the Bible Christians, from the Encyclopaedia Britannica dated 1911, can be found on:
http://21.1911encyclopedia.org/B/BI/BIBLE_CHRISTIANS.htm.
There is a link to this document on:
www.billybray.com.

I said to him, "We must give account of that one day."[12]

Mocking me, he said, "Shall us go to the Bryanites meeting?"

I said, "It is better to go there than go to hell."

I came home that night sober the first time for many years, for we always got drunk on our setting day and payday. My wife was greatly surprised to see me come home so soon, and sober too. She said, "How are you home so soon today?"

I said unto her, "You will never see me drunk no more, by the help of the Lord."

And she never have since, praise the Lord. The Lord can, and do, cure drunken wicked men, praise his holy name. That night I went upstairs and prayed until we went to bed.

The next day I did not go to work. I took the Bible and Wesley's hymnbook and went up the stairs into the bedroom. This was the Saturday, and there I read and prayed all the day. Sometimes I read the Bible and then the hymnbook, and then asked the Lord for mercy.

When Sunday morning came it was very wet. There was a class meeting a mile from our house, called Bible Christians. I went to the house where the meeting was held, but because it was wet none of them came. I had a mind to meet with them, but when I saw a little rain would keep them from the house of God, I said, "I shall not meet here if a drop of rain will keep them home."

I went home from the meeting house, went up to our bedroom, and took the Bible and hymnbook again. Sometimes I read, and then prayed, and asked the Lord to have mercy on me. I felt the devil very busy with me, and he tempted me that I should never find

12   This seems to be good-hearted banter between work col-
     leagues, with Billy giving as good as he got and making a
     serious point at the same time. But Bourne changes the
     word *we* to *you* in *The King's Son*, and makes Billy sound
     holier-than-thou.

mercy. But I never believed him, for I knew that the Lord said. "All that seek shall find." And that is true, bless his holy name for ever and ever.

CLASS MEETINGS

Developed by John Wesley from a meeting in 1739, Wesley declared that Class Meetings were for, "A company of men having the form and seeking the power of godliness, united in order to pray together, to receive the word of exhortation, and to watch over one another in love, that they may help each other to work out their salvation." There were several rules, of which the main ones were: To see each person in his class once a week at least, in order to inquire how their souls prosper; To advise, reprove, comfort or exhort, as occasion may require; To receive what they are willing to give toward the relief of the preachers, church, and poor." (General Rules of the Methodist Class Meetings, 1808.)

The Bible Christians adopted a very similar type of meeting. When Billy says they meet in a house or dwelling house, he means a family home. The model is used throughout the world today by all denominations in home groups. For more information make an internet search for "class meeting" + Methodist.

On the Monday I was all the forepart of the day in my bedroom, some of the time reading, and then asking the Lord for mercy. Then I had to go to the mine, for we was afternoon core.[13] We went down underground, four of us, and went to work. While working, I was always asking the Lord to have mercy on me.

The men that I worked with me was wisht to see me so, for I used to tell lies to make them laugh. But now I was not like Billy Bray, for

13   Shift

last week I was a servant of the devil, and now I was determined to serve the Lord, by his help. And I believed he would help me.

So that stem, or core as we miners call, passed away and we came up. I went home asking for mercy all the way, and the devil was often putting in my mind that I shall never find it. But bless God, I never believed him, for the Lord gave me strength against him. When I came home after that night core it was eleven o'clock, for we left work about ten o'clock.

I used to ask my wife, "What is for supper?" But that night I did not, for I had something else to look for: the Lord to speak peace to my soul. I went upstairs into my room asking the Lord for mercy, but I had it not that night. So I had a little supper and we went to bed.

That night I dreamed a very wicked dream, and when I waked in the morning, I said, "Because I have dreamed this wicked dream, I will not go to bed to sleep this night."

I went to the mine, and we went down to work at our two o'clock core. I was always asking the Lord for mercy. I never spoke to my partner that worked with me, except when he asked a question. This was Tuesday. So this core passed away, and we came up and went home.

My wife's mother told me I must not be out of heart if I did not find God's mercy in twelve months. I told her I should not be so long as that, though the devil tempted me hard that I should never find it. Thanks be to the Lord I found him a liar. I was glad that I had begun to seek the Lord, for I would rather be crying for mercy than living in sin.

By the help of the Lord I shall write my Journal, simple as it is, for I am a simple man as a great many people know. At that time we had a little pig, and this was the Wednesday. While in the bedroom looking to heaven with all the powers of my soul, it appeared to me I had almost laid hold of the blessing. But the pig came up to our door and I thought I never heard a pig cry so in all my life. I should have been very glad if some person had drive him away, if I never saw him no more.

I did not get the blessing then, though it seem so nigh me. By the devil and the pig, I got it not then: with the pig downstairs crying and the devil tempting. For want of a little more faith I got not the blessing, and it was come time for me to go work to the mine.

I went asking the Lord for mercy all the way. We changed our clothes and went down in the mine underground. My partner was in the end breaking the stuff,[14] and I was wheeling it away to a place we call a pleat or shaft. There was at that day a horse whim[15] that drew up the stuff to the surface that we men broke.

As I was wheeling out the barrow the devil tempted me that I shall never find mercy. When the devil tempted me, I said to myself, for my partners did not hear me, "Thee art a liar, devil." As soon as I said so, I felt all the weight go off my mind. Glory be to God, I could praise the Lord, but not with that liberty I could afterwards.

I called out to my three comrades, or partners, for there was two men in the eastern end, and my partner in the western end, and said to them, "I am not so happy as some is, but sooner than I would go back to sin again I would be put in that plat[16] there and be burnt to death with faggots."

When I came home I went upstairs, not staying for supper, for I wanted something better. And bless God I soon had it. I stayed up in my bedroom with my face to the west, and I said to the dear Lord, "Thou hast said they that ask shall receive, and they that seek shall find, and they that knock it shall be opened unto them.[17] Open unto me, my dear Lord. I have faith to believe it."

---

14 A miners' term for the rock and ore.

15 A horse-drawn windlass.

16 A plat is a flat area, either inside or outside a mine, for storing rock and ore. It seems that heat is being used here to break the rock within the mine.

17 Luke 11:9

When I said so, the dear Lord made me so happy that I cannot express what I felt. I shouted for joy and praised God for what he had done for me a poor sinner, for I could say my happy heart felt experience that the Lord had pardoned all my sins. And it seem to me I was in a new world. I think it was in November 1823. What day of the month I do not know, but everything looked new to me: the people, the fields, the cattle, the trees. I was like a man in a new world.

Glory be to God, I was so happy that I was the greatest part of my time praising the Lord. I could say, "O Lord, I will praise thee, for thou wast angry with me but thine anger is turned away, and thou comforts me."[18] Or like David, "The Lord brought me out of the horrible pit and mire and clay, and set my feet on the rock, established my goings, and put a new song in my mouth of praise and thanks given to God."[19]

I was a new man altogether. All that I met I told what the Lord had done for my soul. I heard some say that they have hard work to get away from their old companions, but I had hard work to find them, for I was glad to meet them to tell them what the Lord had done for me.

Some said I was mad, and some said, "We shall have him again next payday."

I always got drunk on our mine payday, and they thought I should go back again. But praise the Lord, there is more than forty years gone and they have not got me yet. They said I was a mad man, but they meant I was a glad man, and I have been glad ever since. Bless and praise his holy name for what he have done for we poor sinners that was once servants of the devil and now are the servants of the Lord; once in the road to hell but now in the road to heaven.

18   Isaiah 12:1

19   Psalm 40:1-3

Bless and praise his holy name, I never shall forget the day when Jesus took my sins away.

Billy quickly begs his wife Joey to return to the faith she once knew. Bourne tells us that about a week later, in Hicks Mill Chapel, Joey "regained the blessing she had lost." But not all Billy's friends are pleased to hear what has happened.

Billy continues:

We used to go to Capson[20] a great many of us. Before I was converted I was their chairman, for I was most of my time telling of lies to make them laugh, and make fun as we called it. But now I could tell them a new tale about heaven and heavenly things, and what the Lord had done for many, and what the Lord would do for them, and what he had done for me.

But all this did not please them. They was better pleased with me when I told them lies, when I was in the road to hell with them. Because I told them about the Lord and heaven and heavenly things, they called me a mad man. But I was only then in my right mind, praise the Lord. Here we may see what blind men is that live in sin, to call a man or woman that is born again mad. In the day of Pentecost, they that was not converted said the Lord's children was drunk with new wine.

It was not long before some of the men was as mad as me. There were men that professed to be converted before I was, but did not love their Lord well enough to honour him in the mine, and did not love we well enough to tell us that the Lord would make us happy. They never prayed with me, nor told me that I must pray or go to

20 Billy twice mentions going to Capson and at the top of this section in the *Journal* he has written *chairman at Capson* referring to himself. Clearly the men are going there to drink. Perhaps it should be spelt *Capstan*, which is part of the winding gear in a mine, and may have been the name of a local alehouse. Another possibility is *Capstone*.

Hick's Mill chapel
redrawn from an engraving in *The Kings's Son*.

hell.[21] But when I was converted, the Lord gave me power to tell all that I met with that I was happy and was going to heaven. I told them that what the Lord had done for me, he would do for everyone that ask him.

There was no one that prayed in our mine where I worked, but when the Lord converted my soul I used to pray underground with the men before we go to our different places to work. Sometimes I felt it a heavy cross, but the cross is the way to the crown. Sometimes I have had as many as six to ten men down with me, and I have said to them, "Now if you will hearken to me, I will pray for you before we go to work. For," I said, "if I do not pray for you before we go to work, and anyone be killed, I should think it was my fault."

Some of them would say, "You pray and we will hear you."

21   The word *hell* is lightly crossed out.

Then I should pray in what the people call simple words, and in the way that I hope the Lord would have me. I used say when praising God, "If anyone must be killed or die today, let me. Do not let no one of them die, for they are not happy, but I am. And I shall be in heaven if I die today."

When I did rise from my knees I should see the tears running down their faces. Soon after, some of them became praying men themselves.

There was a man that was up in Devonshire with me. He was called Justin Thomas, and he and me was two drunkards up there together. We came home to Cornwall together and I was converted before he was. When I used to tell the wicked men what a bad state they was in, and where they must go if they die, he was one of them.

They would persecute me and call me a fool, but Justin Thomas would say, "You shall leave that man alone and say nothing to him, for the Lord hast done great things for him. I knew him when he was a bad man, and now he is a good man, and I wish I was like him."

When Justin said so, I felt great love to him and felt to pray for him. I was out one day in the field turning dressing to teal my 'taters.[22] I kneeled down in the field and prayed for Justin, and while I was praying the Lord spoke to me in my mind, and said, "I will save him very soon."

I believed it was from the Lord, and so it was. That day I was afternoon core and went to the mine at two o'clock. I was going down and Justin was coming up. He had a pick in his hand coming

22   *To teal*, or *teel*, is old Cornish meaning *to plant*, similar to the expression *to till* which in most of England means to prepare the ground for planting. In parts of Cornwall *to till* is still understood to mean *to plant*. *'Taters* are potatoes.

up the ladder and it was knocking against the staves and making a noise, and I heard him before I saw him.

It was said to me in my mind, "Justin is coming. Tell him of it."

So when he came up, I said to him, "I have good news to tell you. While I was out in the field praying for you, the Lord told me you should be converted soon."

And so he was, for he was converted, and taken sick. I saw him many times when he was ill, and he told me he was happy and going to heaven to praise God in glory. So Brother Thomas is now with Abraham and Isaac and Jacob in the kingdom of heaven praising God, and will praise him for ever and ever. The Lord Jesus said in the days of his flesh, "Many shall come from the east and the west, and from the north and the south, and shall sit down with Abraham and Isaac and Jacob in the kingdom of heaven."[23]

Reader, you may say, "How do you know that the Lord spoke to you?" Very well, the blessed Bible and New Testament tell us that the Lord spoke in the days of old by the mouth of his servants the prophets, but now he speaks in our hearts by the Spirit of his Son. And I know that is the truth, for the Lord never told one lie, bless his holy name, nor made one mistake. What I have heard and felt and seen, with confidence I can tell.

23   Matthew 8:11

CHAPTER 2

A NEW LIFE

BILLY IS NOT at all happy with his own lifestyle, and changes need to be made. This next account comes from *The King's Son*. It is told in Billy's words, but is not in his *Journal:*

> I heard that Mr Teare[24] was coming to Hicks Mill to lecture on teetotalism. I thought I would go to hear him, but that I would not sign the pledge, for a little drop, if a man does not take too much, will do him good.
>
> As I listened to what Mr Teare had to say, the darkness was removed from my mind and I thought I would sign the pledge. Before Mr Teare had finished speaking, I shouted out to friend Tregaskis,[25] "Thomas, put down my name!"

In a time of low wages and much poverty, the abuse of alcohol and tobacco led many families into ruin. It is therefore not surprising that Billy, a converted

---

24 Almost certainly this is James Teare who was well known in Cornwall at this time as a temperance reformer.

25 Born in 1785, Thomas Tregaskis was one of the founding members of Hicks Mill Chapel. He was a Bible Christian class leader, a local preacher and an active supporter of the temperance movement.

Bourne writes:

I well remember how wisely and faithfully, yet lovingly, Billy dealt with a Christian whose life was being ruined through drink.

Billy told the man he must be on his guard against his besetting sin, and keep beyond the length of the devil's chain. He went on to say that a crafty fox down his way managed, though chained, to devour some foolish chickens.

The fox kicked a few grains of corn a long distance away, which the chickens quickly picked up without thought of danger. Then a few more grains, but not quite so far off. Then a few again a little nearer, and then a little nearer still, until the unsuspecting birds came within reach, when he at once sprang upon them and devoured them.

"Satan would serve someone like that," said Billy. "Only one glass, *that* he might take without danger; two glasses even, and yet be quite safe. He might think, perhaps, he could take three or four. But if he got on such dangerous ground he was putting himself in the devil's power, and he would drink until he got drunk again. Then the devil would say, 'That is your religion, is it? You may as well give up your hopes and professions at once. No one will believe in you any more.'"

We now return to the *Journal*. In it Billy tells us:

I was, before I was converted, a somkerd[26] as well as a drunkard. I used to smoke and I loved smoking almost as well as I loved my meat, and would rather go down in the mine without my dinner than without my tobacco and pipe. But now I have a new master, better than tobacco and pipes. Everyone in Christ Jesus is a new creature; old things is passed away and all things is new.[27]

In the days of old the Lord spoke by the mouth of his servants the prophets, but now he speaks in our hearts by the Spirit of his Son. So I had not only the believing part, but I could hear the small still voice within that speaks to me. When I would take the pipe to smoke, it would be applied within, "It is an idol, a lust. You are lusting after an idol and I want you to give it up and to worship me with your whole heart."

For so it was, and when I used to put a little tobacco in my mouth it would be said to me, "Worship me with clean lips."

Then I would take the tobacco out of my mouth and throw it on the ground. And after a little time I might forget, and put some in my mouth again, but as soon as it was in my mouth it would be, "Worship God with clean lips."

The Lord told me it was not right to smoke nor chew, but this did not do, so he sent a woman called Mary Hook to convince me. I went into a house and took the pipe out of my pocket and went to light it. And Mary said to me, "I see that you smoke. Do you not feel (bad – or guilty) from smoking?"

"Yes, I feel something inside telling me that it is an idol and a lust."

She said with a very loud voice, "That is the Lord."

---

26 Probably Billy intended to write smokerd (or smokard) – a word he has perhaps coined to rhyme with drunkard. Billy does occasionally transpose letters and even words in the *Journal*.

27 2 Corinthians 5:17

Then I said, "Now I must give it up, for the Lord is telling me of it inside, and the woman outside. So the tobacco must go, love it as much as I will."

So there and then I took the tobacco out of my pocket and threw it in the fire, and put the pipe under my foot and said, "Ashes to ashes, dust to dust."

Thanks be to God I have not smoked since, and that is forty-one years ago now. But I found old habits hard to be broken, and I was forced to pray mightily to the Lord and ask him for help. Bless his holy name, he helped me. The Lord said, "Cry to me in the time of trouble and I will deliver you."[28] And I was the man that wanted help.

When I gave up the pipe, the day following I had the toothache so bad that I did not know what to do. I said, "If I had not gave up my pipe, I should not had this pain in my teeth." But I said, "I will never smoke no more, if I lose every tooth in my head."

I prayed to the Lord, and bless his holy name he helped me, for I said, "Lord, thou hast said that thy yoke is easy and thy burden is light."[29]

When I said so, all the pain in my teeth left me. Sometimes the thought of the pipe would come into my mind so sweet that it would put me to feel my pocket, and I used say, "Lord, keep it out of my mind." Then the Lord would bless me and make me happy.

So I asked the Lord for strength against that habit, for it is a bad one, and it is not everyone that can give it up, for it do enslave a man. It takes a firm mind to conquer that, and then he must ask for help of the Lord.

28   Psalm 34:17
29   Matthew 11:30

CHAPTER 3

VERY NOISY TIMES

THIS CHAPTER MAY come as a shock to readers who think that Sunday services in Victorian England consisted of gentle organ music, a prim-and-proper choir, and a handful of people dozing in the pews during a long and boring sermon. Some of the chapels that Billy attended were packed – and calling the people boisterous would be an understatement.

Billy continues his *Journal*:

I was born in the fire and could not live in the smoke, for I was happy in my work and could leap and dance for joy. I could do it in the mine underground, as well as up to the surface.

My master persecuted me, and would say that it was no religion to leap and dance and make so to-do – there was no need for it. My master, or captain, was down in the mine where I was, and we was working an end, and we had a little water standing in. He began to speak against me, and I looked to the Lord. Then power of the Lord came upon me and I began to jump and smash the water up in his face and his eyes, and put out his candle. He went out shaking his head and asked my comrade, where he hid, "Is this a mad man with thee?"

But he made a mistake. I was not a mad man but I was a glad man, and the Lord made me so, bless his holy name. David was not a mad man when he danced before the Lord with all his might, though his wife called him so. She said he was like one of the wild fellows, shameful, uncovered. But he told her he would be more vile yet, for it was before the Lord that he leaped and danced.[30] It was the Lord that made me so happy as to make me dance and leap for joy. And David's Lord is my Lord, bless his holy name. If a man will not leap and dance for heaven, what will he leap and dance for? There is no better prize than heaven, and we are heaven born and heaven bound.

The sinner says, "We think there is no need for as much to-do as to leap and dance and make so much noise, for the Lord is not deaf and he know our hearts."

And you must know that the devil is not deaf neither, yet his servants make a great noise. But the devil would rather see us doubting than hear us shouting. We believe without a doubt that Christians have a right to shout, but the lukewarm professor will say there is no need for so much noise.

OLD PROFESSORS — THE CONVERTED AND UNCONVERTED

Billy divides the spiritual state of people into distinct categories. First there are the *unconverted*. Although Billy sometimes uses this word, he usually called them the *wicked*. When their lives are especially bad he calls them *very wicked*.

Then there are *professors*. These are not academic professors, they are people who profess the Christian faith but do little about it. It seems from some of his descriptions that Billy sees *lukewarm professors* as having a valid Christian faith, albeit a powerless one. There are also *dead professors*, who have apparently lost their faith to some degree, and the *old dead professors* whom he sees as active enemies of God.

Converted people Billy calls *happy*. He occasionally uses the expression *born again*. It is important to realise that when Billy calls people *happy*, he is usually referring to their relationship with Christ – happy in the Lord. In other words, he sees them as living an outwardly active and joyful Christian faith.

I heard a preacher say one day there was no need for all that ado, and he did not like it. No, nor the devil neither.

> That preacher would have done to be on the Pharisees' side, where they said, "Master, rebuke thy disciples."[30] He would not do to have been on the disciples' side, nor on Christ's side. I have heard more than one preacher speak against the power of God.

Billy is certainly not alone in living out his faith so enthusiastically. James H Rigg (1821-1909), a Methodist minister who spent some time in Cornwall as a young man in 1846, describes the Methodism of the miners in his book *Wesleyan Methodist Reminiscences* (Robert Culley, London 1904):

> Theirs is a realising religion – a religion of deep solemnity and of intense fervour – fervour rising sometimes into extraordinary excitement. All the relief, the refreshment, the congenial excitement of their life above ground they found in the preaching-house or the classroom. There they let themselves go; they shouted, they wept, they groaned, they not seldom laughed aloud with a laugh of intense excitement, a wonderful laugh.

Rigg says this form of worship was to be found in the mining areas, but not anywhere else in the Penzance Circuit. He describes the experience as:

> "Not to be forgotten. I have never witnessed such excitement and such responses from that day to this."

The Rev Mark Guy Pearse, who was born in Cornwall in 1842, became a Methodist minister and was known simply as Mark Guy in later life. He died in 1930. In his two books of short stories, *Daniel Quorm*, he takes many of the events that he observes in Cornwall and hangs them together with tales of the imaginary Daniel Quorm living in the fictional village of Penwinnin. In *Series Two*, Pearse tells of a rock fall in a local tin mine, and the rescue of Mat the miner. I have

30   Luke 19:39

no doubt that this is based on a real and typical event. Mat (sic) decides to go to chapel, and on the third Sunday:

> The preacher was quietly going on in a somewhat drowsy way, when suddenly the congregation were startled. Without a sign of what was coming, Mat leapt from his seat high into the air, and clasping his hands, gave a shout that seemed to shake the place. "Hallelujah!" he cried again and again. "I can praise thee now, my Lord, and I will," he cried, as the place rang again.

> The preacher, a quiet, argumentative brother, stopped and looked over the high pulpit. Then he coughed, bewildered. The joy spread through the congregation until a score of voices rang with loud thanksgiving. The power of the Lord was present to heal, and others who had gone sorrowing for many days found joy and peace in believing.

> The service was turned into an inquiry meeting, and anxious seekers stayed on hour after hour, so that the chapel could not be closed until late at night. Each evening of the week meetings were held, and scores came under the Power that transformed them completely.

This next excerpt from Billy's *Journal* illustrates the way some chapel services were conducted at this time, not only in Cornwall but also in other countries around the world. Certainly Billy would have felt comfortable with the form of Afro-American worship described here. It comes from page 235, near the end of the *Journal*. It is in a different handwriting to Billy's, and superficially it resembled the handwriting of Martha Bowden, the Quaker who persuaded Billy to write the story of his life. On the first page of the *Journal* it says: *This is the property of Martha Bowden*. A closer examination shows slight differences in the formation of some letters. Schools at this time taught children to write in a fixed style. However, the writing is definitely not Hendy's

The words are from a hymnbook by Richard Allen, a black slave born in Philadelphia in 1760. After his conversion and subsequent freedom, Allen published a compilation of hymns in 1801 specifically for African-American congregations, entitled *A Collection of Spiritual Songs and Hymns Selected from Various Authors, by Richard Allen, African Minister.*

These verses are a conversation between two characters called Methodist and Formalist, speaking in turns. The writer who copied the hymn into the *Journal* has not put these names to the sections, so to make the reading easier I have put (M) for Methodist and (F) for Formalist as in Allen's original. Entering the phrase "good morning brother pilgrim" on an internet search engine brings up more information on this hymn and on Richard Allen.

I have transcribed the words exactly from the *Journal*, and they do not always agree with the American version. Interestingly, *the* and *they* are spelt as *the*, and the pronoun *I* never has a capital, as in Billy's own handwriting. Here is the entry:

The substance of a conversation between two persons, one going to and one returning from a camp meeting.

(M) Good morning, brother pilgrim, what marching to Zion,
What doubts and what dangers have you met today?
Have you found a blessing in your joys increasing?
Press forward, my brother, and make no delay.

Is your heart glowing, are your comforts flowing,
And have you an evidence now bright and clear?
Have you a desire that burns like a fire,
Or hope in the hour when Christ shall appear?

(F) I came out this morning, and now I'm returning
Perhaps little better than when I first came;
Such groaning, such shouting, it sets me a-doubting,
I fear such religion is all like a dream.

The preachers were stamping, the people were jumping
And screaming so loud that I neither could hear;
Either praying or preaching, such horrible screeching
'Twas truly offensive to all that was there.

(M) Perhaps, my dear brother, while they prayed together
You sat and considered and prayed not at all;
Would you find a blessing? men pray without ceasing,
Obey the advice that was given by Paul.

For if you should reason at any such season,
No wonder if Satan should tell in your ear,
"The preachers and people, and only a rabble,
And this is no place for a reflection or prayer."

(F) No place for reflection, I am filled with distraction,
I wonder how people could bear for to stay?
The men they were bawling, the women were squalling,
I wonder for my part how any could pray.

Such horrid confusion, if this be religion,
It's something so new as never was seen;
For the sacred pages that speaks of all ages
Do nowhere declare that such ever has been.

(M) Don't be so soon shaken, if I'm not mistaken
Such things have been acted by Christians of old;
When the ark it was coming King David came running
And dancing before it in scripture we are told.

When the Jewish nation had laid the foundation
And rebuilt the temple at Ezra's command,
Some wept and some praised, such noise there was raised
'Twas heard afar off perhaps all through the land.

(M) And as for the teacher, Ezekiel the preacher,
He was taught for to stamp and to smite with his hand;
To show the transgression of that sinful nation
And bid men repent and obey the command.

By scripture's quotation in this dispensation
The gracious Redeemer permits them to shout;

Saying, if they cease praising we have been proclaiming
The stones to reprove them would quickly cry out.

(F) Then scripture is rested, for Paul has protested
That order should be kept in the house of the Lord;
Amidst such a chatter who knows what's the matter
Or who can attend to what is declared?

To see them behaving like drunkards are raving
Or lying or rolling prostrate on the ground,
I really felt awful and sometimes was fearful
I should be the next that would come tumbling down.

(M) You say you felt awful, you ought to be careful
Lest you grieve the Spirit and bid him depart;
For by your expressions you felt some impressions,
The sweet melting showers have tendered your heart.

You fear persecution, and there's the delusion
Brought on by the devil who turned you away;
Be careful, my brother, for blessed are none other
Than persons that are not offended in me.

(M) When Peter was preaching and was boldly teaching
The ways of salvation in Jesus' name,
The Spirit descended and some were offended
And said of the men they were filled with new wine.

I never yet doubted that some of them shouted
While others lay prostrate by power struck down;
Some weeping, some praising, while others were saying,
"These are drunkards and fools and in falsehood abound."

(M) Our moments are flying but time is expiring,
We are called to improve it, and quietly prepare
For that awful hour when Jesus in power
Will come into judgement all states to declare.

Methinks there'll be shouting, and I am not doubting,
But crying and screaming for mercy, in vain;
Therefore, my dear brother, let's now pray together
That your precious soul may be filled with the flame.

(F) Sure praying is needful, I really feel awful,
I fear that my time of repentance is passed;
That I will look to my Saviour his mercy for ever,
These storms of temptation will not always last.

I'll look for his blessing and pray without ceasing,
His mercy is sure to all them that believe;
My heart is now glowing, I feel his love flowing,
Peace, pardon and comfort I now do receive.

Billy mentions three times in his Journal that he was singing, *When the ark it was coming, King David came running,* possibly indicating that this American hymn was in use in Cornwall at the time, which would account for it being here in the *Journal.* However, Billy always adds the words: *and leaping and dancing for joy.* These are not in Allen's words, nor are they a direct quote from the King James Bible, yet they scan well and seem to be part of a hymn or poem. Maybe there was another hymn in use in England, though it is not in Wesley or Bourne's standard hymnbooks.

I heard a story in Cornwall that sums up the gap that existed between the supporters of tranquillity and the advocates of animation in the Cornish chapels and churches. Billy told the Rev Saltern Rogers, the vicar of Gwennap from 1856-1893, "Look 'ere, Passun Rogers, you do love a peace and quietness religion, but I do dearly love a noise!"[31]

Bourne tells us:

Billy was once asked, "Why can't you worship the Lord without making so much noise?"

"It's not my fault," said Billy. "If a person above was to pour water into a basin already full, standing on that beautiful tablecloth, and it was

---

31   I am told this is a written record, but I have not yet been able to trace it.

splashing all about, you would not blame the basin. You would tell the person to stop pouring the water, as it was splashing all about and you could not enjoy yourselves. I am only the vessel. My Heavenly Father is pouring down the water of life freely, and if you can't bear it, call to him not to pour so much."

This next account of Billy jumping for joy is typical of what will become the subject of many disagreements between Billy and some local preachers. Billy gives no indication as to who these people are, nor the identity of the chapel, but there was a man called Richard Sedwell connected with Hicks Mill at the time. So Hicks Mill may be the place, since all Billy's accounts of his early Christian life seem to be connected with this Bible Christian chapel.

Billy writes:

One of our preachers said, if I did not stop cocking[32] up my leg he would tell Brother Sedwel of it. And if he would not stop me, he would tell Mister O'Brian[33] of it. And if he would not stop me, he would turn me out of the communion.

I told him to go and tell that gentleman that Brother Sedwel nor Mister O'Brian did not pardon my sins, for Jesus Christ had pardoned my sins and set my soul at liberty. And while he will give me the power, he do know if they cut off my legs I should cock up

32 Possibly Billy means *kicking*, but I think he is using an old word meaning *lifting*. Modern usage would be *cocking* an eyebrow, or a dog *cocking* a leg to answer a call of nature. Bourne quotes Billy saying at a meeting in the Plymouth area in 1867: "If they were to cut off my feet I should heave up the stumps.""Heave" may be the result of Bourne's coy rewording

33 This is Billy's spelling. Does Billy mean the preacher was prepared to take the matter to the founder of the Bible Christians, William O'Bryan, who was still in Cornwall at this time?

the stumps — and the dear Lord is able to do so, for there is no limits to his power. For in him there is everlasting strength.

In that blessed name of Jesus Christ, the cripple was made strong in the day of Peter. When he went into the temple, walking and leaping and praising God, the people greatly wondered. But Peter did not tell the lame man that he cock up his leg too high. If a lame man could leap for joy, a man that never was lame ought to leap.

You may say, "It is no wonder for him to leap, for it is a new thing to him." And so it was, and it is new too, for there is no old thing in heaven. It is always new, and the last blessing is the best.

Justification is a great blessing, but sanctification is a greater one.

I remember being at Hicks Mill Chapel one Sabbath at class meeting, and a stranger led our class that morning. The leader asked one of our members whether he could say the Lord had cleansed him from all sin or no. And he said he could not say that the Lord had.

I said, "That is sanctification. I will have that by the help of the Lord." I bowed to my knees at once, and said, "Lord, am I sanctified?"

The Lord said unto me, "Thou art clean through the word which I have spoken unto thee."

I said, "Lord, I believe it."

Billy's understanding of sanctification seems to be a second blessing that immediately, or almost immediately, follows salvation. Sanctification is an issue that has challenged theologians, leading to divisive schools of thought on whether it is instant or progressive. At the end of the nineteenth century this led some followers of the Wesleyan tradition to form Holiness and later Pentecostal movements.

The schools are as follows: Positional, stressing 'who we are' in Christ after justification. Sometimes called imputed, the emphasis is that believers have an imputed (given) righteousness from Christ. The Progressive school stresses that sanctification is a life-time call beyond conversion, as the believer co-operates with the Holy Spirit and chooses obedience.

To cover the topic in any more detail would require a whole chapter by a theological expert. Billy mentions the subject several times. Here are three separate quotes from different parts of his Journal. Unfortunately, they may raise more questions than they answer!

> Justification would not make you happy to shout and dance. Sanctification might, and if that would not do it, you may have the sealing of the Spirit. Then you may have a joy unspeakable and full of glory, for the dear Lord told us to ask and receive, that our joy may be full.

> The women that was ashamed to pray, or to speak their experiences, was not ashamed when the dear Lord sanctified them and baptised them with the Holy Ghost sent down from heaven. They had perfect love, and that cast out all fear. The Son had made them free, and they was free indeed.

> We must not only be justified, we must be sanctified and made holy in the Lord. Then we can say, "Lord, thy will be done and not mine." Then we shall hear that beautiful small still voice within.

The ninth verse of hymn 361 in Wesley's 1779 Methodist Hymnbook (410/332 in the Bible Christian Hymnbook), *My God! I know, I feel thee mine*, may help understand the Christian yearning. The words are appropriate whether the Christian is expecting instant or progressive sanctification. The preceding verses call for the Holy Ghost, the Spirit of burning to come.

> Refining fire, go through my heart,
> Illuminate my soul;
> Scatter thy life through every part,
> And sanctify the whole.

John Wesley acknowledged sanctification as the second stage in the Christian life. In his *Plain Account*, sections 24 and 25, he writes that although for many people sanctification takes a lifetime, for some people it can be a sudden event.

Billy continues:

When the leader came to me to ask me the state of my mind, I had good news to tell him. I said, "Four months ago I was a great sinner against God, and since that time I am justified freely and sanctified wholly, for the dear Lord have sanctified me while I have been here this morning. And now, if I was to die this minute, I should be in heaven and be happy for ever, praise the Lord."

When I'd done telling what the Lord had done for me, the leader said to me, "If you can believe it, it is so."

Then I said, "I can believe it." When I told him so, what joy I felt in my heart. I cannot find words to tell of it. O how happy I was.

After our meeting was over that morning I had to go through a railroad. It was a new road. The road seemed to me full of glory, so that it took of my sight. I had a joy unspeakable and full of glory.

Reader, you may say, "How can a man bring forth good things out of his heart?"

Because Christ have took possession of our hearts, and he rules there. And he is all good and no bad, bless and praise his name. Where the devil have a man's heart it is all bad and no good. The devil is a bad master, as so many have found him. You will too, if you do not repent and turn to God. When we are born again we shall know what they enjoy that is born again.

I was so happy and felt such love to God, that I said, "What can I do to be more acceptable in thy sight than I have already done?"

The Lord said in my heart, "Fast this day for my sake."

I said, "I will, Lord."

I did not eat any meat before eight o'clock that night, and that was a good day to me — the best that I ever had for twenty-nine years.[34] Since that day I have had many blessed days, thanks be to God. I

---

34   Billy's age at the time of this event.

went on to fast every Sunday, two meals. I did not take anything from Saturday night till Sunday afternoon four o'clock.

When my neighbours knew about it, they said I shall starve myself. There was a man called Richard Verran. He said to me one day, "The devil is trying to starve thee, for he knows that the Lord have done great things for thee." He was good man, and I believe he said it out of a pure motive.

I said to Richard, "The devil shall not starve me, by the help of the dear Lord, for I can soon know. I will ask the Lord, and he will tell me whether I am right or no."

So I waited until the next Sunday morning, and I came downstairs and left my wife and our two children in the bed. I said, "Now I will ask the Lord whether I must fast or not."

I took my little stool and kneeled down on it, and I said, "Lord, thou knows what the people is telling of, how I shall starve myself. Now, my dear Lord, if I must eat meat, make me happier than I have been."

But I did not feel happier than at other times. Then I said, "Lord, must I fast?"

The power of God came on me so that I fell off the stool. I said, "I do not care what they say, for now I know fully it is the will of the Lord that I should fast."

Some of my brethren used to say to me it would not do for me to fast, for I should be always thinking about the meat. I told them that I would as soon that the devil should tempt me about the meat as any other thing, for he cannot work with me two places at once. If members of the churches was to mortify and not gratify, they would be a great deal happier than they now are. Christians in the days of old used to fast. There was set days for fasting and for praying. John Nelson used to fast Fridays.

Billy finishes by quoting Matthew 6:16 where Jesus tells the people to fast in secret, and not show off about it in public. When he writes in the days of old Billy is probably referring to the time of John Wesley rather than New

Testament times. As he is mentioned in the same breath as *the days of old*, I am assuming that John Nelson is the stonemason from Yorkshire who was converted under John Wesley while working in London in 1739. John Nelson (1707-1774) was in a small team that visited Cornwall with John Wesley in 1743. Nelson soon returned to the north of England, and became well known there and in the Midlands.

These early Methodist preachers must have made an amazing impression on the Cornish people because Billy, writing over 120 years later in 1864, is able to mention John Nelson's name without feeling it necessary to explain who he was.

CHAPTER 4

STRONG AS A LION

BILLY NOW HAS a problem with working in the mine on Sundays, a problem that is nearly going to lose him his job:

At that time we worked in a shaft eight of us together, four cores, two in a core. Our shaft was dry at the bottom where we worked to the ?ninth (nineteenth would be more likely in this account) fathom level, but at the twenty-six there did a stream of water come out of the north wall. There was a fork at that level, and that fork was full in twelve hours. The water was drawn to the surface by a horse whim every twelve hours, and one of we men used to land it.

It was drawn up Saturday nights at six o'clock, at Sunday mornings at six o'clock and in the evening at six o'clock. One Sunday out of eight it was my core to land the water

On the day it was my Sunday to land the water I was at Hicks Mill Chapel. It came into my mind to go to the mine to land the water, and the Lord said unto me, "Stay here and worship me this day."

I said, "I will, Lord."

So I stayed there that Sunday and let the water go to the bottom of the shaft, and it did not hinder no one.

On the Monday morning I went to the mine at six o'clock to land the water. After I had done it, I was going into the other mine. There was two mines there, one was called Cusvey and the other Wheal Fortune, and two captains used to look after both mines. Us worked at Cusvey, and I was going into Wheal Fortune.

I met Captain Hosken coming out, and he said to me, "Where wast thee yesterday, that thee wast not here landing the water?"[35]

I said to him, "It was not the Lord's will that I should come."

He said, "I'll Lord's will thee. Thou shalt not work here any more."

When my captain said so, the Lord spoke in my heart. I said, "I have the Lord of rocks and mountains for my friend, and I do not care who is against me."

When I told him so, the power of the Lord came on me so that I shouted for joy. Then he went before me like a man afraid, for "One shall chase a thousand, and two shall put ten thousand to flight."[36]

Then William Roberts, my comrade that worked with me, said, "Captain Hosken hast turned me away too, and you know that it is not my fault."

I said, "No, you shall not be turned away, for it is my fault, not yours. I will go to him with you and tell him."

I said to the captain, "You must not turn away William Roberts, for it was not his fault. It was my core to land the water, not his,"

Then the captain said to me, "That must be done away in thee, for here in the mines we must work Sunday."

I said to him, "I have a new master, and he is a good one, bless and praise his holy name. And he tell me that I must not work on the Sabbath day, but keep it holy. I shall do as he tell me, by his help, and shall not work any more on the Sabbath day."

The clerk that was in the counting house, he was called Mister Mitchel, said, "If I feel like William Bray do, I would not work Sunday neither."

Then the captain said, "Thee should go to work if thou wants."

I said to him, "That is no good, for I shall not work Sundays. Have you any place else to put me to work?"

He said, "Thee may go down to the engine and wheel away the ashes from the engine if you will."

---

35 This is Bourne's spelling. Billy spells the mine captain's name both Hosken and Hoskin.

36 Deuteronomy 32:30

I was glad when he said so, for I could go to meetings or preaching every night. If I was working underground I could not, for us work underground some cores by night.

So I took my wheelbarrow and went to the engine and wheeled away the ashes, and they that I seed I told them what the Lord had done for me. One man cried for mercy, and a revival began at Twelveheads Chapel. I asked the Lord whether I should go down to Twelveheads or not, and the Lord said to me, "Go."

Bourne's comment is worth including here:

Whatever people may think about Billy's statements that he heard the voice of God forbidding him to do this, and directing him to do that, or about his belief that God would not allow any harm to be done by the water on the Sunday, surely all must admire Billy's fidelity to his conscience and to God, and his courage in acting up to his convictions of truth and duty, whatever the result might be to himself.

Billy continues:

So I left my barrow and the ashes pile, and went away to the chapel. And there I was wanted, for the old professors[37] was very dead at that time, and would come into the chapel with their hats under their arms and look very black on us.

But the Lord was with us and he tore a hole in Satan's kingdom, for I have seen people crying. The young converts have said to me, "William, there is someone crying. Go and speak to him."

And I said, "Let us give a good shout."

We gave a shout and he would fall down, and six or seven more. The Lord would give me power that I could leap for joy when I saw so many fall down and cry for mercy. I think we had nearly a

---

37   The men presumably professed to be "born again" by going to an evangelical chapel, but Billy sees no evidence of this in their lives and attitudes. See box on page 40.

hundred converted in one week, and that was the first week that ever I worked for the Lord. I was twenty-nine years old then, and now I am three score years and ten, and I have the Lord this day in my heart, the hope of glory. Bless and praise his holy name for what he done for me and many more.

It was setting day at our mine on Friday that week, our taking day once a month.[38] When I was at Twelveheads Chapel it came into my mind, "I have a good mind to go to the mine as it is taking day, and try to take on." But I said, "No, I will work this week for the Lord."

It was not long after that, in that same day, that two or three men came to the chapel to call me out. They said, "You are going to work with we in Chapels Shaft, for Captain Hosken hast told us to take you with us."

Now this Captain Hosken was the same man that turned me away. So I worked that week for the Lord (at Twelveheads), and we had a blessed week. We had a hundred converted to God, and the revival went on. I may with boldness say that there is many up in heaven praising God now that was converted in that revival, bless and praise his holy name.

I went on Monday morning to the mine to see the place that the Lord had got for me, for I believe he got that place for me while I was working for the Lord. It was a good one too.

The miners said, "Bray will be forced to work Sundays now he is gone in Chapels Shaft. For they that sinked from the hundred-and-twenty to the hundred-and-thirty,[39] they have a hundred barrels of water in a core. So Bray is into it now."

38 When miners bid for contracts and took on men to work with them.

39 These are fathoms. There are 6 feet (nearly 2 metres) to a fathom, making the mine 780 feet (247 metres) deep at this time.

But they missed,[40] for the Lord got that place for me. My comrade and me was the first of the pair that begun to work under the hundred-and-thirty. We was eight men and four boys, working six hours a core. Two men and a boy in one core, the boy to draw the stuff, and we was all happy.[41] We always prayed before we went to work, and after we had done. The Lord was with us, bless and praise his holy name, for he is good.

So we pecked our shaft, and when the engine was idle the water would come back up through the level and fill up our shaft. As soon as the engine go to work, the water would be all gone again. We did not draw one barrel of water in all the way of sinking to the other level. The place that I was turned away from, because I would not work Sundays, I got about two pounds in a month. In this new place I got five pounds in a month, or more, and I did not work as hard by a great deal as I did before.

So the Lord cleared my way for ever from working Sundays. When I have been going to my plan I have met with the sump shaft men singing for men to go to Capson. They have said to me, "It is no use to press you, for you will not go."

"No," I said, "I shall not go, for I am going to work this day for the Lord."

So I did not lose by serving the Lord, for I got three pounds a month more than I had before, and done the will of the Lord. And that is better than all the money in this world, for: It is a heaven below, our Jesus to know; and while we do his blessed will, we bear our heaven about us still.

40 Here, and in other places, *to miss* means to get it wrong.

41 Many times Billy writes about people who are *happy and die happy*. As we have seen, Billy considers someone with a deep, outwardly demonstrated faith to be happy, as with his companions here. It is important to bear this in mind when reading some accounts, where the ending is not so much a happy-ever-after story, as an indication of a person's deep Christian faith.

After we had sinked down the shaft to the other level, we went in further east to sink that we call a winze.[42] We began at the same level that we pecked the shaft, and my comrade said to me, "We pecked the shaft and had good luck in the shaft." My comrade was working in a pool of water when he said so.

I said, "We shall have good luck in the winze too. For if the Lord would save Sodom and Gomorrah for ten righteous, he will give us a dry winze for two."

By the time the word was out of my mouth my comrade threw in the pick, and down went all the water in a moment. We done well there too, so we can see that the Lord can work miracles as well as in days of old. He is the same Lord, and there is no limits to his power, bless his holy name.

To have that God for our enemy, what shall we do? It was better for us that we was never born. But to have the Lord for our friend we are right, and all is well. Live or die, we are the Lord's. Underground or to grass,[43] the Lord do know where we are. He is with us, and he knows when danger is near.

I never shall forget that day when the Lord saved the lives of my comrade and me. As I said before, we always prayed before we went to work, and after we left work we always prayed the last thing. At that time we were underground cutting what we call a winze plat,[44] and we was working away and it came into me at once to go back in the level and pray.

As soon as the thought took my mind I took my comrade by the hand, and said to him, "Let us go back and pray."

---

42 A vertical shaft connecting passages within a mine, but one that does not come through to the surface.

43 A miners' term for the surface.

44 A flat area at the top of the winze (internal shaft) for storing rock and ore.

We went back to pray, and while we was praying the Lord threw down two rocks, and we thought them to be ten hundredweight[45] a rock. At this time I had a new comrade and he was not converted. I said to him, "If the stones had fell upon me, I should have been in heaven by this time."

My poor dear comrade, how wisht he did look. And well he might, for he was very near hell and I was very near heaven. It seem clear to me that if I had not been converted we should have been killed, both of us, for prayer was the very thing that called us away from that danger. Prayer do belong to heaven and to heavenly-minded people, and it is the Lord that puts it in their minds. You may ask, "Why did the Lord put it in your mind to pray?"

Because he is good, and would not the death of one sinner, but rather they would all repent and come to heaven. The dear Lord was not willing to send my comrade to hell, and he had more work for me to do. So he spared both our lives. While we went back to pray, he thrown down the rocks, and we was spared.

Bourne quotes Billy as saying:

Soon after I was converted, the devil said to me, "Billy Bray, you'll be a great man." But I sunk into nothing, and in that way slipped through the devil's hands.

Bourne tells us:

A year after his conversion[46] Billy began to speak publicly, telling people to repent and turn to God. Towards the end of 1824 his name was put on the local Preachers' Plan, and his hard work led to the conversion of many souls.

45 Ten hundredweight = half a ton. Billy clearly has an innate belief in the sovereignty of God.

46 Billy was converted in November 1823.

PREACHERS' PLANS

The Bible Christians, in common with the Methodists, did not have a minister in charge of one chapel. A minister was appointed to run a group of chapels, and had a list of preachers to call on. The Bible Christian list included women as well as men.

These preachers travelled from chapel to chapel, often visiting more than one chapel on a Sunday, so the congregation saw a range of preachers throughout the year. A 'fixture list' called a plan was drawn up to cover several months. The group of chapels was known as a Circuit, and this system is operated today in the Methodist Church. Billy was a preacher, but he was never ordained.

Billy did not usually select a text, but sometimes began his address by reciting a verse of a hymn, or telling a little of his own experience. He had such a way of speaking that young and old, all social classes, the rich as much as the poor, and the worldly as much as the committed Christians flocked to hear him, and he retained his popularity until the last.

As he travelled around the Circuit preaching, Billy wore the clothes he had before his conversion. He tells us:

As I have said in this Journal, before I was converted I was a bad drunkard. I had not much best clothes, for it cost me too much money in tobacco and drink to buy them, and my best clothes was very poor. As the dear Lord had converted my soul, I felt that he called me to try to convert others. The dear Lord gave me power to do his will, and my poor clothes did not keep me home.

I had a very poor low price fustian[47] jacket for best, and a poor suit of clothes. I went in these clothes as they was, to Flushing, Penryn, Falmouth and Camborne, and to other places as the dear Lord opened my ways. These clothes was better than I deserved, for I deserved to be down in hell fire with the devil and his angels. But O the mercy of our God, he did not let me wear these clothes long.

He put it in the heart of servant girl, and she went to one of the Quaker Friends and told him that she knew a man, and she believed he was a good man but he was very poor, and he wanted a coat and a waistcoat. She asked him whether he had a coat laid by that he could give to a poor man.

The Quaker said he no such thing as a coat in his house laid by, but he said to her, "I will give him the coat that I wear, and waistcoat."[48]

Then he took off his coat and waistcoat and gave them to the girl, and the girl brought them to me from Falmouth, and that was nine miles from our house. Now who the Quaker Friend was I do not know, but the dear Lord do know, for he put it in his heart to give them to me. If he done it to God's glory he will have his reward, for they that give to the poor lend to the Lord.

When the servant girl bring the clothes to me, the clothes suited me as if they was made for me. The clothes that good friend gave me ?hould me for years. The Quaker Friends have been good friends to me all through life, for they have gave me clothes to wear, and clothes to cover me in my bed, and shoes on my feet when I do want them.

47 Fustian cloth was a thick cotton twill, rather like the material of jeans, usually dyed to a dark colour.

48 The coat is probably what we call a jacket, not an over-coat. Billy gets an overcoat later.

Billy has continued the Sunday fast he started at Hicks Mill Chapel, on the Sunday when he had his experience of sanctification:

Many times while going to my plan I have been so happy that I would not exchange my dinner that I have had from heaven, not for the richest dinner on the earth. I used to go Penryn, Flushing and Falmouth to my plan in one day. Flushing in the morning at half past ten, and noon to Falmouth for half past two, and then it would be between four and five o'clock on the Sunday evening.

I always went with the first friend that asked me to their house, and when I have taken tea[49] I have gone to my evening plan at six o'clock again. When we had done our service it would be near eight at night, and then I had nine or ten miles to walk home – and all the food I have had is one meal from Saturday night till Sunday night, ten or eleven o'clock. I spoke three times and walked nearly twenty miles. It was not because I could not have it, for I had good friends and I might have what meat I would – and it was a great deal better than I had at home to my main table. But I had better still than any of their rich tables would afford, for it is better than meat or drink to do the will of the dear Lord.

I remember one time that I was planned to Flushing in the morning at half past ten, and that was nine miles from our house. I walked there and supplied my plan, and after the service I was asked to a friend's house to dinner. I did not go, for I went to Penryn to hear friend Tregaskis preach, not knowing I was planned at that time.

I took my plan out of my pocket and saw that I was planned at Mylor Bridge by half past two, and it was already near half past two. I said, "Now I must run in the Lord's service, for I used to run

49   Billy has already said, *"I went on to fast every Sunday, two meals. I did not take anything from Saturday night till Sunday afternoon four o'clock."* It looks as though the fast was often until teatime but sometimes much later, and always involved missing the first two Sunday meals. Maybe Billy is only referring to drinking tea here.

in the devil's service. I have a new master, and I must run for he. He will help me, and so he did, bless his holy name.

When I came to Mylor Bridge it was twenty minutes after the appointed time, and the people was waiting for me. I told them what the Lord told me to tell them, and I had a very good time, for the Lord was in our minds to make us happy and bless us. Some friends asked me to go to tea with them, but I did not. I went to Penryn again, for I was planned at Falmouth that evening at six o'clock.

As I was going from Mylor Bridge back to Penryn through the fields, I thought myself almost as strong as a lion. When I came to Penryn, I took tea at a friend's house, and then I went to Falmouth to my appointment that evening where we had a good meeting. From there I had nine miles home and had to walk. I wish to honour the blessed Lord, for I could not have done it if he had not helped me. I walked between twenty and thirty miles that day, and had meat but once, and did not want it. I had better food there than this world could give me, for I had mine from heaven.

I am sorry there is a great many dead professors in our world that is not alive to God. There was a man that I knew and his name was John, and he was up in Devonshire when I was. We both came home to our own county, Cornwall, and went to meet with the people. He went to meet with the Methodists, and I to meet with the Bible Christians where I was put on the plan to exhort the people to turn to God. And many did turn to the Lord and was made happy, blessing and praise and glory and honour be to him that sits upon the throne for ever and ever.

When I was planned to the chapel near where John lived, he always came to hear me. When I had done speaking he would take his hat and leave the chapel. The reason that John left the chapel was because, after I had done speaking and come down out of the pulpit, we that was happy had what we call a Victory through the blood of the Lamb. Some of us singing, some of shouting and some dancing: that is what we call a Victory. It is not through a pope or a priest, but through the blood of that Lamb that was slain on Mount Calvary.

THE VICTORY

This is not a term that is generally known today. It seems to be an ecstatic outpouring of faith. Billy writes about an occasion when the preacher orders the people to stop their meeting, and there may be a connection. *I said unto him, "How did you come to stop our revival?"* The preacher tells Billy, *"Because they was offering of strange fire. They was making a noise for nothing."*

In the early editions of *The King's Son* Bourne mentions the Victory, but puts the excerpt from Billy's *Journal* in the third person. *"Some singing, some praying, some shouting, some dancing; scenes to be frequently witnessed when the Cornish people get what they call the 'victory' through the blood of the Lamb."* In later editions of *The King's Son* Bourne omits the words *through the blood of the Lamb*. I find myself asking why.

The chapter in the later editions that contains the shortened reference to the Victory ends halfway down a page, so space was not a problem. (A chapter is often shortened during editing to prevent it over-running a page by a line or two.) Towards the end of the nineteenth century the Bible Christians were making moves to merge with the Methodists, and might not have wanted to put too much emphasis on their past exuberance. But why omit only Billy's last few words? Perhaps Bourne did not want to imply a scriptural authority for the *Victory*, but was unwilling to remove the whole account.

We had the blessed heavenly shower of divine love, and some called us fools and some called us mad men and women, but bless the Lord he made us glad and happy men and women. We did not care what they said, and John was one of them that had a bad attitude.

One Sunday I was planned to the chapel near where John lived, and John dreamed that same morning that he was going through a village, and there was in that village three houses. He thought in his dream that it was a Sunday, and it was.

When John came through the village he saw in his dream one house door open, and he looked in and thought he never saw so many plain looking people in a class meeting in all his life. One of the members came out of the house and walked along the road with him.

John said to him, "You are some plain ?partey class of people back there. What do you call yourselves?"

He said, "We are some of the old primitive Christians, and there is none like us in all the earth." Then he stopped, and said, "Accept little William Bray down at Twelveheads."

So I came to my plan that day to the chapel near where John lived, and spoke to the people in my usual way. When I had done speaking, and came down among my brethren, we contended for the Victory again. Some of us was singing, some shouting and some danced. But John did not go away, for the Lord had convinced him that we was right and he was wrong.

After our service was over that Sunday afternoon John came to me, and said, "Will you go home with me and have some tea, and see Jane my wife? For she want to see you so."

I went home with John and he told me how he liked to hear me speaking, but he did not like to see me dance and hear me shouting and seeming so. He said, "But the Lord hast convinced me in a dream that you are right and I am wrong."

John came many times to the chapel after that when I had been planned there, but he did not go away, for he joined with us in praising God. John lived a good life and died a happy death. I may say he is now in heaven, for I saw him when he was near death and I asked him whether he remembered the dream that he dreamed about me.

"Yes," he said," and if thou hadst thrown me over thy head I should think thee all right."

Reader, you may ask, "Who made you right?" Not Peter nor the pope nor the cardinal nor the priest. There was but one that could make us right, and that is the dear Jesus that died on the cross. He will make you right, as well as John and me, if you are willing to be made so. John is not tempted against shouting now he is in heaven, for there is ten thousand times ten thousand, and thousands of thousands in that happy place, saying to him that hath loved us and washed us in his own blood, "To him be glory and honour and power, to the Lamb for ever and ever." [50]

So John have done with the doubters and he is got up to heaven with the shouters. They that love the dear Lord will praise him, because they feel his love in their hearts.

50   Rev 5:13

CHAPTER 5

BETHEL CHAPEL

BILLY NOW STARTS to build his first chapel, which will be called Bethel. Bourne says some of Billy's friends who lacked his faith told him he had better build it with a chimney – because it would be easier to turn it into a cottage if it did not succeed as a chapel.

To this Billy retorted, "No, I will have no chimney in it, except it be to drive the devil out through!"

Billy built Bethel Chapel around 1830, possibly slightly earlier, between Cross Lanes and Twelveheads close to the house where Billy was born. There is no official indenture, because the land belonged to his mother. Very few buildings remain in the area today, but the shell of Billy's family home is still standing and can be seen in a nearby farmyard.

Here is Billy's account from his *Journal*:

> In the neighbourhood where we lived there was a great many uneducated, dark, wicked people, and chapels there were very few. The Lord put it into my mind to build a chapel. My mother had a small plot of land, and by one of her little fields there was piece of common. The dear Lord opened my mother's heart to give us a place in that piece of common to build a chapel, or house to worship God in.
>
> I begun to work as the dear Lord bid me, and take away the hedge and clean out the foundations. Many will have to praise God that ever Bethel Chapel was built, for many is in heaven already that was born there.
>
> In that day there was but one little small chapel in our neighbourhood that is called Twelveheads, and it did belong to the

Wesleyans.[51] Our people had a place in the little old spams house[52] to preach. The place where our people preached would hold a score or thirty people, so we wanted a place to preach, and the people wanted a place to hear.

Paul had a thorn in the flesh and so had I, for I had not only the wicked ones against me. We had a little class in the little stamps house where we preached, and most of them turned against me and tried to turn our preachers against me. But with all they could do they could not hurt me, though they made me a little uneasy at times when I saw them so cross.

So I got out the foundations of the Lord's house, and we had preaching on the foundation stone.

John Ashworth in *Strange Tales Volume 5* published in the 1870s, says Billy stood on the stone and told the people, "If this new chapel, which they say is to be called Bethel, stands one hundred years, and one soul be converted in it every year, that will be one hundred souls – and one soul is worth more than all Cornwall." Billy then danced on the stone, and shouted "Glory, glory, bless the Lord!" This was probably noted by an eyewitness. In *The Ship Where Christ Was Captain* (1926) Pearse repeats the story. Billy is going to write more or less these same words in his *Journal* in relation to Kerley Downs.

Billy continues:

One of our neighbours said, "I will not give William Bray anything toward that chapel he is building."

He had two horses that drew the whim around at the mine, and one of them was taken lame in the field and lost many days' work. Then

---

51 Presumably the chapel that Billy's grandfather had helped build.

52 This is Billy's spelling. Probably it was a converted stamps house (see later), where ore was once crushed.

the people said, "It is because he would not give anything to William Bray's chapel."

But the people must know it was not William Bray's, it was the dear Lord's chapel. The Lord might punish him because he was greedy, for the chapel was not much good to he. He died very soon and the Lord enabled me to build the chapel without his help.

When I had took down the field hedge, and had cleaned out the foundations, and had some stone hauled to the place where the chapel was to be built, and the masons had built some of the walls, I had one pound fifteen shillings given to me by friends towards the building of the chapel.

Then the devil entered into some of my classmates, and they said that the chapel ought not to be built there. When they saw that they could not stop me from building the chapel, they went to our preacher and tell him that he ought to stop me from building the chapel there, for that was not the place for the chapel. They told him it ought to built at Twelveheads, or at Tapta Stamptes.[53]

Then our preacher came to me and told me how the class had been to him, to stop me from building the chapel there. I told the preacher that the Lord had put me to build the chapel there — and the dear Lord did.

When the class had been so hard at me, sometimes I said, "I have a good mind not to touch the chapel." But the minute I said so, I have felt my mind dark and very unhappy.

53   Above the words *Tapta Stamptes,* in another handwriting, is *Teppets Stamps,* with a possible dot over the first e. I can find no trace of a similar name today, but Bourne calls it *Tippets Stamps,* so maybe he knew the place. I am copying all Billy's spellings, as they may help identify the area that must have been large enough to have the potential to require a chapel. Nowadays there are so few houses remaining that it is impossible for visitors to appreciate that anywhere around here could ever have supported a chapel.

When I have felt so dark, I have said, "Yes, I will build the chapel, my dear Lord." And then I should feel happy again. I write this to let you know that the Lord helped me in building the chapels that I have built, or they would never be built.

Now to return to my tale again. I showed the preacher what I had done already towards building the chapel.

He said, "They be telling me that the chapel ought to be at Twelveheads or Tapta Stamptes. It is our preaching night, and will you be willing to cast lots whether you shall build there or not?" [54]

"Yes," I said. "If it is not the Lord's will that the chapel shall be built there, I do not want to build it."

So in the evening we went to preaching, and most of our little class was there, and the men that was against me. After preaching, our preacher wrote three lots: Twelveheads, Tepa Stampes and Cross Lanes. Now Cross Lanes was the place where I was building my chapel. When they drew the lots, the lot came out for Cross Lanes to be place. Then they said to our preacher they would help me to get on raising stones for the chapel. But telling about it that night was all they did to help me.

The following day one of them came me, and said, "We shall not help you, for Cross Lanes did not ought to be the lot."

So I was as well off as I thought I should be with them. Then I worked away and rose stone and mortar, and put the mason to work. The Lord helped me, for I was very poor and had no money of my own. But the dear Lord rose up friends and sent me money to pay the mason, and we got the chapel walls up, and got timber for the roof and got it sawed and got it up, but we had not timber

---

54 Drawing lots was a practice carried out by Charles and
    John Wesley, as was opening the Bible at a random page
    to read a verse in order to get a message. In the book of
    Acts the Apostles chose between Matthias and
    Barsabbas using lots, a practice carried out by some
    Christian groups today after a time of much prayer.

enough by one sile.[55] So I asked my Heavenly Father to send me some timber or some money to make or buy a sile.

That morning there was a Wesleyan local preacher at home praying, and the Lord said to him while he was on his knees, "Go down and give William Bray a pound note."

Until 1971 the British currency consisted of pounds, shillings and pence (£–s–d). There were 20 shillings (s) to the pound (£) and 12 pennies (d) to the shilling, making 240 pennies to the pound. 'Sovereign' was the name of the coin whose face value was £1.

In the time of Billy Bray (the first part of the nineteenth century) an annual wage of twenty-five pounds (£25, or ten shillings a week) would support a mining family if they had a small amount of land for growing vegetables. The tribute system, where individual miners bid for work at the mines, meant the pay varied considerably month to month. This often led to severe poverty if the tribute was badly judged by the miner.

At that time there was no sovereigns. There was a one pound note on paper. It was drawn on the banks, and was worth twenty shillings. So when the preacher had his breakfast he came down to me by the chapel, and he said to me, "What do you want a pound note for?"

I said unto him, "To buy timber to put up a sile on that end of the chapel."

He said, "I never felt such a thing in all my life. While I was home praying this morning, it was always coming into my mind to go down and give you a pound note. And here it is for you."

55 *Sile* is Billy's spelling. The word is probably *sill,* but clearly not something as small as a window sill. Bourne uses the word *principal,* presumably meaning a main beam for the roof. Whatever it was, it was obviously an expensive item.

So I had the note, and I went to Truro and bought a sile, and put it up on the chapel. And there it is to this day. When the timber was up on the roof, I went around and gathered two pounds toward covering the chapel.

At that time we had children, and the youngest of them was taken very ill. When my little maid was taken ill, Satan tempted me that it would take seven pounds to cover the chapel, and I had but two pounds, and our little maid would die. It would take one pound to bury her, and then I should have but one pound left.

The devil tempted me very much on that point. If I wanted it, I had a right to take it, for the dear Lord and me in this place kept but one purse. I paid my money that I got at the mine to the chapel when I wanted it. So I had but one to give my account to, and that was the dear Lord, the very best comrade that man can ever have.

So the devil tempted me that the child would die, and it would take one pound out of the two to bury her. While he was tempting me so sore, for it was sore, it came into my mind: I shall be paid for building this chapel.

Then it came into my mind, "Yes, because thou hast build this chapel, I will save thy child's life."

I said, "Where is this coming from?"

It was said to me, "I am the God of Abraham, Isaac and Jacob. Be nothing doubting. It is me, said the Lord."

I believed it, and it was so. I went home to my house and said to my wife, "Our child (the words "will not" must be missing here in the Journal) die for the Lord told me so."

My wife said, "Do not say so, William. The neighbours say she will die, for she is very bad."

I went to work to the mine, and when I came home the child was not anything better and had not eaten any meat. All that night the child wasn't anything better, and all the forenoon of the following day she was very ill. When I came in to dinner the child was nothing better.

I was afternoon core at the mine, and ever since the dear Lord converted my soul I always felt it my duty to pray with my wife and children before I leave my house to go to work. We knelt to pray, and the child was lying down in the window seat. We had what was very plentiful in that our day, and that was fish and 'taters for dinner.

In my prayer, I said, "My dear Lord, thou hast said that my child shall live, and she have not eat any meat yet."

She begun to eat meat there and then, and she is living now. She is the mother of ten children, and she is well to this day, bless and praise the dear Lord for it.[56] So here the dear Lord made the devil a liar, for I did not want one pound out of the two to bury my child, as the devil said I should. The old devil did not do me any hurt, he only made me the bolder. But I had only two pounds, and the chapel would cost seven.

When the roof was on, I went and borrowed a horse and rode ten or twelve miles from where I lived, up among the farmers. I asked one of them whether he had any reed to sell, for I wanted three hundred sheaves. He told me he had, and it was two pounds for a hundred sheaves. I told the farmer to bring three hundred sheaves to me as fast as he could, and some spears for them. But I did not tell him I had no more than two pounds.

He brought down one hundred at the first and some spears, and I had three pounds when he came. I paid him for the hundred sheaves of reed and the spears. Then I had a few shillings left, and that was all I had. I told the farmer to bring away more reed as fast as he could. I did not tell him I had not money to pay him for it. I had no need to, for before the farmer was a mile off from our place

56   "Well to this day" is 1864, the time Billy is writing his
      Journal. Billy's youngest daughter was called Grace. In
      1846, at the age of eighteen, she married William Davey,
      a labourer from St Neot. The 1861 census shows seven
      children. There may have been more born later, or
      perhaps Billy is including some who died young, for
      there are enough gaps in the birth dates to allow for this.
      See Appendix 3.

the dear Lord sent a friend with two pounds to me. So as the reed was brought by the farmer, the Lord sent me money to pay him.

I put the thatcher to work to cover the roof, and that cost one pound ten shillings, with a little other work. When he came to be paid I had but one pound, and wanted ten shillings more to pay the thatcher.

There was a high road where a great many people go up and down to work, and dear Lord put it in my mind to go down in the road. I came in the road and the first person I saw was PB.[57]

I said to him, "PB, you have not gave me anything yet towards my father's house."

"No, nor I shall not," says he.

I said to him, "What, are you amind for the Lord to say to you in that day, 'You saw me a-hungered and gave me no meat, and saw me athirst and gave me no drink, and a stranger took me not in'?"[58]

He said to me, "I do not care if I do give you ten shillings."

I said, "That is the money that I want."

So he gave me the ten shillings and I went and paid the thatcher. Then I wanted timber for the door and windows, and for the forms.[59] There was a mine, and that mine was stopped, and they was selling off the timber. There was a bargain of timber that would cost one pound six shillings, and I had not money to buy it. A friend came and asked me whether I'd been to the mine and bought any timber.

I told him no, for I had no money. That friend gave me one pound, and with some money the dear Lord sent me from other places I

---

57 Billy often uses initials and gives no other identity. Bourne sometimes uses initials, even where Billy has given the full name in his *Journal*. Where a name is given, I am always using it.

58 Matthew 25:35-46

59 Benches.

was able to buy and pay the one pound six shillings to the mine and have the timber. Then I wanted the timber brought home to my dear Lord's house, or chapel.

I wanted a horse and cart, and one our neighbours had a horse. So I went to this neighbour and asked him to lend me his horse. He said to me, "You may have her, but she will not draw anything."

I said, "I will have her and try what she will do."

So I had my neighbour's mare, or horse, and put her in the cart and went away to the mine for the timber. I never saw a better mare in my life. I did not touch her with whip or stick, and we had steep hills to come up over.

So I brought home all the timber, and when I brought my neighbour's mare to him he asked me how she drawed with me.

I told him, "I never saw a better mare in all my life."

Then said he, "I never heard such a thing, for she will not draw with anyone else."

That mare was working that day for a very strong company. If you ask me who they was, they are the Father, Son and Holy Ghost. Horses, angels, men and devils must obey them. If there was no one there of more power than Billy Bray, the mare would have been as bad with him as she was with others. But bless and praise the name of the dear Lord, he said, "The horse shall work, for the timber is to seat my house." And what the dear Lord say shall be obeyed.

In the counting house of that same mine there was a very large cupboard. It was very large and high. There was an old friend of mine that said, "I will buy that cupboard, for he will do for a pulpit for William Bray's chapel."

There was another man that was a landlord, that said, "And I will buy that cupboard."

Then said my old friend, "That cupboard is for a pulpit in William Bray's chapel. If you buy the cupboard…

The rest of this line, and the next ten lines, are crossed out, down to the bottom of the page (page 128 in the *Journal*). It is possible to read some words through the crossing out.

Haslam, Bourne, Pearse and Ashworth tell the story of Billy personally purchasing a large cupboard at an auction sale, and using it as a pulpit. Bourne, Pearse and Ashworth say it was bought for Kerley Downs. Billy writes that the mine was closed, and the cupboard came from the same place, and at the same time, as the timber he bought for Bethel. I explore some possible explanations in Appendix 2, where I give my best attempt at reading the crossed out section.

Billy continues:

Some said I ought to put chembels[60] in my chapel, and some said, "When the chapel is built you shall not have it planned."[61] So I went on and finished my chapel.

When the Lord's house was finished, some of them said, "Now your chapel is finished you shall not have preaching there."

When they said so, I locked up my chapel door and carried the key home to my house and hanged the key to the nail behind the door.

I said, "Lord, there is the key, and I have done what thou hast told me to do. The chapel is built and there is the key. If it is thy will that the key shall stay there for seven years, or thy will that the key shall be taken down every minute in the day, thy will be done, my dear Lord."

That day our preachers planned our chapel more than I should ask if I was there, for they named my chapel and called it Bethel. We had preaching every Sabbath at half past two, six in the evening, and a class meeting in the morning. We got on well there, for the Lord soon revived his work and we had a great many members.

There was a new large chapel built by the old one that is called Bethel. The old is kept for a school and for class meetings.[62] No

60 Chimneys

61 Put on the Circuit Plan.

62 The original Bethel no longer exists, because of the massive depopulation of this area when the mines

wonder for the devil to be against me and put his servants to hinder me from building of Bethel Chapel, for I saw at one time fifteen[63] down asking for mercy, and mercy they had. Some of them is now in heaven praising the dear Lord, and will praise him for ever.

I remember something that took place when I was building Bethel Chapel. There was a brother called R, and he was a very good man, but his wife was a very bad, wicked woman. She was dirty and would sometimes throw water in his face, and she was bad in most every way. One day she provoked him so that he swore. Then he was in a very bad way.

When she had provoked him so that he swore, he found that he had sinned, and he was asking the Lord to have mercy upon him. Satan was very hard on him, telling him that it was no use for him to pray, for no one would believe for him.[64] But good the dear Lord is, for he is not willing that one of his children perish, but he always supply them in time of need.

When I was working about the chapel, the Lord spoke to me, "Go up and restore thy brother R, for he is fallen."

So I throwed down the shovel that I was working with and went away to my brother's house. When I came to his house, he and his wife was there. His wife began to curse him and tell me what her husband had said. When she had done, I told her what the dear Lord told the Jews when the woman was taken in adultery, in the very act.

closed. The replacement is still in existence, and is currently in a good state of preservation and in domestic use . A mound is all that is left of the original chapel, and it can be seen close to the lane, in the field opposite the 'new' Bethel.

63   In *The King's Son* Bourne puts the figure as fifty, but fifteen is clearly written in Billy's *Journal*. It may be that Bourne is right and he recognised Billy's figure as a mistake

64   Presumably Billy means they would not be influenced by his faith.

I said unto his wife, "If you are without fault, cast a stone at him."

Then I asked him to go out with me, and we walked about together, Brother R and myself. I said to him, "Brother R, what is the devil telling you of? Is he not telling of you that no person will believe for you any more?"

"Yes," he said, "it comes into my mind."

"That is the devil," I said. "The dear Lord sent me to you, and the dear Lord is on your side. And I am on your side and you need not fear."

While I was talking to him just in that way, the Lord sent to him another brother to encourage him. That brother was well off in the world and was very liberal with what the dear Lord gave him. This rich brother said to Brother R, "You are better to go to Penryn with William Bray next Sunday."

Brother R said, "I have no shoes to go on Sunday to Penryn."

The rich brother said to him, "You shall have shoes off me."

Then R said, "I will go."

The shoes he had off our dear brother, and he was not the only one that my brother gave shoes to. He have clothed many of the dear Lord's children, and fed them too.

Sunday came and I was planned to Penryn that day. Brother R and me went to my plan and the dear Lord was with us and made us very happy, for the dear Lord blessed Brother R. We came home that Sunday night, light and glad in the Lord, and Brother R was more on his guard afterwards.

Some time after that I was planned to Penryn again. The Lord blessed Brother R in a wonderful manner, for he was with me, and the dear Lord sanctified his soul. So R had to praise the Lord that ever he went to Penryn with me to my plan, for he was well paid for his journey.

But his wife was still his enemy, for she done all to put him back to the world. She was very bad to him, and he came and told me how bad she was.

I said, "Do not beat her on any account, but pray for her, that the dear Lord may convert her and make her happy."

He said, "The Lord hast converted her twice already, and she has gone back again."

I said, "You pray for her, and if she is not better, the Lord will take she from you, or you from she very soon."

It was not long after that before she was taken ill and she soon died. Brother R lived many years after, a very happy man. He married another wife and they lived together happy and died happy,[65] and now they are in heaven praising of that God that they loved and served here on this earth.

---

65 A reminder might not be out of place here of the way Billy considers someone with an outwardly demonstrated faith to be *happy*. So this is not a clichéd happy-ever-after ending, but an expression of the couple's deep Christian faith.

CHAPTER 6

KERLEY DOWNS CHAPEL

NEVER ONE TO SIT around after a hard day's work in the mine, Billy now sees that church planting is something that God is calling him to undertake. However, although he has the energy to dig out the stone and help build the walls, lack of funds is a major obstacle. The problems facing Billy can perhaps be summed up as: no land, no money, no chapel! And not everyone can see things from Billy's point of view.

This is the second Billy's chapel-building accounts. Kerley Downs was probably finished in 1836, but seems to have been started much earlier. The Billy Bray Memorial Trust holds the Indenture for this chapel, and a transcription of the first section is reproduced in Appendix 4 with permission of the Trust. A transcription of the whole document can be found on www.billybray.com.

Billy writes:

A little while after I had done building Bethel Chapel, the Lord said to me, "As I have made thee an instrument in my hands of building Bethel Chapel, so I will make thee instrumental in building a chapel at Kerley Downs too."

When the dear Lord said so, I believed it, and I rejoiced greatly to think that I was so honoured to work for so good a master as the King of heaven and earth and sky.

Kerley Downs was near a mile from where I lived and it was in the same parish, the parish of Kea. At Kerley Downs they had their preaching in a dwelling house, and they had a class meeting in the same house, and it was a small one. There was a house near the house they preached in, and it belonged to a widow woman.

Some of the society friends agreed with the woman to buy her house to make it into chapel, and she agreed with them to sell her house. We had preaching there at the woman's house and made a collection, meaning to make the house into a chapel, but they was deceived. After she had agreed with them, someone offered her more money and she let that man have it. And there was no way opened for near twelve months.

About twelve months after, one of the neighbours that had a farm said to one of the class, "Where is that money you collected so long ago to build a chapel and had not done it yet? If your people have a mind to build a chapel, they shall have ground off me."

When the farmer had offered the brother the land to build the chapel, the brother came to me and told me what the farmer had said. Then I went to the friend,[66] for he was a friend and is still. Because he was good to the Lord's cause, the dear Lord is good to he, and that good old friend is living still.

I went to our preacher and told him that we could have a piece at Kerley Downs to build a chapel. I told him if he did not call a meeting and appoint trustees, I would begin about the chapel myself.

So he appointed a day and got trustees, and one man that was at our trust meeting said what he would do. And he never done anything, for I never saw him there until the chapel was built and opened.

We had piece of a hedge to take away before we could clean out the foundations where our chapel was to be built, and before the hedge was taken away all them that promised to help me left me. So my little son and me went on and got some stone, and the good friend

66 Probably the farmer who farmed the land although Billy's 'friend' here could a Quaker Friend, who is still a Quaker, and was the legal leaseholder who sublet to the farmer. According to the Indenture, the leaseholder was a carpenter. See Appendix 4.

that gave us the land to build the chapel let me have his horse and cart to draw stone. He did not charge anything for his horse and cart or land that I know of, but made it a sacrifice to the dear Lord.

When my little son and me went on and got stone and mortar, the masons was put to work to build the chapel. We got stone and mede,[67] or clobe as we call it, for the masons to work with.

You that read this must remember that this was not the place where I met, for my meeting house was Bethel Chapel.

I was a very poor man with a wife and five small children at that time, and worked in the mine underground. Sometimes I was forenoon core, and when I had my dinner I should go up to the chapel and work as long as I could see, and then come home and have a little supper and go to bed. Then next day do the same.

The next week I should be afternoon core at the mine, and then I should go up to the chapel in the morning and work until the middle of the day, and go home and away to the mine. And so I did when I was afternoon core, and so I done all that week. The next week I was night core to the mine, and then I worked about the chapel by day and the mine by night. Hadn't the dear Lord strengthened me greatly for his work, I could never have done it.

When I was about the chapels I had 'taters to teal in my garden, and every Sunday I was planned. Sometimes I had to walk twenty miles or more, and to speak three times. If I had not the strength from the dear Lord I could not have done it. Many times I have worked twenty hours out of the twenty-four.

I remember that when our chapel was up to the door head, the devil said to me in my mind,[68] "They be all gone and left me and the chapel, and I have a good mind to go and leave the old chapel too."

---

67 Billy almost certainly means *mud,* used to make *clob,* a mortar consisting either of clay and lime, or clay and straw.

68 made me think.

Then I said, "Devil, doesn't thee know me better than that? By the help of the Lord I will have the chapel up, or else I will lost my skin on the downs."[69]

So the devil said no more to me on that subject. Sometimes I have had bladers[70] in my hands by working hard, and when I have looked on my hands and saw the bladers, I have said, "I do not mind this, for if this chapel stand one hundred years, and if there is one soul a year converted, that will be a hundred souls in a hundred years and will pay me well if I get to heaven. For they that turn many to righteousness shall shine like the stars for ever and ever. So I shall be rich enough when I get there."

The chapel was built and the roof put on, but we had no money to buy the windows. I went to my neighbours and they was very kind, for they gave me money to buy the windows. There was trustees that belonged to this chapel. Though I had work to do, I had not much to do in getting the money to pay the masons and others. But I collected the money to buy the windows.

So our chapel was built. The opening day came and we had preaching. But the preacher was a wise man but a very dead man, and I believe there was not much good done there that day, for it was a dead time with preacher and people. He had a great deal of grammar but little of Father.

"It is not by wisdom nor by might, but by my Spirit," saith the Lord.[71] And the dear Lord said the truth, for if it was by wisdom or by might I should have a small part. For my might is little and my

---

69   An unknown saying.

70   *Bladders* is an old English word for *blisters*. Why a miner with work-hardenend hands would be susceptible to these is puzzling. Maybe it was the extra work that caused the problem.

71   Zechariah 4:6

wisdom is less. Thanks be to the dear Lord the work is his, and he can work by weak instruments.

The second Sunday I was planned there after the chapel was opened, and the Lord was with us and blessed us in a wonderful manner. I said to the people that was there, "You know I did not work here about this chapel to fill my pockets, but to glorify God, and for the benefit of the neighbours, and for the good of souls. And souls I must have, and souls I will have."

Then two women said, "Lord, have mercy on me."

When the women each said so, I said, "Now the chapel is paid for already."

The Lord worked there, and there was about fifteen members when the chapel was built. The Lord revived his work and soon made them thirty members. Here you can see how good the Lord is to me. I spoke for one soul a year, and he gave me fifteen souls the first year.

Our chapel had three windows, two on one side and one on the other. Then Satan, or the old devil that is no friend to chapels, put his servants by way of reproach to call our chapel Three Eyes, because it had but three windows in it. But blessed be God, the chapel is become too small for that place and it is now made larger. There is six windows now instead of three, and some that have been converted there is now in heaven.

It is interesting that Three Eyes, a name once used as a form of ridicule, has become one of affection. Bourne adds Billy saying: "They may call the chapel Six Eyes now if they will." Visitors may like to know that the chapel was lengthened by extending it backwards. Looking from the car park today, only the centre and left hand windows are part of the "Three Eyes". It is generally believed that the third eye was on the far side where there are now three windows, the three windows on each side making the "Six Eyes".

Bourne gives the following, but does not name the chapels. There can be no doubt that Billy's chapel building took not only his time, but also much of his money. Billy's financial troubles in the first account below are probably the result of a bad tribute contract:

At a time when wages were low, Billy was still using his own money to support the chapels as well as his family. He came home one payday from the mine without any money, and his wife Joey reproached him for being the cause of their poverty and trials.

He said to her, "The Lord will provide."

Just then a neighbour, who had heard of Billy's circumstances, came to the house with a basket of provisions containing all that Billy and his family needed.

On another occasion Billy took some of the money that he had earned in the mine to pay for something wanted for the chapels. His wife declared, "We shall be brought to the union if you go on in this way."

"Never mind, my dear Joey," he assured her, "the Lord will provide."

This incident from *The King's Son* is in Billy's words. Bourne does not say whether Billy wrote it or told it, but it sounds like Billy's writing. In his writing Billy always refers to Joey as "my wife", but Bourne may have changed this:

At one time I had been at work the whole of the month, but had no wages to take up when payday came. As we had no bread in the house, Joey advised me to go up and ask the captain of the mine to lend me a few shillings, which I did, and he let me have ten shillings.[72]

On my way home I called to see a family and found they were worse off than me. For though

---

72 One week's pay. See Box on page 71 for the value of money.

we had no bread we had bacon and 'taters, but they had neither. So I gave them five shillings and went towards home.

Then I called on another family and found them, if possible, in greater distress than the former. I thought I could not give them less than I had given the others, so I gave them the other five shillings and went home.

Joey said, "Well, William, have you seen the captain?"

"Yes."

"Did you ask him for any money?"

"Yes, he let me have ten shillings."

"Where is it?"

"I have given it away."

"I never saw the fellow to you in my life. You are enough to try anyone."

I said, "The Lord isn't going to stay in my debt very long," and I then went out.

For two or three days after this Joey was mighty down. But about the middle of the week when I came home from the mine Joey was looking mighty smiling, so I thought there was something up.

Presently Joey said, "A lady we know has been here today."

"Oh?"

"And she gave me a sovereign."

"There, I told you the Lord wasn't going to stay in my debt very long. There's the ten shillings, and ten shillings interest."

CHAPTER 7

IDOLS AND A RAG DOG

AS WE WILL SEE BELOW, not everyone in the chapels is able to identify with Billy's active faith, although some members seem to go beyond even Billy's love of noise. There are plenty of preachers who prefer what Billy calls "a peace and quietness religion", and this is going to bring both groups into sharp conflict.

Bourne writes:

Billy and a like-minded preacher were holding a mission meeting at F. Billy opened the meeting with prayer, and the preacher and others fervently responded to many of his petitions. Observing this, Billy began to be more detailed and pointed in his requests. "O Lord, help the people to give up their idols."

The preacher said, "Amen."

"May thy children be saved from the love of the world's fashions."

"Amen," said the preacher again.

"Help thy people to give up their ribbons and feathers."[73]

"Amen," was still the response of the preacher, and again, "Amen."

---

73 Billy is showing his disapproval of women who go to chapel to show off their fine clothes. He will soon be criticising the men!

Then the preacher added, "And their cups and drinks."

"And their pipes and tobacco," said Billy, but to this there was no "Amen" from the preacher.

Billy immediately said, "Where's your Amen, Brother B? Why don't you say Amen to the pipes as well as the cups? Ah, you won't say Amen to the pipes."

Billy then proceeded with his prayer, but the preacher afterwards found fault with Billy for rebuking him in public.

Billy justified himself by saying, "You were hearty and loud enough with your Amens for others to give up *their* idols, but you are not willing to part with your own. Bless the Lord, I have given up *all* for my Saviour."

Bourne tells us that more than twenty years after Billy had abandoned smoking, he said, "God has given me just enough money to pay my way through life, and nothing for the pipe. If I had spent only sixpence a week on the pipe, I should have been at this time about thirty pounds in debt."

We now return to the *Journal*, where Billy writes:

We had an old man that met with us and he was an old professor,[74] and he dearly loved his pipe. He loved those idols too much to be a good man, for it was told that he loved other women more than he ought, besides his own wife. One night it was our preaching, but I was not there. There was a great many young converts there, and they was praising God for what he had done for them. And so they ought to. That old professor told the preacher that he ought to stop the young converts from praising God, for it was a false fire.

74 A professing Christian whose faith was not evident in his lifestyle. See box on page 40 for details on 'professors'.

I do not know how the preacher came to do it, for he was a noisy man himself and was sometimes very happy. But that night Satan got around them both, and this old lukewarm professor told the young converts that they must be silent, for the Lord was not deaf. So then the young converts quenched the Spirit and stopped our revival, and we had no more converted for some time.

On the next day, when I met with some of the young converts, they told me what the preacher and the man had done. I felt much from it. So I went after the preacher and found him, for I knew where he was. I said unto him, "How did you come to stop our revival?"

"Because they was offering of strange fire. They was making a noise for nothing."

I said, "The Lord made them happy, and they was praising him for it, as you and I ought to praise him too."

Then the preacher was very rough with me.

So I said, "How did you feel when you stopped them from praising God?"

He said he would do it again.

I said to him, "I hope I shall never be in a revival with you."

I went away and left him, and we had none converted there for a great while.

Now there was a preacher and an old professor that ought to help us on, but they tore us down. I believe the preacher felt from it, for he was very kind the next time I met him. But our revival was stopped, and both men must appear before him who sent that revival, to give their reason for stopping his children from praising him. For the preacher said many times in his preaching that the dear Lord ought to be praised from morning till night.

When the dear Lord's children begin praise him, these men will try to stop them if they can, but we are not afraid to meet these preachers in the great day of his coming. We know we are right, for

God's blessed book the Bible tells us that the people shall say in that day, "Oh Lord, we will praise thee, for thou was onest angry with us, but thine anger is turned away, and thou comforts us."[75]

We will praise our God and give glory to his blessed name, for in the revival we had near a hundred converted, so we are sure that the dear Lord done that. All the men on the earth, and all angels in heaven, could not convert one soul. The dear Lord converted a hundred souls, but the preacher and that old professor did not want them praising God for the great good he had done.

In the days of our Lord's flesh he tells us that he could not do many mighty works because of unbelief, and so it is in our day. The dead and lukewarm and proud and greedy professors is the Lord's enemies to this very day, and do hinder the work of God in all his houses. But bless God, he is on our side and shall conquer soon. We shall be able to praise the dear Lord without anyone to hinder us, with Abraham and Isaac and Jacob in the kingdom of heaven. We shall have no smokers there to hinder us from praising our dear Lord that we love so well.

Billy has plenty more critical statements to make about 'professors' in his *Journal*. This is only a foretaste of what is still to come:

Now we must have a full joy ourselves to know what a full joy means. Some professors get poor tempered when the Lord makes his children happy, and instead of praising the Lord with them they speak against them. It is no new thing to hear preachers, as they call themselves, speak against the power of God: such as shouting and dancing, and praising with a loud voice. The reason is because they do not feel it themselves, and then they condemn it in others.

Some time ago I was in a Primitive Methodist chapel, and there was two men in that chapel so happy that they was shouting and dancing for joy. The dear Lord had made them very happy, and that was not the first time. If we do not shout and dance for heaven,

75   Isaiah 12:1

what shall us shout and dance for? I was very glad to see them so happy, and I was happy with them.

I came into a house in the town and there was two preachers there. One of them was a superintendent of a connexion and the other was a local preacher of the same connexion. These two preachers was speaking evil of these two happy men.

When I heard them saying so, I mocked them, and said to them, "You bore a hole in a stick, and put some powder in it, and put a little fire to it, and the powder will heave the stick up in the air. Is not the Lord so strong as a little powder? And I have heard them say that if you take hot loaf of bread and make a hole in it, and put a little quicksilver in it, it will heave the loaf of bread around the table. Isn't the Lord so strong as a little quicksilver? David said that the Lord had turned his mourning into dancing and took away his sackcloth, and girded him with gladness.[76] And Jeremiah said, 'Then shall the virgin rejoice in the dance, both young men and old men together, for I will turn their mourning into joy and will make them rejoice from their sorrows.'"[77]

When I said so, the superintendent preacher began to speak some bad words and call me a foolish old man, for I said some things when I was at Redruth that I ought not to have said. He gave me a great many words of abuse, but the dear Lord kept my mind in peace.

When he had done speaking, I said to him, "You cannot preach the gospel from this text: 'Cry out and shout all ye inhabitants of Zion, for great is the Holy one of Israel in the midst of thee.'[78] You cannot preach from that text, for you never shout yourself. And you cannot preach from this text: 'I would that men pray where you are, and would hold up holy hands without wrath and doubting. And in like

76   Psalm 30:11
77   Jeremiah 31:13
78   Isaiah 12:6

manner women would adorn themselves with modest apparel and shamefacedness, not with gold and pearl and broided hair, but as women professing Godliness with good works.'[79] You cannot preach from that text, for you are proud yourself."

So he said no more to me. He was a proud man just at that time, for long beards came in fashion and he had one of the newest fashion. He was proud and he could not be happy, for the Lord will fill the humble with good things and the proud he will send empty away.[80] The two men that was in the chapel was happy with the love of Christ in their hearts, and the love of Christ will make men and women and children happy. For he said in the Bible, "Young men and maidens, old men and children, praise the name of the Lord."[81]

The two preachers was like the dog in the manger. The dog could not eat the oats himself, and he would bite the horse's nose if he did. The preachers could not shout and dance themselves, and they mocked them that did. These preachers would have done to be on the Pharisees' side when Christ rode into Jerusalem on the ass colt. They would be with the Pharisees that said, "Rebuke thy disciples, for they are making too much noise."[82] The preachers would be on the devil's side, for they that were on the Lord's side said, "Blessed be the king that cometh in the name of the Lord. Peace in heaven and glory in the highest."[83]

Bourne tells us that Billy objected not only to men who grew long beards just to show off the latest fashion, he was also critical of women who had hats full of flowers, commenting that, "Flowers only grow in soft places!"Bourne says that Billy also criticised young women who, he said, pretended to pray in chapel, but were

79   1 Timothy 2.8

80   Comment based on Luke 1:53

81   Psalm 148:12

82   Luke 19:39

83   Luke 19:38

peeping through their fingers to see if their special man was there; and criticised the young men who leant forward as though in prayer, but were proudly reading the label that said their hats were waterproof and made in London!

Here is an example of Billy's dislike of the type of chapel service he loves being 'hijacked' by what seems to be a puppet play and drama. It comes from this entry in his *Journal*. But the sight of the young men smoking at the front may help us understand Billy's disapproval

I do not agree with the fashion of the day, for it once was sing in the Spirit and pray with the Spirit of the dear Lord. But now the people have another spirit, the spirit of pride and vanity. If they have a school tea they must have a band, and they are wicked young men in general. I was invited to a chapel anniversary, and the people was so many that the chapel would not hold them, and we had the services out of doors.

A man came to our meeting riding in a carriage, and he brought three or four young men with him. He and they that he brought with him stood on our platform, and the young men at first told some verses. Then they had some rags made up in the form of a dog. They played with that, and the people was laughing to see them.

After they had done with the dog, there was two of these young men that dressed themselves in some clothes that they brought with them. They had a seat, and they sat one against another. They had a pipe and they smoked one against another, and they looked to my friend and me much like a Christmas play, for the congregation was laughing to see the four. Now if they was happy I could laugh with them, for I love to see people happy, shouting and laughing for joy. But not after wicked works. I trusted in the dear Lord and he brought me through, bless and praise his holy name.

The day after, my friend and me was asked to a teetotal meeting. We had a good time while speaking, for there was some praying people there that loved the Lord. I think there was as much as five hundred people there while we was speaking, and the Lord was with us to make us happy.

When we had done speaking, one of them said, "The singers is going to sing a piece."

There was five or six of them that could sing that piece, and all the congregation did not know what they was singing of. Soon after they began to sing their piece, the people left the place. So when the singers done singing, and when we came to pray, we had not fifty to pray to. All them that could worship the Lord in Spirit and in truth had left the chapel, and there was only Satan's servants left.

Singing is one part of the worship of our God, and we are told to sing in the Spirit as well as pray in the Spirit. God's children have been blessed many times while singing in the Spirit, but when Satan's servants sing the piece we cannot get happy, for we do not know what they are singing of. But if the preacher give out hymns we can sing to, that spoils Satan's worship.

When we, the children of God, sing in the blessed Spirit, Satan do not like us, nor his servants neither. The preachers tell them they have eyes and they see not, and they have ears and hear not, and have hearts and understand not.[84] Now, my brethren, these people cannot worship that dear holy God aright in Spirit and in truth.

84   Mark 8:18

CHAPTER 8

GREAT DELIVERANCE
CHAPEL

WE ARE GOING to visit a miser in Helston in an attempt to get a donation towards building another chapel. To quote Billy, this miser: "Has never been known to give anything to anyone." And we are also taking a trip with Billy to St Ives, a picturesque fishing village on the north coast of Cornwall.

Billy built three chapels. The third, Great Deliverance in the village of Carharrack, was opened around 1840. From this account the work seems to have been well underway in 1838. This time the people are generally supportive, especially the folk at St Ives. Little is left of the Great Deliverance now, but the covered shell can be seen in a field where it is currently in use as a cowshed.

Here is Billy's account:

> The dear Lord told me to go and build another chapel, in the parish of Gwennap, and I lived in the parish of Kea. I was instrumental in the hand of the Lord in building two chapels in the parish where I lived: that was Bethel and Kerley Downs chapels. The Lord told me to go in another parish and to build a chapel, and he would help me.
>
> I went to a gentleman, and the Lord opened his heart and he granted me a piece of land to build a chapel, or a house, for the Lord. There was another man that said he would help me get out the foundations and raise stone, and so he did, but he was paid for all he done.
>
> We got out our foundations for building the chapel, and then we wanted a quarry to raise stone. The Lord put it in my heart to

go down by the railway, and there we went. Some person had already been there trying to raise stone, but their quarry was poor. They had worked to the east and to the west, and left a piece in the ground in the middle. And there we went to work.

Some wonder at it to see what a quantity of stone I had. But I was working for a strong company. If you wish to know who the company is I will tell you, my dear friends. It is the Father, Son and Holy Ghost. This company will never break.

I used to work in the mine eight hours out of the twenty-four. When I was forenoon core, and came up at two o'clock, I should have a little dinner and then work in the quarry until that night, and then sometimes go to a meeting. When I was afternoon core I worked in the quarry in the forenoon, and also when I was last core by night.

I was very poor in this world's goods, and had a wife and five children, and I lived a great way off from where I built the chapel. Here the dear Lord helped me again, for he put it in a gentleman's heart to give me five shillings a month while I was raising stone for the Lord's house.

There was a coffee house near our quarry. When I came up from the mine last core by night I would go to the coffee house and have my breakfast for six or seven pence, then pray, and then away to raise stone for the house of my dear beloved Lord. Here you may see that the Lord helped me by giving me my breakfast. You may ask, "How did he help you? You had not anything for building the chapel."

But I was well paid. We have a hundred-fold in this world, and they that turn many to righteousness shall shine for ever, so the more good we can do the greater our reward will be.

We rose away our stone and got it where the chapel was to be built. The foundations was got out, as we thought, forty feet long and twenty-four wide (12.2m and 7.3m). Then the masons began to build, but I had no money in hand and had no bank to go to but the bank of heaven. But thanks be to God, that is a strong bank. I had often to go there by faith.

Great Deliverance chapel
redrawn from an engraving in *The King's Son*

When our chapel walls was up about five feet high (1.52m), the man that was with me said, "Our chapel is wider and longer than you say. For he is forty-five feet long (13.7m) and he is wider too. Shall they take down a piece of the end and make it shorter?"

"No," I said. "If the Lord will give us money to cover the short one, he will give us money to cover the long."

And so it was. The Lord sent Mister T to me before the chapel was up, and Mister T said to me, "You will want timber, and lime and slate for your chapel, will you not?"

I said, "Yes, sir, we shall."

He said, "Come down to our store and have what you want for your chapel."

That was the way the dear Lord helped me. When the masons wanted money I went away collecting, and got money to pay them. Some friends was very kind and gave me kind words and money, but some was very rough. I went to one man, and he was well off in this world for he was the manager of the mine. I asked him to give me something to help me build the Lord's house. He was in the mine counting house, and as soon as I asked him he got into a great passion and drove me out. Now that man is dead long ago, and I believe there was no hope in death.

When he drove me out of the counting house, and gave me nothing, I went into a gentleman's house that was nigh by, and asked him for something to help to build the Lord's house. That gentleman said, "Yes, I will give you ten shillings."

I had ten shillings there and then, and that gentleman is living and done well, and he is an old man.

Billy goes to other friends, some of them Quakers, who also give money. Because Billy never uses a capital F in his writing it is not always possible to tell when he means Quaker Friends – members of the Society of Friends – and when he means everyday friends. For this reason I am only using a capital F when *Quaker* directly precedes the word *friend*, or it is reasonably likely from the context.

We went around Camborne and some Friends was very liberal. Then we went to the west to a great many places, and I went to Helston.

One of the Friends said to me, "There do a man live in that house that is worth a deal of money. But he is a great miser, and he has never been known to give anything to anyone."

I said, "I will go in and see him."

The outside of his house looked like a miser's house, and when I came in there was an old man sitting down to a meal to a little old wisht table. He had an old chair and an old stool or two, and all the clome[85] that I saw was on his table. And that was not much.

So I asked him for something, and he said, "I cannot afford to give you anything."

I said, "You can give me some money, and if you do not you may die and leave it all behind. Job was very rich but he was soon made poor. I am begging for the Lord's house, and if you do not give me some of your money you may die."

Then he wiped his mouth and put hand in his pocket, and took out his hand again. I told him that the gold was the Lord's, and his life was in the Lord's hand and he could take it away, and then the gold would be no good to him.

Then he said, "Go around the town and come again to me by and by."

I said, "You have got money and I must have it now." I talked to him and told him what the dear Lord would do by greedy people.

He wiped his mouth and put his hand in his pocket four of five times and was talking away. At last he put his hand in his pocket and took out two shillings and sixpence and gave it to me. It was a hard job to get the money from that old miser. I do not think Satan let him sleep that night, for the dear Lord helped me take away a half of a crown of his god. I believe money is his god and he love it dearly.

When I came to the friends, they said, "He have not give anything, have he?"

"Yes," I said. "He gave me two shillings and sixpence."

Then they said, "That is the greatest miracle that was worked in Helston, for he was never known to give anything before now."

85   Earthenware crockery.

I went to another gentleman and asked him for some money to help to build the chapel. He asked me how long and our chapel was. And I told him, "Forty feet long[86] and twenty-five feet wide."

Then he said, "And how high are you going to build it?"

I said, "Sixteen feet high." (4.9m.)

The gentleman said to me, "If you will build the chapel eighteen feet high (5.5m) I'll give you two pounds. If you build the chapel eighteen feet high you can put a gallery into it, for it always a good thing to have a chapel large enough to hold the people."

Then I said, "Yes."

And so it is, for he said, "You may have missionary meetings there, or teetotal meetings, and no doubt a large chapel will be good."

I told him, "What you say is very right, sir, and we will have the chapel walls built eighteen high."

Now here the dear Lord helped me for he put in that gentleman's heart to build the chapel higher, for it was wanted, and the dear Lord said he would help – and that you will see as I write. Before the chapel was up for his ?frithe the Lord sent a carpenter. He was the master, and had men working under him. He came where the chapel was building, and I was there at that time.

When he came, he said, "You have a good chapel here."

---

86 It seems that accurate measurements are not one of Billy's strong points. This is the original length. Surely the foundations were dug too large on day one, making a length of 45 feet (13.7m). A little later Billy says it ends up *five feet longer and three feet wider than we meant to build it*. On this basis the chapel should be 45 feet by 27, but the building has been much altered and enlarged in the past. It is now in a very poor condition, and the exact size of the original would be extremely difficult to measure today with any accuracy.

I said, "Yes, we have, and I hope there will be great good done here."

Then said the foreman carpenter, "You will want someone to do the carpentry work for your chapel, won't you?"

"Yes," I said, "we shall." Now the dear Lord helped me in sending these friends.

Then he said, "If you will let me do it, I will put on the roof for nothing. That would cost you, if you was to pay for it, three pounds. I will do all the rest of the carpentry work, only you pay the men's wages if you will let me do it."

I said, "I cannot go from that, and I thank you for your offer."

He was as good as his word. He done as he said, and the dear Lord will reward him for it.

When our chapel was up and covered we had no mind to have gallery, but we had a mind to have rising seats in one end of our chapel.[87] One day the carpenter said to me, "If I was you, I would have a gallery, for sometimes you may have large congregations at missionary meetings and teetotal meetings. The same timber that will do to put in the rising seats, will do to put in a gallery. There is only a girder and two pillars wanted, and then there will be room for a hundred up overhead in the gallery."

Then I said, "Yes, we will have a gallery."[88]

So the chapel was built and gallery was in, and I owed the masons and carpenters twenty pounds.

87 Seat on an upward sloping floor.

88 Presumably the original two feet (0.6 metre) extra height, if that is all that was needed, was to allow a gallery to be added at some time in the future when funds became available. The carpenter's offer to do it now is impossible to turn down.

There was a man that lived at St Ives. He was the master of a vessel and he used to come to Penryn and Falmouth. He was called Captain John Havey[89] and he was a teetotal advocate. He and me used to go to the teetotal meetings together.

I used to tell him I was building a chapel for teetotal meetings, and was in debt on the chapel twenty pounds or more for labour to the masons and carpenters. I asked what sort of people St Ives people was, whether they was liberal or no. He said they was, and they gave a deal of money to the cause of God, and they would help me.

John Wesley and his brother Charles visited Cornwall on many occasions. Their influence on Cornish life was dramatic, as can be seen from the large number of Methodist chapels in the county today. Apart from bringing the message of salvation, the Wesleys had a genuine concern that the people should work hard and save for the future, and break free from the grip of alcohol and gambling that was wrecking so many lives. John Wesley made his first visit to Cornwall in August 1743 and his last (his thirtieth) in 1789. Here is an entry from John Wesley's diary during his first visit: *Tuesday August 30. In the evening we reached St Ives. At seven I invited all guilty, helpless sinners who were conscious they "had nothing to pay", to accept of free forgiveness. The room was crowded both within and without, but all were quiet and attentive.*

My friend told the St Ives people about me, so they knew me before I came there. At that time I had a plan to St Just in the west, and when I had done my work for the Lord in St Just I enquired of a friend my way to St Ives. He told me the way to go

89 This is Billy's spelling, which is not reliable. Both *Havey* and *Harvey* are surnames from St Ives at the time, but *Harvey* was the usual spelling.

and told me who to ask for in St Ives. It was a good man and his name was Bryant.

When I came to St Ives I enquired where my friend Bryant lived, and they told me, "Down by the quay near the sea."

At that time the main street led down on the quay or seashore. St Ives was a very little small place about the year of 1838, but now it is a brave town and greatly improved.

I found my good friend Bryant, and when I told him that I was William Bray he was glad to see me. He asked me how my wife and family was, and they was well. Then I told him what I was come for, and he told me that I was come in a very poor time, for they taken but little fish for the year. There was some of the people almost wanting bread.

He said, "It is a poor time to come to St Ives now."

But he did not know that it was poor times with Peter – till his dear Lord told him to let down the nets on the other side of the ship.

My brother Bryant missed, for I came in a very good time. We went up to the Wesleyan chapel, and there was a great many happy members there. We had a good meeting and prayed for the Lord to send them some fish. After our meeting was over in the chapel we went into the coffee house. After we had a little refreshment we began our meeting and continued until midnight, and we prayed for the dear Lord to send in fish.

When our meeting was over in the coffee house we came out to go to our lodging, and there was the dear and poor women with pilchards on their plates. The fish was shining by the moonlight, for it was a pretty moonlight night. The dear women was smiling, the moon was smiling and we was smiling. And no wonder, for the dear Lord put bread on many shelf that night, and blessed many families.[90]

We asked the dear women what fish was taken. They told us they was ten thousand hogsheads taken in many driving boats, and in some there was twenty thousand taken. The next day, if I make no mistake, there was eight thousand hogsheads taken.[91]

Here I must speak it to their praise. Though they had so much fish in those seas, and the people were so poor, they rested on Sunday and left it till Monday before they went about their fish. And they losed none.

Some men that belong to the fish seine, said to me, "Now you shall have some money for your chapel. If you can get a boat and come out to our seine we will give you some fish."

There was a carpenter with me and he was used to the sea. He said, "I will bring him out to your seine."

90   The pilchards would be preserved with salt and oil, and packed into barrels to be taken by ship for sale in Spain and Italy. In that way they provided bread.

91   A hogshead was a barrel containing 54 gallons – 245 litres, each holding over two thousand pilchards. A catch of thirty-eight thousand hogsheads sounds excessive. However, in 1834 a massive catch of pilchards was made in St Ives, and in 1846 "over 30,000 hogsheads were taken at one time".
(Source – http://west-penwith.org.uk/ives6.htm).
1846 cannot, of course be the date when Billy visited St Ives, as Great Deliverance was completed long before this. I think Billy has become confused over the number of hogsheads, or maybe the men, being fishermen, exaggerated the size of the catch to Billy! Driving boats had a crew of four or five men, with four to eight driving boats controlling the extensive net, called a seine. Wilkie Collins in *Rambles Beyond Railways* (Richard Bentley, London 1861) has a detailed chapter on Cornish pilchard fishing.

He got a boat and he gave me some clale.[92] I changed my clothes and he rowed me out to the seine where the fish was. They was looking pretty, for they was shining and leaping about the seine. Then the fisherman dipped up the fish out of the seine, and threw them in the boat where we was. The fish was alive and leaping about our boat, and I thought about the church ministers how they take the tithe of the corn, and I took tithe of the fish.

So when we had done our fishing we came away to land, and there we sold our fish. The carpenter told them up to the people that bought them, and I took the money. The fish money was six pounds fifteen shillings. So the dear Lord helped me as he said he would.

There was another friend that kept a druggist shop. He told me that he would give me all the gain he got by the all the medicine that he sell for the week. He gave me two pounds two shillings, so that was well.

The friends in St Ives was very kind, for I had seventeen pounds to bring home. I should have more if I was much about the money, but I was going from one to another telling the people what a good master I had. And who is your master? Why then, that dear Saviour that died upon the cross. Some of St Ives people love that dear Saviour and are with him before now. So I came home from St Ives with seventeen pounds, and paid it to the masons and the carpenters.

That chapel was built to house our teetotal meetings in, for when teetotalism first came it had many enemies – and it was those that professed religion. Some them would not love[93] a

---

92   An unidentified word. Maybe it was some sort of water-proof clothing. In an early twentieth century paperback edition of *The King's Son*, there is an engraving of Billy in the fishing boat wearing his top hat!

93   Billy probably means *leave*, as in *allow*.

teetotal advocate to come inside their chapel door to advocate that good cause, and some of the preachers would not give it out from the pulpit for a teetotal meeting.

Now here you may see how good the Lord is to me and to the dear neighbours, for the chapel is five feet longer and three feet wider than we meant to build it, and there is a gallery and all. I have seen the chapel full, and some out of doors. If we had built the chapel in our way, it would be too small. But our dear Lord knows better than we.

We had good meetings and class meetings, and we had teetotal meetings. We had some converted in our teetotal meetings, for the dear Lord is able to save souls in teetotal meetings as well as in other meetings, and we have had many blessed times in that chapel.

After I went out as a missionary,[94] some unfaithful class leaders led the class. Unfaithful preachers was among the people, and the glory departed. When the power of the Lord was gone they said that the chapel was not in the right place. Some of them have gone so far as to say that I was moved by a bay[95] spirit when I built the chapel there. It was he that said so, and the rest of the preachers and the leaders, that lost the power. And they lost the congregation. Then they said the chapel is not where he ought to be.

Now Solomon's temple was built right, for his Lord blessed him in a wonderful manner, for he sent the glory down on Solomon. When he opened the house the dear Lord blessed them so that the priests could not minister, for the Lord sent down so much glory from heaven that all can see that the temple was built right. But Solomon and they that was with him went out of the way, and then the glory departed. The people might

---

94   Members who travelled around the local area, holding missions, were known as missionaries.

95   An unknown word. Perhaps it means dark, as in a *bay mare*, or maybe Billy meant to write *bad*.

have said the temple was not built where it ought to be, but it was they that was not right, not the house.

Now the preachers is gone out of the way, as well as the people, and they have not that power that the dear Lord told them to have. It is a rare thing now to hear preachers say, "Praise the Lord." And many of them do not like we that do.

Some time after I built that chapel I went up eastward to live, to a place called St Neot. When I came home and went to see my friend, I went up to the Deliverance Chapel, for that was the name of the chapel, for the Lord worked out great deliverance for me to build that chapel, a poor man that had no money.

When I came home, a superintendent preacher was planned there that Sunday. He asked me to speak in his place, and I did. That preacher could not bear for the people to praise the Lord with a loud voice. He used to tell them, when they was praising God with loud voices, that they must be silent.

When I began to speak I felt that my great and good Master was with me. While I was speaking, that preacher got the Bible and sat down behind me. The dear Lord gave me power to tell them, "Miriam, a sister of Aaron, took a timbrel in her hand, and all the women went out after her with timbrels and with dances. And Miriam answered them, 'Sing ye to the Lord, for he hath triumphed gloriously. The horse and his rider hath he thrown into the sea.'[96]

"David danced before the Lord with all his might. So David and all the house of Israel brought the ark of the Lord with shouting and with the sound of the trumpet. As the ark of the Lord came into the city of David, Michal, Saul's daughter, looked through the window and saw King David leaping and dancing before the Lord. And she despised him in her heart. If she had gone out and hugged her husband around the neck, and said, 'My dear

96   Exodus 15:21-22

David, I will dance with you, my dear husband, and your Lord shall be my Lord,' then she would be a good wife. But she called him a vain fellow.[97]

I have not written down here all that David's wife said to David, but you can read it in the Bible at your own leisure. I said that the Lord set a mark on her, for Michal had no child to the day of her death, and that was a great curse on women in that day.

While I was telling all this, the preacher was sitting behind me with the Bible in his hand. As I did tell them where to find it, he would turn over the Bible and find it. Then I said, "In the last Psalm it is said, 'Praise ye the Lord in his sanctuary. Praise him in the firmament of his power. Praise him for all his mighty acts. Praise him according to his excellent greatness. Praise him with the sound of the trumpet. Praise him with the psaltery and harp. Praise him with the timbrel and dance. Praise him with stringed instruments and organs. Praise him upon the loud cymbals. Praise him upon the high sounding cymbals. Let everything that hath breath praise the Lord. Praise ye the Lord.'"[98]

Now after that preacher heard me say what I have set down here, my friends told me he was better and would help them bless and praise God. But there have been unfaithful leaders and members, as well as preachers, but thanks be to the dear Lord we hope the best is all to come. For the chapel is there still, and there will be more good done there yet. The Lord did not put me to build that chapel for nothing, bless and praise his holy name.

I went out begging for that chapel down in the west, and one of our friends told me that I was ?wanten six weeks, and I brought home seventy-two pounds and paid all my expenses. So the dear

---

97   2 Samuel 6:14-16,20-21.

98   Psalm 150

Lord blessed me. Before the Lord put in my heart to build that chapel we had no place that we could call our own to hold our teetotal meetings in, for the professors was very shay[99] in that day to open their chapels to hold meetings in. Many of the preachers as well as the people was against it. When there was a bill in the pulpit to announce a teetotal meeting some of the preachers would not give it out, for they loved the drink themselves and did not like to give it up.

I remember a school tea, and we had a chapel full of people. We had a Wesleyan in our chair at seven o'clock. and we had another Wesleyan on our platform. They was good men, and friend Hoper, our superintendent, and another friend and myself. They told the teachers that they must be converted, or they could not teach the children right. They all seemed to speak with power, for the dear Lord was there in our midst.

There is a society and a good Sabbath school there. So I think the chapel is built right after all. I am well pleased with the chapel and the place, and praise the dear Lord that he ever put it into my heart to build that and other chapels.

May the Lord bless all his chapels.

99   Maybe *shy*, as in *shy away from*.

CHAPTER 9

THE DEVIL IN THE HEDGE

THERE ARE SEVERAL photographs of Billy dating from the 1860s, including some with the top hat he is said to have worn at times in later life – but not in fishing boats! When Billy was young, of course, photography had not been invented. Even in the late 1840s, when transportable cameras were available, the pioneer photographers would not have made their way to the wilds of Cornwall to photograph a tin miner. Although a picture is alleged to be worth a thousand words, the addition of a written description will help us understand just what the people saw when they went to chapel on Sunday.

In *The Story of Billy Bray* from *Short Stories and Other Papers* (1886) Pearse, who knew Billy well, gives us this eyewitness description:

> From one end of Cornwall to another, no name is more familiar than that of Billy Bray. On Sundays, when one met crowds of strangers making for the little whitewashed chapel perched up amongst the granite boulders, or when one found the quiet town church thronged by the well-dressed people, the usual explanation was that Billy Bray was going to preach.

> If you had joined Billy on the way, you could not have been long in doubt as to who he was. A little, spare, wiry man, his dress of orthodox black-and-white tie indicated the preacher. The sharp, quick, discerning eyes that looked out from under the brows, the mouth almost hard in its decision, all the face softened by the light that played constantly upon it, and by the happy

wrinkles round the eyes, and the smile that had perpetuated itself – these belonged to no ordinary man. With the first suspicion that this was Billy Bray there would quickly come enough to confirm it.

If you gave Billy half a chance there would certainly be a straightforward question about your soul, in wise pithy words. And if the answer was what it should be, the lanes would ring with his happy thanksgiving.

It is a shame that the standard portrait of Billy, familiar to many readers, is an old engraving of his head, copied from a photograph where he is sitting upright in a chair. The photograph was taken near the end of Billy's life. Not only does Billy look too smartly dressed to seem like the man we are reading about here, but he has lost his teeth. This has made his mouth draw in, giving an unexpectedly dour expression.

For the cover of this book I am using an informal photograph of a younger-looking Billy. He is dressed in more ordinary clothes and at least some of his front teeth seem to be in place. I am pleased to see that the photographer has not persuaded Billy to brush his hair forward in an attempt to make it look fuller. It cannot date earlier than 1852 and is more likely to have been taken around 1860 when Billy was in his mid sixties. It is either an ambrotype or a tintype, as the picture has been reversed left to right, a failing of this early type of photography. This can be seen from the coat buttons in the original. I have corrected this. Bourne tells us:

> I once heard Billy speak with great effect to a large congregation, mostly miners, in a neighbourhood where there were two mines. One was very prosperous, where good wages could be earned. At the other the work was hard, and the wages low. Billy presented himself to the congregation as working at this second mine, but on payday going to the prosperous mine for his wages. But had he not

been at work at the other mine? the manager would inquire. He had, but he liked the wages at the good mine better

Billy continued to act out this play to the congregation, pleading with the owner of the prosperous mine very earnestly, but in vain. He was dismissed at last with the remark, from which there was no appeal, that he must come there to work if he came there for his wages. Then he turned to the congregation, and the effect was almost irresistible: They must serve Christ here if they would share his glory hereafter. If they would serve the devil now, to him they must go for their wages by-and-by.

Bourne writes about someone, whom he refers to only as "Mr Maynard", who first met Billy in 1844. This is probably John Maynard, 1820-1912, who was converted around 1840 and entered the Bible Christian ministry in 1844. Mr Maynard was in the pulpit of Great Deliverance Chapel when, he says, "I noticed a small man come in. Everyone turned to look, and noting the pleasure on their faces I thought, 'This, then, is the famous Billy Bray about whom I have heard so much.'"

After the service, Maynard says Billy dragged him round the pulpit pew to the amusement of the people, shouting and jumping all the time.[100] When he let Maynard go, Billy asked him whether he could stand it or not.

100 It seems that carrying people around was a habit of Billy's. There are several accounts of him doing it. Bourne says that when they first met, Billy carried him round the room many times. Bourne says he was much too disconcerted, half amused and half frightened, to be able to say anything. I doubt if there was any religious significance in this. It was probably Billy's way of showing his joy at meeting another Christian.

"Yes, much more than that," was the answer.

"All right, friend Maynard, praise the Lord!"

Maynard continues in his own words:

If people told Billy he praised God too loudly, he would point heavenward and say, "Up there we shall praise him more sweet, more loud."

Many a time, when Billy and I have been leaving my home together, he has said to me, "Now, friend Maynard, let us pray a minute before we go, or else the devil will be scratching me on the way. If I leave without praying, this is the way he treats me. But when I get on my knees a minute or two before leaving, I cut his old claws, and then he can't harm me. So I always like to cut his claws before I go."

This account is in Billy's words, but told only by Bourne in *The King's Son*. It has all the marks of Billy's writing:

I was once asked to go to the reopening of a chapel where we had large congregations. I spoke in the forenoon, and Brother Coles[101] spoke in the afternoon and evening. He had the mighty power of God and preached two very good sermons. The people was very kind in giving their money for repairing God's house.

On the Monday they had a tea meeting, and I had to speak at three o'clock. The tea was at five. I believe we would be better off if we were to *fast* and pray, and give the money without a tea, for then we would have more of the glory in our souls.

In the evening we had a meeting, and one of our friends took the chair. He called on the superintendent to speak first, and after that he

---

101 Possibly James Coles, 1822-1909. He was converted by a woman preacher and entered the Bible Christian ministry in 1850.

called on me. I told the people that the dear Lord had given them a pretty chapel to worship in, and now he wanted good furniture, for bad furniture looks disgraceful in a good house.

I told them that good furniture for the house of the Lord was *sanctified souls*. We must be pardoned, sanctified, and sealed, and then we shall not only be fit for the Lord's house on earth, but we shall be good furniture in heaven.

I am letting Bourne conclude this chapter:

Billy knew how to fight the devil and his agents with their own weapons. Returning late from a revival meeting on a dark night in a lonely road, some men tried to frighten him by making all sorts of ghostly sounds. But he went singing on his way.

At last one of them said, in a bloodcurdling voice, "I'm the devil up here in the hedge, Billy Bray."

"Bless the Lord, bless the Lord," retorted Billy, "I did not know thee wast so far away as that!"

To use Billy's own expression, "What could the devil do with such as he?"

At a house in Truro, a friend's wife read the account of the temptation of Jesus at family prayers. Billy listened quietly until the verse was read in which Satan promises the Saviour all the kingdoms of the world, and the glory of them, if he would only fall down and worship him.[102]

Then Billy jumped to his feet. "The old vagabond. The old vagabond. He give away all the kingdoms of the world, when he never had an old 'tater skin to call his own, the old vagabond!"

102   Matthew 4:8 and Luke 4:5

CHAPTER 10

AN OLD MAN OUT OF TEMPER

THE FERVOUR THAT filled the chapels whenever Billy was present was certainly not a short-lived occurrence. But as time went on, most branches of the Methodist church in the mining areas of Cornwall became more staid, drawing away from some of the Bible Christians in their form of worship. This does not suit Billy, but in this chapter he is objecting to the conduct of some Methodist preachers rather than their denomination. Certainly Billy identifies with the teachings and practices of John Wesley, but not necessarily Wesley's successors. Later Billy says about a group of Methodists with whom he has a falling-out: "I am the son of a Methodist and I love them, but these was no Wesleyans."

Bourne writes:

> If you did not join Billy in praising God he would tell you that he thought you were dead. I went with him one day to see a dying saint whose character had been unblemished for many years, but whose natural disposition was modest and retiring almost to a fault. His face wore a look of indescribable dignity and repose, lit up with a strange, unearthly radiance and glory. He was just on the verge of heaven and could only speak in a whisper.

> He said, "I wish I had a voice so that I might praise the Lord."

"You should have praised him, my brother, when you had one," was Billy's quiet, but slightly satirical comment.

Billy tells us in his *Journal*:

I was invited to an elderly man's house to lead a class, and there was no chapel near that place. A man that lived in the house had been a Wesleyan, and he was a very wise man. The worst was that he knew it, and I was very foolish compared with him. We had our class meeting Sunday morning, and when at first I went to lead the class at this house we was five or six. The old man and his wife made two of them.

After I was at his house a week or two and led the class, he said, "The people is telling that you are a fine silly man, and are not fit to lead a class well."

I said, "I do not mind that, nor what they say. Will you stand with me? If you will stand by me, we shall have them that speak against us converted, and then they will be on our side."

He said he would stand by me, but not very cheerful. I have reason to believe it was he that spoke against me, for his behaviour showed so. Then the dear Lord poured out his blessed Spirit and our class was increased to twenty.

Blessed meetings we had, and we had our class meetings in the old man's parlour. When we had our revival the old man of the house got so offended that, while we was in the parlour enjoying of our meeting, he was up in the kitchen and was very poor tempered.

When my class saw the old man so out of temper, the members said to me, "Let us get another house to meet, for the old man do not like to have us here."

I said to them, "Let us not go till he tell us to go. We should bear the cross as long as the Lord wish. If we go away and he tell us not to go, we shall be cowards."

So we went on, and the old man was up in the kitchen and we in the parlour.

It was not many weeks before the old man said to me, "I did not feel for to tell you to leave my house before, but now I wish you to get another house to meet in."

I said to the old man, "Then now we must go, for it is the Lord's will."

It was after our Sunday class meeting that the old man told me so. When the Monday morning came I went to our preacher and told him that if he please he must get a place for the class to meet, for the old man had told us to get another place.

The preacher said to me, "You must get a place, for you know the people better than I do."

I went away to the houses of all the members that same day, and told them we was going away to meet in some other house on Sunday mornings. They was all glad for that. I went and got a place at another man's house. There was a good man and his wife in that house, and the dear Lord blessed us there. At the old man's house we meet in before, we had a class meeting on Sunday mornings and preaching Monday evenings. That Monday night it was preaching at the old man's house.

While the preacher was preaching, I was down on my knees praying and asking the dear lord what we must do with the Monday nights' preaching.

The Lord said unto me in my mind, "I will rid my people out of this place."

And I believed it.

When our preacher had done preaching I told the people, "The Lord told us we must get a place to meet Monday. Next Sunday morning our class meeting will be down to Brother M, and the preaching on Monday next will be down to Brother M."

When I told the people so, the old man of the house said before all the people that I was a hard faced liar; that he did not tell me to go.

I said to him, "Did you not tell me yesterday, after our meeting was over, that we must get a place to meet?"

The old man did not say much more. He was well off in this world's goods, and he would give the preacher a meal when he came round.

One of our members, a woman that had a long tongue and that minded other people's business more than her own, said that I had done what was very bad, to take away the meeting from the old man's house. She said the preacher would now have no place to go to, and the class would come to nothing.

I told my class that we could not stay there any longer, for the old man had told us to get another place to meet, and I had done what the Lord had told me to do, and I was clear.

Then she said that my class would be all broken up. But she missed, for the Lord poured out his Spirit and our class was increased to near sixty, and the house where we met was nearly filled with happy souls. And that was a miracle, for they that had idols gave them up, and they that had pride gave it up. And some that drank gave it up for the Lord's sake. And so they ought to, for everyone in Christ Jesus is a new creature. Old things is passed away and all things is become new.[103]

But we had our trials too, and we had it from professing people that had a name to live and at the same time was dead. I remember a man that was a class leader and he was well off in this world. When we was in the meeting house, and the dear Lord made us very happy — some was shouting and some was dancing for joy — the class leader began to say, "Why are you making so much noise?"

I said to our young converts, "Do not mind to quench the Spirit of the Lord for no man."

And we did not mind, though the class leader was well off in this world. When he went out of the door of our meeting house I was on my knees praying, and I did not see him going out, but found my faith increasing and my mind getting light. I said as he was going

103 2 Corinthians 5:17

out, "The devil is going out." And as he went out, I said, "The devil is gone."

That class leader went out and said, "I never saw such a man as William Bray in my life, for when I was going out of the house, he said, 'The devil is going.' And when I went out, he said, 'The devil is gone.'"

Now you must remember that I did not see that class leader going out of the house, but felt a greater power to pray. I believe he carried away some devils with him, for our dear Lord in the days of his flesh could not do many mighty works because of unbelief.

There was men that lived there near the house where we had our class meeting, and they was members of another society. They had been professors for a great while before we came there, and they came to me and asked me whether they shall meet with me or not. I told them they might, if they would. But I think Satan sent them there, for they could not believe for us.[104]

When we had a good meeting, and we was very happy, they would speak against us and try to stop us. When we was praising of God, the old devil got his ends at first when he sent them there, but afterwards we did not mind them or their bad tempers. We held fast and praised our dear Lord.

After some time one of the men thought that the rest of the class was more happy than he was, and he left speaking against us and began to pray. He was soon made happy and could praise the Lord as well as we. He was filled with joy unspeakable and full of glory. That man was a good man, and now I believe that he is in heaven with Abraham and Isaac and Jacob, and all the prophets in the kingdom. It was well for him that he got the power to praise God, for he is with a noisy company now. All that is up there can praise God with loud voices, and so they ought, for the dear Lord have bought for them that is there a royal city, and that is a pretty place for old

---

104 Presumably they could not agree on matters of faith and/or worship.

miners like he was. Now he have a crown on his head and a palm in his hand, and he is rich for ever, and will be poor no more.

The other man was still opposed to the power of the dear Lord, and tried with all the power that the devil could give him to stop us. But he could not, for angels and men before our dear Lord fall, and devils fear and fly. So he that is for us is more than they that is against us.

This man used tell me that I brought the people there to vex him and one or two more, but if my praising my dear Lord will make them poor tempered they will all be poor tempered where I am. I mean to praise the Lord as long as I live, for when the ark it was coming, King David came running and leaping and dancing for joy. And if the king leaped so much under the law, how much ought we to leap that have the gospel? If David leaped we ought to leap for joy as well, for David's Lord is our Lord.

So that man tried all he could do to hinder the work of the Lord and to stop us from praising God with loud voices. If we ever had what we call a dead meeting, he and the old dead professors would be pleased and say what a good meeting they had. But that was not often that they could say so. We see how blind these must be. When we had a dead meeting they would say it was a good one. These is the lukewarm ones that the dear Lord will spew out of his mouth, for our dear Lord said that he would that they was hot or cold. And because they was neither hot nor cold, but lukewarm, that he will (spew them out of his mouth).[105]

One man did love his father's house well, and he would be found often there, and there he would get drunk.[106] He would come home and beat his dear wife that he ought to love. She was a good woman

---

105   Rev 3:15,16

106   From the context this seems to be a public house that either his paternal father, or his 'father' the devil keeps, rather than God's house, even though the man must be a member of the chapel.

and did meet with us, and she was happy. And he beat his wife more than once.

When he beat her again, I went to him and told him, "The next time you beat your wife I will bring you before our preacher."

It was not long before he beat his wife again, and I brought him before our preacher. He was to be turned out of our society if I was willing for it to be, but he told the preacher so many lies against me.

The preacher asked me, "Shall we turn him out of the society?"

"No," I said. "If he had not told so many lies against me, I should have said, 'Turn him out of the society.' But now the hand of the Lord shall be on him, and not me."

There was another class meeting put on in the week, and another leader, and this man went in to meet with him for a little time, and then he went off to another part of the world. So we got clear of him.

There was another man that met with us in the same place, and he had a brother-in-law who had been a soldier in the battle of Waterloo with Lord Wellington, and our member asked the soldier to our meeting. The soldier told his brother-in-law, which was our member, that he would go one day. He told him so to keep him quiet, for he did not mean to go.

But his brother-in-law would not let him rest. He went to him time after time, and the soldier promised to go with me to our class meeting.

I was the leader of the class, and I well remember when the soldier came to our meeting for the first time. We made it our rule not to speak to a stranger the first time they came.[107]

When the meeting was over, for we had a very good one for the dear Lord was with us and blessed us in a wonderful manner, the soldier

107 At these class meetings the members would be encouraged to share their experiences in the Christian life. Presumably visitors were made welcome on arrival, and Billy means they were not picked on during the meeting, so they could sit there and feel more at ease

said, "I came here this morning to please my brother, and to come here no more. But I shall come again, for this is prettiest place that I was ever in, in all life."

Then the soldier began to seek the Lord, and before the next Sunday came he was converted. When he found his dear Lord he was not ashamed to tell of it, for he came to our meeting on the next Sunday and told us what he had found. He thanked the Lord that his brother-in-law had asked him there.

He met in my class and was a good soldier for Christ. He was not ashamed to own his master in no place. He was a soldier for the Lord, for he fought the Lord's battles. Before he was converted he drank and smoked, and after he found the dear Lord he gave up his drink and he gave up his pipe, and told others that they ought to give up their drinking and smoking for Christ's sake. Jesus done more for we, when he died on the cross, than we do for him when we give up our drink and our smoking.

There was a market town not far from where this soldier lived. When he was in the market town, and he saw the professors, he would ask them how they was. They would complain and say it was not all well with them, and then he would say to them, "How can it be well with you, when you have neither given up your drinking nor your smoking for the Lord? And how can you be happy with so many idols about you? And you are ashamed to speak a word for the Lord."

Now this soldier, after he was converted, became a new creature: for old things is passed away and all things is become new. He was a diligent soldier for Jesus Christ and was not ashamed of no man, for he had a new master and he loved him. He gave up all his old idols to please him, and now he is reaping the benefits of it, for he is in heaven. He was in the right of it, for it do not look well to see a man who say he is called and appointed by the Lord, to tell others to give up their idols when they have idols of their own.

When they bear the vessels of the dear Lord, they ought to be holy. May the Lord make us holy, and may we follow that dear brother as far as he followed Christ. Then we shall reach heaven and we shall be happy for ever and ever.

I lived some years ago in a little village where there was a Methodist chapel,[108] and they had a class leader there who loved the public house. He was found there very often and would get drunk sometimes, and there was two or three more with him that had a name to live and was dead. One of them said that if a man got so happy as to dance for joy, it is the work of the devil.

If he had been in David's day, when David danced before the Lord with all his might, he would have said it was the work of the devil. It is my opinion that the devil would not desire a better leader to lead a class than such men as them.

That man was a very great smoker, and the men that worship idols in this our day is much to be blamed. The old pipe is an idol, and you smokers do know it. He that know to do good, and do it not, to him it is a sin.

There was another man that met in that chapel, and he could not bear to hear the dear Lord praised with a loud voice, for he could not praise God himself, and he tried to hinder those that could. He and me could not agree, for I could praise God myself and I tried to get others to do the like, and he was much against the noise as he called it. He said he knew of a revival where there was a great many converted. They made no noise, for they was all quiet.

When that revival was in the day of Pentecost there was great noise then, and they said the people was drunk with new wine. They made a great noise because: Jesus had revealed his power and sin destroyed; such bliss, such happiness they feel, has made them shout for joy. If it made them shout it will make we shout, for their Lord is our Lord, bless and praise his holy name.

---

108 At the top of the page Billy has written Neot, so presumably the chapel is in St Neot.

Our people the Bible Christians had not any chapel in that village, but we had our meeting and preaching in a dwelling house. A poor man opened his door for us, and it was not in vain. One night we had a meeting and our dear Lord began to work. We had a revival, and a good revival it was. When the revival began some of them offered us their chapel to carry on our meeting.

You might say that was very well with them, and so it would be if they was like Mister Wesley. He asked for a thousand tongues to sing his great Redeemer's praise. There is many Methodists that I know that is very happy people, and I believe I shall meet many of them in heaven.

Our revival went on, and we had many converted every night for a great while. I remember at one time we had some down on their knees asking the dear Lord for mercy, and two of them was daughters to one of the men that met at the chapel. He came to the house where the revival was, but the house was so full of people that he could not get in.

He stayed outside the window and said to one of our brethren that was inside the window, for the window was open to give the people air, "If you do not end your meeting I will come in and take up my two maidens."

The brother said to me, "WC[109] is out here, saying if we do not stop our meeting he is coming in to take up his maidens."

Then I said, "We shall not stop our meeting. If he will take up his maidens, he may."

He made so much ado that we let him come in. He and his maidens went away, and as soon as they was gone there was two more down in their place. We went on with our meeting, and the Lord was with us. After the man and his maidens went away, we had many others made happy in the Lord. They came to our meeting the children of the devil, and they went home the children of the dear Lord .

109 Billy only gives these initials.

The two maidens, that the father put away, was very bad in their mind all the day after. In the evening four people that was converted took them up to their chapel and prayed with them. But the maidens was not converted. After they kept them some time, and could not get them converted, they was brought back to our meeting. They was not long this time before the dear Lord converted their souls and made them very happy, and they praised God with loud voices.

We could help them because we had learnt to praise the dear Lord for many years. We had not forgot it, but if they was made happy in that chapel, they would have no one to help them there. The class leaders and four men that belonged to that chapel was better men, for they bear quart and the public house, and for the tobacco pipe, than they was for praising the Lord.[110]

I am the son of a Methodist and I love them, but these was no Wesleyans. If they was, they would love to hear the dear Lord praised. But they had a name to live and was dead.

In another place we had a revival and there was many converted, and they was made very happy when the dear Lord had converted their souls. Some of them shouted for joy and some of them danced for joy, and we had a Pentecost shower. They said we was fools and mad men, but we was wise and glad men. David danced and shouted before the Lord, so he told his wife. The lame man done it because his ankle bones received strength, and he was made from a

110 This is a difficult sentence. Remember that at the start of this section Billy writes: *I lived some years ago in a little village where there was a Methodist chapel, and they had a class leader there who loved the public house. He was found there very often and would get drunk sometimes, and there was two or three more with him that had a name to live and was dead.*" It is possible Billy means to say that the class leader and four other men from the chapel work, or spend their time, in the public house. Whoever they are, it seems they are better at drinking and smoking than they are at praising the Lord.

cripple to a sound man. We dance and shout because we are born again. And if you was newly born of the Spirit you would shout, and might dance too.

Justification would not make you happy to shout and dance. Sanctification might, and if that would not do it, you may have the sealing of the Spirit. Then you may have a joy unspeakable and full of glory, for the dear Lord told us to ask and receive, that our joy may be full.

In that revival we had a young woman converted, and the young woman was very happy. The young woman's mother was in the chapel where her happy daughter was, and the old mother was unconverted and a wicked woman. When her daughter was praising God for what he had done for her, the old woman was so full of the devil and envy that she wanted to get to beat her daughter, and I had to keep her back from doing of it.

I said to the old woman, "If you was converted you would not look to beat your daughter, but would love her and help her to praise her dear Lord."

There was a man called JS with me in the revival, and a good man he was for he laboured well. The people said JS and William Bray converted the people. But thanks be to God it was not so. If we had done it, it would be a bad conversion. There was one that converted them that was stronger than JS or William Bray. Then who was it? It was Jesus Christ, the Saviour of the world. They and we are the purchase of his blood.

That old woman, the night after she was going to beat her daughter, she was converted. She went around the chapel praising the Lord for what he had done for her soul. Then she loved her daughter well enough to take her in her arms and hug and kiss her.

There was many people in the chapel and when the old woman went to sit down, I said to her, "Why did you make that great noise?"

She said, "The Lord have made me happy."

I said, "That is right. Cast your burden on him, for he is able to carry it now." Then I said, "The charge is taken away from JS and William Bray, for this woman says the Lord have made her very happy."

And so he did, and many more was made happy in the Saviour's love. Some of them no doubt is now in heaven, in a better land than JS or William Bray could provide for them, and JS and William Bray do hope to meet them there.

Billy writes about another lively incident that attracts criticism:

One day I was asked by a Wesleyan Methodist brother whether I would come over to his house on the next Monday evening to carry on a meeting.[111] It was a mile from where I lived, and I said I would come over. When the Monday evening came I went and got two of my neighbours, a man and his wife, and my own mother, and we went away to the Wesleyan brother's house.

When we came over, there was eight or ten women, and no man but the brother that went with me. The women was members of the Methodist society, and there was no one to begin the meeting but me. I am a poor singer and there was no one to set a tune, but I had learnt some little light tunes and one was: "We are travelling home to heaven above, where Zion's pilgrims rest in love."

So I pitched my little tune, and they helped me. When we had done singing I prayed to the Lord, and he was with us. When we had sung another little tune I asked one of the sisters to pray, but they would not.

Then said I, "Let us tell our experiences." And I told them what the Lord had done for me. When I had done speaking I wanted them to tell theirs, but they did not. So we sung another little tune, and then I went to pray.

111 Presumably in his absence.

I said in my prayer, "Lord, our meeting seems to be almost over and we all seem to feel well, except John upon the bench by the screen." For there was a screen in the house where we was.[112]

When I said so, the power of the Lord came down so on John that he fell to the ground, and he began to kick the screen with his feet. When his wife saw her husband so happy she began to shout, and my mother began to leap and dance for joy.

Then another woman began to leap and dance, clapping her hands and saying, "Is this what the Bryanites is beleaguered for?" — or persecuted for, she meant.

I began to sing and to leap and dance, and I singed: "When the ark it was coming, King David came running and leaping and dancing for joy." As I was singing, the power of the Lord came down in such a manner that most all that was in that house could leap and dance for joy. And the more I singed, "When the ark it was coming, King David came running and leaping and dancing for joy," the more we leap and dance, and the happier they was. The same God that made David so happy that he could run through a troop and leap over a wall, and turned his mourning into dancing, he was with us to turn our mourning into joy. And he did too.

Mary, the sister that lived in the house where we had the meeting, did not get into the dancing Spirit that night, but she greatly wished to have it. The next evening, which was the Tuesday evening, there was a class meeting some way off from her house. Mary went there determined for the blessing, and the blessing she had.

There was an old man in that class meeting and he was a very happy man. He took Mary by the hand and I laid my hand on her shoulder, and she and we cried to the Lord. The Lord heard us, and sent the power down on every one of us, and we was all happy.

112 This must be the neighbour who came with his wife.

Mary was so light in the Lord that she leapt for joy so high that her head struck the floor every time she leaped.[113] She was filled with the power of God and had a joy unspeakable and full of glory. And so we all had, bless and praise the name of the Lord our God, for he is good and he delights to make us children happy.

The women that was so happy met in the class with Mary. The next Sunday morning they went to their class meeting, but their class leader was one of old dead professors. They begun to leap happy, and he did not like it and tried to stop them, but he could not.

On the Monday their class leader came to their houses to try to stop them from shouting and leaping for joy, but he could not. He could not withstand the dear Lord, for the Lord is too strong for him.

The next Sunday they went to the meeting again, and the Lord made them very happy. Their class leader would not lead them, for he was angry because they was happy, and would not lead them because the Lord was with them.

They went on the third Sunday, and the dear Lord made them so happy again that their leader said he would not lead them any more. The Lord made his word good, for he died soon. And what he die for? Not because he was happy, but because he was not happy himself, and he was not willing that his class should be. So he was on the devil's side for: "He that is not for me is against me,"[114] said the Lord, and he could not bear to hear the Lord praised.

I am sorry to say that there are many preachers and leaders that will say the Lord ought to be praised from the rising of the sun to the going down of the same, but they never do it. They pay the dear Lord off with what ought to be done, and if a woman or a man should praise the Lord aloud, the preacher would say, "I wish, I

---

113 Presumably Billy means the ceiling (the floor of the room above), or underside of the balcony if the meeting was in a chapel.

114 Matthew 12:30 and Luke 11:23

wish that man or woman would keep silence there and not make such noise." When he ought to say, "That is right, my brother or sister, we all ought to be praising God with loud voices."

We are told to, "Quench not the Spirit",[115] and the Lord said, "If they should hold their peace, the stones would cry out."[116]

The women that was ashamed to pray, or to speak their experiences, was not ashamed when the dear Lord sanctified them and baptised them with the Holy Ghost sent down from heaven. They had perfect love, and that cast out all fear. The Son had made them free, and they was free indeed. They was not afraid of their class leader, though he did not like leaping and dancing, and shouting and praising God with a loud voice. He was one of the blind leaders, and, "If the blind lead the blind, they shall both fall into ditch,"[117] so our dear Lord said. I know what he said is the truth. Heaven and earth shall pass away, but his word shall not pass away, bless and praise his holy name.

When their old leader was dead, they had another leader. He was with them a great many years, and they had many happy meetings together. They lived good lives and they all died happy in the Lord. They and their leader are all in heaven praising of that God that made them so happy while down here, but they are happier up there.

That same Lord that made David happy, made the women to dance. I believe they may dance and shout now without any interruption. There is no old dead class leader in heaven to stop them from praising the Lord. There is no one there saying, "Rebuke thy disciples, for they be making too much noise."[118] They, and many

115 1 Thessalonians 5:19

116 Luke 19:40

117 Matthew 15:14

118 Luke 19:39

more that I know, is now up with Abraham and Isaac, and Jacob and David.

You preachers and class leaders did not ought to find fault with the happy members. You ought to find fault with the Lord, for it was the Lord that made them happy and not they themselves. The dear Lord have said, "Quench not the Spirit." [119] Quench not the Spirit is a command from God, and we must not break it.

There was a preacher in a chapel one day and his text was, "Quench not the Spirit." So he preached away from this text, but he was a bad hypocrite and the Lord never sent him there. These sort of preachers can talk well. He said a great many good things about the Spirit, and there was many happy people in the chapel that knew about the Spirit. They was glad to hear about the Spirit, for the Spirit of the Lord was their best friend, for he was their all and in all.

They came for the very purpose to meet with the Spirit, and the Spirit and the Lord was there. But not for that preacher. He drew nigh the Lord with his lips, when his heart was far away. We that is happy should think that this preacher gave great encouragement to we shouting and dancing Christians, but the tree is known by his fruit.

When he was preaching and telling so much about the Spirit, one of our sisters felt so much of that happy Spirit that she shouted and praised the Lord with a loud voice. We should think that our sister would please him, but she did not. And the reason was that he had not that Spirit himself.

Reader, you may ask, "How do you know that the preacher had not the Spirit?" Because he told the people to quench not the Spirit, and then he told them to quench the Spirit.

119 1 Thessalonians 5:19

Then the preacher said, "I wish that woman would keep silence there."

And that good sister, to please him, quench the Spirit for the time. So the preacher preached away from "Quench not the Spirit." Then the same sister felt so much of that blessed Spirit that she was forced to praise God with a loud voice. So did another sister, and a brother, that the dear Lord made so happy and gave them as much of that blessed Spirit that the preacher was telling about. They shouted aloud for joy, all three of them, and praised the Lord with loud voices.

The preacher that preached from "Quench not the Spirit" was very poor tempered because they done what he told them to do, but he meant for them to quench the Spirit all the time. As soon as they began to shout, he got angry with them, and he would not preach any more. A good brother that belong to that chapel, that lead the class, gave out a hymn and they sang. Then he prayed for the Lord to convert the preacher.

Now that class leader was a converted man and knew what he was telling of, for he was born twice: once of the flesh and once of the Spirit. He and his class could say, "Lord, I will praise thee, for thou once was angry with us but thine anger is turned away, and thou comforts us." They could say with John Wesley, "O for a thousand tongues to sing my great Redeemer's praise, the glory of my God and King, the trophies of his grace. My gracious master and my God, assist me to proclaim, to spread through all the earth abroad the honours of thy name."[120]

---

120 This is hymn 1 in J. Wesley's 1779 *Methodist Hymnbook*. Charles Wesley wrote it, but John would have used it at meetings. Bourne reports Billy referring to it (i)"Many of you don't sing with the one tongue you have. A bird that can sing and won't sing, ought to be made to sing."; (ii) to disarm objectors, "Wesley wanted nine hundred and ninety-nine tongues more than he had, and it is very hard if Billy Bray cannot use his one!"

That preacher would make a poor companion for John Wesley, for John Wesley wanted a thousand tongues to praise God with: that was nine hundred and ninety nine tongues more than he had. He wanted to praise the dear Lord, and he wanted to spread the name of the Lord all over the earth. And he wanted a thousand tongues to do it.

So John Wesley loved to hear the name of the dear Lord praised. If that preacher did not love to hear the name of the dear Lord praised, there is many of the Methodists that do – and he would too, was he happy. These sort of preachers will find themselves under a great mistake when they come to die.

In the Shaw Collection, in the Courtney Library at the Royal Institution of Cornwall in Truro, there is a revealing fragment someone has copied from the records of an unnamed preaching circuit:

Local Preachers Minutes 1855 – that Brother Bray's name come on the plan as an accredited local preacher.

Quarterly Meeting 1857 – that William Bray be informed that the meeting is grieved by his having allowed an unauthorised person to preach in his stead and that he is desired not to do so again.

Local Preachers Plan March 1858 – that William Bray's resignation be received.

Quarterly Meeting September 1858 – that William Bray, Bible Christian local preacher, be not allowed to take any active part in our public services.

This is almost certainly the result of a falling out with the local circuit leaders, a not uncommon event at this time for many preachers. Note how Brother Bray becomes William Bray, and he is finally identified beyond any possible doubt!

We continue with Billy's *Journal*. There is no suggestion that this account is linked in any way to the preaching circuit just mentioned:

There was a local preacher and he lived in same circuit that I did, and he was called a very great preacher. The people would flock to hear him, for he was a very great orator and could talk well. One Sunday, after preaching in the afternoon, a happy sister asked him to go home with her to have a cup of tea. The preacher went home with her, and she was a very happy woman, for I know her well. She asked him whether he believed in the power of God, whether he believed in shouting and dancing or no.

He said he did believe in it, but he never felt it. Now you may say, "See what sort of preacher he was, that told others so much about the power of the dear Lord and know nothing about it himself."

Then said our happy sister to him, "How can you believe in it and never felt it?"

He said, "Down in the town where I live, in our chapel there was a man back in the end of the chapel among the sinners.[121] This man was called WS. He was shouting and praising God with a loud voice, and there was an old woman by me. She said to go back and stop WS from making such a noise.

"When I was going back to stop him, the Lord said, 'Cry out and shout all ye inhabitants of Zion, for great is the Lord in the midst of thee.'[122] When the Lord said so to me, I did not go to where WS was, but went back where the old woman was.

"Then WS was shouting and clapping his hands, and praising of God. The old woman said, 'Go back and stop WS from making such a noise.'

121 *Among the sinners* may be Billy's own term. It sounds insensitive nowadays, but visitors to a chapel service could be asked to sit at the back until their spiritual status has been checked out. It seems that this converted man, identified only as WS, is also sitting there, so the area is obviously open to all. Maybe he is viewed as troublemaker and has been put as far back as possible!

122 Isaiah 12:6

"I was going back to stop him, and the Lord said to me, 'Clap your hands, all ye people. Shout unto God with the voice of triumph.' That is in the forty-seventh Psalm. When the Lord said so to me, I could not go back to WS, so I went back to the old woman again.

"Then WS was stamping with his feet and he was making a great noise. The old woman said to me, 'Go back and stop WS from making that noise, for he will frighten all the people.'

"There is no scripture for stamping. As I was going back the third time to stop WS, the Lord spoke to me, and said, 'Stamp ye the residue of my people.'[123] When the Lord said so to me, I could not go back to WS."

WS was a very good man and was not ashamed to own his dear Lord, and his dear Lord was not ashamed to own he. Now here you may see what a state this preacher was in. After telling others so much about Jesus Christ, and what he would do for them, at that very time he knew not Christ himself.

We must remember that this was the Lord speaking to a man, and he ought to have been a converted man, for the office he held was a preacher. The old woman and he ought to have helped WS to praise God. And they would, if they was converted.

That preacher had the telling part and not the feeling part. He was like a watch that have good wheels but a bad mainspring. Now if he had a good mainspring it would have been a good piece of machinery. Jesus Christ is our mainspring. Had the preacher and the old woman been sanctified, they would have helped WS praise the Lord, and would be glad to do it.

123 There is no Bible verse that supports this exact state-
     ment. The preacher may have been thinking of Ezekiel
     6:11 where the remnant, or residue, of the scattered Isra-
     elites are told to clap their hands and stamp in sorrow
     and repentance.

A preacher that have a good gift for preaching and no grace is like one that have knives and forks and plates, and no meat. But knives and forks and plates and meat is best, and gifts is great blessings. You may say, "When preachers have grace, then you need not say anything about gifts, Beley,[124] for you are a very blunt man."

That is all true, and I know that I am a very blunt man. Thanks be to God I have a good mainspring, even if my wheels is poor. And thanks be to God I have good meat, even if my knives and fork and plates is poor. Thanks to God I can get along, and I should have helped WS if I was there. I would not try to stop him, I would shout with him. If he clapped his hands for joy, I would clap mine too. If he leaped for joy, I would leap for joy too.

WS's God is my God, and there is a parcel of great blessings promised to us in the Bible. They are all ours through believing, and we may have enough of the love of our God in our hearts to make us shout and dance for joy. That preacher did not try to get it, though the Lord told him plain enough that was he not right. The preacher told our happy sister that he believed in it, but never felt it. What a miserable man, preaching to others and knowing nothing about it himself. And it is not likely that he ever did, for he is dead, and I hear that he died out of his mind. It may be a good thing that he is gone, for if the blind lead the blind they shall fall into the ditch.

The happy sister that he told it to is living still, to tell others of it. And, thanks be to God I am still living, to tell and write about it. If that wise preacher was sanctified he would know better than to stop WS from honouring God, for he that praises God do honour God, and he that honours God, him will God honour. There is none but them that is born again that can honour God. An unconverted man or woman cannot honour God, no matter how great his talent is.

Gifts is not grace. The old devil will carry away a great many with different sorts of gifts, but he cannot carry away one that have

---

124 Billy's spelling of his own name varies throughout the *Journal*.

grace. The word of God tells us that the devil carried away the rich man, with all his riches and his gifts.[125] Down in hell he lifted up his eyes, being in torment. But the devil could not carry away the beggar, because he had grace. The beggar knew what it was to eat that bread of life that came down from heaven. And the beggar knew what it was to eat that flesh that was meat indeed, and to drink that blood that was drink indeed.

Knives and forks and plates would not please the beggar. He wanted meat, and good meat he had. God is love. I know he fills us with joy unspeakable and full of glory, for there is no limits to his power. We ask and have whatever we want, for there is a great plenty in heaven.

125 Luke 16:19-31

CHAPTER 11

THE MISSION GOOSE AND THE WHIRLWIND

BILLY IS STILL working underground as a miner, although later in this chapter - around 1848 - he is employed on the surface. This may have been due to temporary ill health, as shortly after he seems to be underground again. There was no official retirement age, but mining underground became too arduous for many men as time went on. On the surface we would expect to find children, women, less active men and older miners.

Surface work included work indoors operating the various crushing mills, and work outside such as wheeling away the ashes – a job that Billy was once given because he refused to work on Sundays. Even surface work was not without its unexpected danger, as Billy is to tell us later in this chapter.

First, Billy tells in his *Journal* about a mining family called Sando. It is not clear if the old man is Billy's uncle, or the miners know him as Uncle William as a term of affection. Billy writes:

> There was an old man and his son that worked by me underground in the mine, and he was called William Sando. He and his son worked in the western end, and my partner and me worked in the eastern end. So we worked to the same level and wheeled our stuff to one plat. The old man and his son was not converted, so I used to tell them about the Lord and what he would do for them. Then I would kneel down and pray for them.
>
> I said, "Lord, if any one of we must die today, let me die. Do not leave Uncle William Sando, for he is not happy."

When he rose from his knees, for they would kneel down with me, the tears would be running from the old man's eyes. But what power the devil have over poor sinners. The same old man that the tears was running from the eyes of, was in a short time in the end swearing at his son.

When I heard him swearing I used to think I would not pray for him again, but this was a temptation of the devil. Thanks be to God I did not hearken to the devil, but always prayed with him. And thanks be to God, I did not pray in vain. The old man was made very happy before he died, and now I believe he is up in heaven praising God, while I am here writing his Journal.

Bless and praise God for converting Uncle William Sando. One soul is worth more than all this world. William Sando is rich, and he will be poor no more. The Bible tell us that we cannot pray in vain.

Another account by Billy shows his burning desire to share his faith:

I worked with a man before I was converted called William Bray,[126] and he was like me a very wicked man. The blessed Lord promoted both of us at one time, for he was put captain into a mine and I was adopted in the royal family and made a prince. For now are we the sons of God, and it do not appear what we shall be. But one thing we know, when Christ do appear we shall be made like him. We shall see him as he is.

After some time the mine that William Bray was captain in got poor, and stopped. Then he came to the Great Consols mine, as captain over boys and girls. I had not seen him for a great while. One Sunday I had been to my plan and it was late when I came home. When I waked on the Monday morning William Bray came into my mind. It was said to me, "If thee wast rise and go to Carharrack, I will give you his soul."

I said, "Where is this coming from?"

126 A common combination of names at the time.

It was said to me again, "I am the God of Abraham and Isaac and Jacob. Go nothing doubting, it is me."

Then I said, "I will go Lord."

I rosed, and as soon as I had breakfast I went away on the Lord's errand. On the road there I met a man. His name was Blaney. He asked me where I was going, and I told him.

He said to me, "Go on, that is from the Lord."

I went on and found William Bray's house, and found him home with his wife. I said, "I have a message from God for you."

And his wife cried out.

I said it was a good message and not a bad one.

The Lord would not the death of one sinner, but rather all would come to him and have life, for the dear Lord have shown us what he have done for us. There is no man that will buy a premises at a dear rate in which to mine and work hard, and suffer much to pay for it, and then go away and leave this place behind. Now we are the Lord's premises, and he has paid very dear for us. He is not willing to lose us, for there is joy in heaven in the presence of God and his angels when sinners are brought to God.

I said to William Bray, "The Lord has told me this morning that he will give me your soul. If you will begin to pray, you will soon be converted and made happy in the Lord. I have no need to tell you what sort of man I was, for you know all about that when we worked together. But now I am happy in the Lord. If I was to die this minute my soul would be in heaven, and I would rather die this minute than you should. You can be as happy as me, if you find the Lord."

He seemed to look at me with surprise, so we all kneeled down before the Lord and I prayed with them, and asked the Lord to bless them.

That same day, in the evening, William Bray sent for me again. I did not go until the day following, for I was night core in the mine.

When I came to his house the next morning, I said to him, "What do you want of me?"

He said, "I did not feel much when you was here yesterday, but after you went away I felt much about my soul, and I feel determined to serve the Lord."

It was not long before he found him. The Lord soon made him happy in his love, for I saw him many times while he was sick, and he was happy. The day before he died he sent for me. When I came by his bedside he told me, as well as he could speak for he was very weak, that he wanted to see me to tell me that Christ was his.

Then he had a good praise, and said to me. "Christ is mine, and I am his."

These are the last words that he spoke to me, and soon after this he was taken up to his reward where sin nor sorrow can never come. Since then four of his children is gone to meet him. His wife will not be long, for she is an old woman and in the road to heaven, and she will no doubt be there soon, praise the Lord.

It might seem from Billy's accounts that as soon as someone is converted they die. Other people seem to die, in Billy's opinion, because they turn down the offer of salvation. It is likely that many of these people know they are acutely ill, and this makes some of them more ready to seek God. The following is an exception to this 'rule':

I well remember when we that was the children of the Lord went to see a sick woman, and she was so bad that the doctor said she must die. While we were at her bedside kneeling down, and one of my brothers was praying, I was asking the Lord, "Will she recover or not?"

The Lord said to me, "Rise up and tell her, that she may know that I am above doctors and physicians, tell her I will restore her to her perfect health again. And tell her to sin no more, lest a worse thing come upon her."

When we had done praying, I said to her, "The Lord has told me to rise up and tell you, that you may know that he is above all other doctors and physicians, that he will restore you to your perfect health again. But you must sin no more, lest a worst thing come upon you."

When she heard me say so, she cried aloud for joy. But when we came out of the woman's house, one of my brethren said to me, "What did you tell her so? For she may die."

I said, "The Lord told me to rise up and tell her what I have told her, and I have done the will of the Lord. If she die this time, you may call me a false prophet."

So it ended there.

The day following I went to see her again, and she was downstairs by the fire. She is living still, and that is more than twenty years agone. By what I have heard she have not kept that which the Lord commanded her to keep, for I have been told she have been a bad woman and is still. So her worst is to come if she do not repent and give her heart to the dear Lord. She is an old woman, and she must soon die and give up the ghost. If she is not right while we are on the earth, she cannot get back again, for if she die unholy she will be for ever unholy.

We must be born again, or die. It is heaven or hell, and that for ever and ever. You that read, and me that write, must be in one of those places. But thanks be to the Lord, we may get where Abraham and Isaac and Jacob is, and the prophets is in the kingdom of heaven, and that is our heaven as well as theirs.

Bourne tells us:

Billy always insisted that the best should be given to the Lord, and not the blind, the lame, or the sick. At one mission meeting Billy became upset because he saw something in the report about money received for rags and bones.

When he rose to address the meeting, he said, "I don't think it is right, supporting the Lord's cause with old rags and bones. The Lord deserves the best, and ought to have the best.

"I knew a woman down at St Just some years ago that had two geese," he continued. "Though she might have a good flock to begin, she could never rear above two or three. At last she

Cornish miners breaking ore
redrawn from an engraving in *The Mine*

promised the Lord that if he would increase her
flock, she would give every tenth goose to the
missionaries.[127] Now I reckon you will say that
that woman had a good heart, but I don't think
so. If she gave every fifth goose to the
missionaries she would still have more than she
had before.

"But the Lord took her at her word, and the next
year she had eleven, and they all lived until they
grew up nearly as big as old ones. And then the
Lord tried her faith. One of her geese died, and
what do you think the devil said? 'That's the
mission goose!'

127 Preachers travelling locally, holding missions.

"That's how the devil would serve the missionaries. He would give old, dead, stinking geese to them to eat. What do they want of an old, dead, stinking goose? But she knew him, and she said, 'No, devil, I have ten left now, and the missionaries shall have one of them.'

"The next year she had eleven again. They was out swimming about the pond, with their great long necks and their beautiful white feathers. They was the most respectable looking geese I ever saw."

We now come to the danger. Billy writes in his *Journal* about his surface work as a dressing captain somewhere around 1847 or 1848:

He is a God of all power, and sometimes men see his mighty wonders on the earth that cause them to fear and tremble. When it is loud thunder and fierce lightning, and in some places earthquakes, these are showing the wicked inhabitants of our earth that there is a God of all power, and they must stand before him, and that very soon.

I am about to write of something that I saw of the wonders of the great King of kings and Lord of lords. When I was at St Neot,[128] at a mine called Wheal Sisters, I was what they called a dressing captain that looked to the boys and maidens, to keep them to work.[129] One day when we was at the mine we saw in the distance a whirlwind. It appeared to us to be from twelve to fifteen feet wide (4 to 5m).

You might say you could not see the wind. True, we could not see the wind but we could see the effects, for it was tearing the bushes

128 Billy and Joey's daughter Grace was married at St Neot in 1846, when Billy was aged 52.

129 Children as young as seven worked above ground at the mines. Some had to leave home at five in the morning and walk long distances to work. Fourteen was the usual age for boys to start work underground, although large boys as young as nine could be allowed below.

out of the hedges. There was a shaft they was sinking a little time before, but as it happened the shaft men was not there. And thanks be to God they was not, for there was a timber house over the shaft.

The whirlwind thrown down the house that was over the shaft, and the shaft was not far off from we. The wind had a great power. There was as much as fifty boys and maidens with me, and the whirlwind seemed to be coming in a right line unto us. When the boys and maidens saw that, they fell down on their knees and cried to the Lord to have mercy on them. And the dear Lord heard them and had mercy on them, for he turned the whirlwind another way around the barrow.

After it left where we was, it over-seat a farmers cart house, so if our dear Lord had not turned the whirlwind it would be bad for us. There was a great deal of timber where we was. There was timber about the shaft and iron too, and the bucking house and the cobbing house.[130] So had not the dear Lord turned the whirlwind, it was looking as though that whirlwind would throw down the great part of it.

But as I said before, when the boys and girls fell down on their knees and cried for mercy, the dear Lord had mercy on us. That whirlwind was the means the Lord used to begin a revival, for there was many converted at that time. Among them was two little boys about twelve years of age. One of them, John Hicks[131], is now a preacher and has been for some years.

---

130 Buildings where the ore was crushed.

131 The 1881 census for St Ive near Liskeard in Cornwall (not to be confused with St Ives on the north coast) shows: *John Hicks, age 45, formerly copper miner, now local Methodist preacher, born at St Neot, living with his wife Jane and daughter Mary.* This John Hicks would have been 12 in 1848, which means he is almost certainly the boy Billy is writing about here, as every detail fits. It gives me confidence that Billy's memory of events in his life, some of them many years before he wrote his *Journal*, is extremely good.

I did not hear that the whirlwind was seen anywhere far off from where we was, for we saw it for a great part of that day up in the air like a ?whining sheet of dust, constantly blowing in the air, clouds of it. It was there for hours, and looked very much to me that the dear Lord, that would not the death of one sinner, sent that whirlwind to awaken some of our wicked boys and maidens, and to stir up me.

If that whirlwind done no more good than to be instrumental in the hand of our dear Lord in converting the two boys, it was a good thing that the dear Lord sent the whirlwind. John Hicks has no doubt been made a blessing to others, for when he was a little boy he went with me on the Sabbath day to my plan. He and me have gone many miles on the Sabbath together, to tell the people to repent and be converted that their sins may be blotted out, that the times of refreshing may come forth from the presence of God.

Bourne tells us that he heard from Mr Gilbert[132] of a meeting where Billy was about to leave Highway Chapel in company with a young boy who had come with him. In the early editions of *The King's Son* Bourne tells us that is John Hicks, who became a great friend:

Billy said, "Johnny and me, we'll make the valleys ring with our singing and praising as we go home."

I said, "Then you are a singer, Billy."

"Oh yes, bless the Lord, I can sing. My Heavenly Father likes to hear me sing. I can't sing so sweetly as some, but my Father likes to hear me sing as well as those who sing better than I can. My Father likes to hear the crow as well as the nightingale, for he made them both."

132. This may be William Gilbert (1821-1885) of the Gwennap Circuit that included Hicks Mill. He started preaching in 1846.

Billy continues:

When John and me went to Liskeard to my plan, the chapel was full of people. They would many of them come to hear the little boy pray. I lived at St Neot at that time and John lived there too. So John was my companion, and he was glad to go with me, or I might rather say ride, for I asked the people for money to buy a horse. And money I had given to me, and the Quaker Friends was very kind in helping to buy a horse for me.

The Friend that gave me the most towards my horse is dead now, and he is not sorry that he gave Billy Bray money to buy a horse for John Hicks to ride on the Sabbath day with me to our plan. The dear Lord knowed that we wanted a horse, John and me, and he provided one for us, for we had a large circuit. We was out every Sunday, sometimes to Liskeard, and sometimes to Looe and Polperro and other places.

I used to speak to the people, and John prayed after I had done. The dear Lord was with him, and though he was so young he would pray with mighty power. We had a chapel full of people wherever we went. They would come to hear John pray, and thanks be to the dear Lord, John can pray still, for he is on the Liskeard plan with the Bible Christians. When he went with me first it is sixteen or eighteen years agone, and John have his Lord still, for he is a good master, for John have found him so. And so have I.

We have had many good meetings together, and many comfortable rides together. The Lord have kept John for the great part of twenty years, thanks be to the Lord for keeping John all that time, and may the dear Lord bless him for ever and ever. The Lord have kept me for more than forty years, and John is well, thanks be to the Lord for it. And I am well. It was never better with me than now, for I am happy in the Saviour's love, and John and me shall surely meet in heaven, with many more that I know, praising the dear Lord.

John was a good boy and he loved to hear the dear Lord praised. There was some that I know that could not bear to hear anyone praise the Lord with a loud voice. But everyone in Christ is a new creature. Old things is passed away and all things is become new. That is why the unconverted man and the converted man cannot agree.

CHAPTER 12

FLORENCE HOSKIN'S STICK

FLORENCE HOSKIN WAS a woman who was known to Billy as Florey. She lived in Porthleven, a fishing village on the south coast of Cornwall. More famous these days as a place for seaside holidays, in 1848 something amazing was being talked about in the streets. This account from Billy's *Journal* is extremely well documented, including a signed witness statement written in another hand. Since the witness statement was apparently first written in 1848, sixteen years before Billy compiled his *Journal*, it seems to have been copied into the *Journal* from the original document and signed by a man called William Hendy. It is not clear if Hendy was also the original class leader, or just the copyist. Florence Hoskin's disability was certainly genuine, having been diagnosed by a surgeon in Helston as incurable.

Billy writes his account first, followed by William Hendy's entry in the *Journal*:

> Dear reader, I am about to write of a woman wherein God's power was made manifest on her in a wondrous manner, and I heard it from her lips twice. I will write down here as near as I can as she told it to me.
>
> Sister Hoskin[133] was hurted by some way in her thigh so that she was a cripple for seven years, and she was obliged to go on a crutch

---

133 The spelling of this woman's name, both by Billy and later in the *Journal* by William Hendy is inconsistent. Mostly it is *Hoskin*, but sometimes it is written *Haskin* or *Hasken*, and even *Hosking* or *Hasking*. The formation of

and a stick. She was so weak that she was forced to drag her foot after her. The doctor said that she would never be sound no more, but the doctor made a mistake, for she was made sound again. He is a God of all power and there is nothing too great for him to do.

She was old when she was converted, and after she was converted some time she felt dark in her mind. I think it was on a Saturday night when she went to bed that she felt very dark in her mind, and she could not sleep. But she prayed to her dear Lord who is able to heal both body and soul, for she wanted a cure for both.

She prayed to her dear Lord, and said in her prayer, "Show me, my dear Lord, whether I am a wheat or a tare."

She prayed away some time like that, and then the cloud broke from her mind and she was made very happy in his love. She said, "Now, my dear Lord, thou hast healed my soul. Why not heal my body, too?"

She meant her sore thigh or leg. When she said so, the Lord said to her, "Arise and go down to my gospel house, and there thou shalt be healed."

She said, "Why can I not be healed here, my dear Lord?" She was in the bed, and it was an easy place for a poor cripple. But when she said so, the dear Lord's Spirit was taken away from her for some time, and she was dark again.

When she found herself like that, she said, "I will go to thy gospel house, or anywhere else, but only let me be healed, my dear Lord."

Then her dear Lord said unto her, "If I heal thee here, they will not believe it. For there is many of them as unbelieving as the Jews was in Jerusalem."

the letters *o* and *a* is inconsistent in clearly identifiable words by both writers. Bourne prints an excerpt from this entry in *The King's Son* and uses the spelling *Hoskin*. Since Bourne probably either knew the woman, or had heard her being talked about, I have adopted his spelling here.

That was true, for if the dear Lord healed her in the bed, many of them would say that she was not healed, for there is many unbelieving people in our country and it is hard to make them believe. But when the dear Lord told Sister Hoskin to go the chapel, there was many witnesses that saw the almighty power of God in healing that woman.

It was Sunday, so she rosed out of bed to go to the gospel house to get healed, for her faith was strong. But when she got out of her bed and had got downstairs, it was as if the devil stood in the door and tempted her to stop and to have her breakfast first.

She said, "No, devil, I will have none. For thee hast many times tempted me to stay for breakfast, and I have had a dead meeting for being so late."

So she left her home with her crutch and stick, and went away for her gospel house, dragging her poor lame foot on the ground. When she came to the chapel it was so early that there was no one there.

When her leader came, he said, "What are you doing here so soon today, Florey?"

Florey said to him, "There is great things going to be done here, for I am going to have a sound leg today, for the dear Lord told me so in the night."

Her class leader told me he thought she was mad, and he said if she had not more faith than he had, she would never have a sound leg.

So the meeting began, and while someone was praying, Florey said, "Pray away, the balm is coming."

Then they heard her leg, or thigh, cracking like a stick and she was thrown in the seat. When she rosed up she could walk the chapel without her crutch or her stick.

Some of the people saw her walking the chapel, or gospel house as she called it, at Porthleven. They went around the little town at Porthleven, and said, "Florey Hoskin is walking the Bryanites' chapel with no crutch nor stick."

When the people heard that, a great many came together to see what a miracle the Lord had done. For the dear Lord Jesus Christ had done it, for no one else could never had done such a miracle, bless and praise his holy name for ever and ever.

So when the people went out of the chapel, Florey Hoskin rosed and went away without her crutch or stick after being a cripple seven years. When she was going out of the gospel house, one of the people said, "Here, Florey, is your crutch and stick."

Florey said, "You may have they if you will, for I shall not want they any more."

Nor she did not want crutch nor stick any more while she lived in this world. And she do want neither crutch nor stick now, for I believe she is in heaven among the blessed where there is no cripples, and she is no doubt singing to him that loved us and washed us in his own blood, and made us kings and priests to God. Some foolish people will say the Lord do not work miracles in these days like he did in the days of old, but the dear Lord do. If we can believe and pray for it, we are sure to have it.

Florey Hoskin believed, and prayed to her dear Lord that he would hear her, and heal her thigh. She believed that he could do it, and would do it, and he did it according to her faith. She went away from her own house a cripple on a crutch and a stick, with her leg drawn after her, and in a few hours she came home to her own house, and did not want neither crutch nor stick.

Her dear Lord made her a sound woman, so it was well for Florey Hoskin that she served the Lord. It was the same Lord that cured Florence Hoskin that cured the lame man in the days of Peter and John, for he have the same power now as he had then. And what that power is, there do none know, but the dear Lord himself.

Billy immediately follows this with a story, told in this book on page 158, of John Sims who became rich and greedy, so it is unlikely Hendy, who writes his entry three pages later, has been sitting there prompting Billy's memory. The different wording and the small details give us a much fuller account. Maybe Hendy was in the area and reminded Billy of Florence Hoskin's healing, and Billy invited him to copy the testimony into the *Journal*, but continued writing in the meantime. The pages immediately after Florence Hoskin are taken up with Richard Allen's hymn *Good morning Brother Pilgrim,* so Billy seems to have had more than one visitor. This is the only place where others have written in the *Journal.*

The signed witness statement and testimony is not in Billy's handwriting, and is presumably that of William Hendy. It is without punctuation and is headed: "1848 March 1st Hoskin". Since the *Journal* was written in 1864 this seems to be a copy of an original statement made by Florence Hoskin to her class leader in 1848:

> My dear reader, this is the experience of Florence Hoskin, the account I had from her class leader from the parish of Sithney in the county of Cornwall, aged about seventy-two years of age.
>
> About seven years ago I was made a cripple by the ill usages of some of my family. I lost the use of one of my legs entirely. I applied to Mister Daniel, surgeon of Helston, for relief.[134] He told me it was quite impossible for him or anyone else to render me any use, and told me that I should not have the use of my leg any more.
>
> For seven years I was obliged to have a crutch and a stick to assist me wherever I went. In 1844, the Saturday night before the first Sunday in July, I went to bed with my mind greatly cast down. I prayed to the Lord that he would disperse the gloom from my mind. I prayed for some considerable time, I believe almost all night. In my prayer I told the Lord that he was able to disperse this darkening from my mind, as he had been so good to heal my backsliding and pardon my sins.
>
> While I was wrestling like Jacob all night, the Lord made my soul happy in the God of my salvation. I could rejoice with joy inexpressible and full of glory. While I was in that happy state of mind I had faith to believe that the Lord would heal my leg, and he will. I was hoping and believing. I heard a voice saying to me,

134 The 1830 Pigot Directory for Cornwall lists Charles and Thomas Daniell as surgeons in Wendron Street, Helston.

"Arise out of bed and put on thy garments, and go to the gospel house, and thou shalt be healed."

While I was moving on my things, a light shone around me and a voice spoke to me the second time, saying, "Arise and go to my house, and I will give my disciples healing and saving faith."

I am very thankful that I went to the house of prayer that day. It was a time of much good to all present. The house was filled with the glory of God. I went to the house of God this morning[135] with crutch and stick for the last time. While in the meeting I had faith to believe that God had healed my leg.

When the meeting was concluded I stopped behind to try whether I could walk. I walked the pew and then the chapel. I left my crutch and stick in the chapel, and went home praising God for what he had done for my body and soul.

The writer adds:

Florence Hoskin's experience is written as it was related to me. I have known this woman about twenty years. Within this seven years I have seen her go to preaching many times with a crutch and a stick. I have likewise seen her many time since she have been healed go without a crutch and stick. I believe the work is of God. Florence Hoskin is a very poor woman but rich in faith.

This was written in the presence of William Bray

William Hendy, Bible Christian

At the bottom Billy has written:

Florence Hoskin is written in two pieces. I had one from her own lips and the other in writing from her class leader, William Hendy.

There are a few more lines in Billy's handwriting on this page, the first verse of a hymn by John Newton. It is hymn 371 in the early Bible Christian Hymnbook, but it is not in

---

135 This account appears to have been first written in May 1848, nearly four years after the healing. So this morning must mean the morning being written about.

Wesley's Methodist Hymnbook. The words show the difficulties in reading much of Billy's *Journal*. The first and fifth lines would be indecipherable without knowing the hymn, but when read aloud the lines sound better than they look:

How teges and taselas the ours
                              [how tedious and tasteless the hours]
When Jesus no longer I see;
Sweet prospect, sweet birds and sweet flowers,
Have all lost their sweetness with me.
The mede samer san but dime
        [the mid-summer sun <shines> but dim – MS omits shines]
The fields strive in vain to look gay;
But when I am happy in him,
December's as pleasant as May.

CHAPTER 13

UNABLE TO SPEAK

IT IS CLEAR from the census records that Billy and his family regularly move around Cornwall and Devon seeking work. Billy is now at Tokenbury Mine near Liskeard, and only a few miles east of St Neot, where we know Billy was living in 1846. He is working underground with his son. The mine opened in 1841 and stopped working in 1849. In 1850 a new company was formed. This may date the following account to the late 1840s when the mine is in financial trouble and the owners are cutting back on the workforce. If this is so, Billy's son James will be in his mid twenties. As always, the Quakers are remarkably generous in supporting Christians of other denominations, providing work, clothes and food as they are able.

Billy writes:

> When my son was grown up to a young man, we went to the east to work under the Quaker Friends, and they was very kind to me. Me and my son was put to work in a mine called Tokenbury, and we had a good captain, and we had a good place. We done well for some time, until the dear Lord had another job for me. Then two captains came up from the west to inspect our mine, and they said where there was two men working they must take away one man and put a boy in the man's place. So me or my son must turn out.

> When our captain told me that my son or me must go and get work, I told my son that I might get work sooner than he, and he must stay and work where he was. So I was out of work, and I went to my Friend to try to get work, but I could get none.

Then I went away into a strange mine,[136] where there was a strange captain and strange men, and there I got work with three more men. They was three wicked men and they was unconverted. We worked two in a core. Two men would go down in the mine by six or seven o'clock in the morning, and up again by two or three in the afternoon. My partner, or comrade, was called George Vine. He and me was forenoon core the first week we went to work there.

When we came down in the mine where we was to work, I said to my comrade, "We must kneel down and pray, and ask the Lord to keep and bless us, and bless the labour of our hands."

My partner said nothing against me praying, so he and me went down on our knees. I prayed to the Lord for his help, for I could do nothing without him. I prayed that the Lord would bless my partner, and that he would convert him and my other two comrades. And I prayed that the Lord would bless us and bring us safe through our labour.

When I had done praying we began to work, and I began to tell him what a good thing it was to serve the Lord, and what peace it gives to the mind, and how happy it makes a man that can say, "O grave, where is thy victory?" And, "O death, where is thy sting?"[137]

George Vine said to me, "What you have said is all true, for it is a blessed thing for a man to be happy and all his sins forgiven. For," said he, "I was once on the Primitive Methodist preachers' plan, and I know what happiness was. But I am not happy now, for I have lost it."

I said, "If you have lost it, you need not stay without it. Why do you not seek it again? The dear Lord have said, 'Come, all ye backsliding children, and I will heal your backsliding and love you

---

136 Strange, meaning previously unknown to Billy, and also
     with the captain and men.

137 1 Corinthians 15:55

freely.' "[138] Then I said, "Begin to pray again, and the dear Lord will help you. I will pray for you, and if our two comrades do say anything to you I will be on your side, and the dear Lord will be for you too. And we shall be on the strongest side."

He and our other two comrades, or partners, was to the public house a few days before, and they was all drunk together. But the dear Lord is merciful, and if the wicked man forsake his ways, and the unrighteous man his thoughts, let him turn to the dear Lord and he will have mercy upon him; and to our God, and he will abundantly pardon.[139]

Then my partner said, "By the help of the dear Lord I will begin again to serve the Lord, for he is the best friend."

George Vine began to seek the Lord, and he soon found him. He was soon put on the plan with our people the Bible Christians.

He asked me to go down to Gweek[140] where he lived, to carry on a meeting on the Tuesday night. So I went to his house to carry on our meeting. As I was a stranger and called Billy Bray, I had a great many to hear me. I did not speak in vain, for the dear Lord soon began to revive his blessed work. The dear Lord's work is a blessed work, and they that do it will prosper.

We had a revival and some were converted to God. Among the rest there was one Mary Bennets (sic) that had not gone to my meeting or preaching for some time. When she heard that Beley Bray was going to speak she came to hear me, and what I say in the name of my great Master convinced her that she was a sinner.

I formed a class meeting in George Vine's house and Mary made one of our class. She was unwell the first time I saw her, in a bad state of health. After I had done speaking Tuesday night we had our class meeting and Mary Bennets used to come. I was the under

---

138 Jeremiah 3:22

139 Isaiah 55:7

140 Probably *Gweek,* but Billy spells it *Quicke* here and later.

leader, but the dear Lord was the Head Leader and he was with we to bless us and to make us happy, bless his holy name.

Mary came many weeks. She was not converted but wished to be so. I used to tell her it was sure to come if she continued to hold fast. And so it was, for the last time that I saw her was to the class meeting, and she told us all that she was happy in the dear Lord and she was going to heaven. She died in that same week and she is now in heaven praising her dear Lord. Her husband was made happy too, and some of her neighbours.

We had a good class at George Vine's house and he was on our plan. He preached with our people, and while we worked there he was in a good way. But after I went away from George he fell back in some way and he went to drink and he smoked the pipe. Drinking is a bad thing for a man that preach the gospel. May dear Lord save preachers from that error.

Men who is employed, or ought to be, by the dear Lord to tell other people about their idols, sometime have a tobacco pipe in their pocket themselves. George Vine did not live long after he began to backslide, for the dear Lord soon afflicted him and took out of this world. He was no good down here, but the dear Lord is slow to anger and of great mercy. He would not the death of one sinner.

George found the dear Lord to be so, for I heard that he cried to the Lord in the time of affliction and the Lord heard him. He died happy and he is gone to heaven for all I know about him, and we see that the dear Lord is willing to save all that is willing to be saved.

We read in God's blessed book that when the eunuch was willing to be saved the dear Lord sent Phillip his servant to help him. When St Paul was in distress the dear Lord sent his servant to help him. And the dear Lord sent me, unworthy me, to Gweek to help them to heaven.

There was a man that lived in the neighbourhood of Porthleven, called John Sims. He was a Wesleyan. He had no father and he was very poor at first. But the dear Lord blessed him, for John worked at the mine and he done well. At first he was very good to the poor, and very liberal to the cause of God.

I remember the first time I ever saw John Sims was at a missionary meeting at Porthleven. We had a very good meeting, for the dear Lord of missions was there. All the speakers spoke with power, and we had a good collection. The people was so liberal that they was throwing the money in through the window.

John Sims said, "Mister R, if you will be one pound, I will give another."

And Mister R said, "Then I will, John."

So Mister R gave his pound, and John gave his pound. John was not very rich then but he was very liberal. But after the dear Lord blessed him with more money, he was very greedy. He had a purse full of money, and the more money John had the greedier he was. He was not married, he had no wife nor child, and he had his hundreds in money and houses and land. He was so greedy that he would not afford shamel meat,[141] but would buy a sheep's head and lungs because that was cheap. John met with the Wesleyans, and they had enough to do to make him pay his quarterage.

Now here we may see how the heart of man do depart from the living God and get a life to the world. John, when he was converted first and he had not much money, he was very liberal and went to see the sick, and he could give them a little to help them along. But when the dear Lord gave him more money to give to his cause, and to give to the poor, the sick, the fatherless and the widow, he hid his talent. But he is dead, and left it all behind.

Here is an experience of Billy's that Bourne records in *The King's Son*. Although it sounds like Billy's writing, it is not in the *Journal*:

When I was in the St Neot Circuit, I remember one Sunday I was planned at Redgate and there was a chapel full of people. The Lord gave me great power and liberty in speaking, but all at once he took away his Spirit from me, so that I

---

141 Meat from a butcher's shop or stall.

could not speak a word – and this might have been the best sermon that some of them ever heard!

"What," you say, "looking like a fool, not able to speak?"

Yes, but it was not long before I told them, "I am glad I am stopped, and that for three reasons. The first is to humble my soul and make me feel more dependent on my Lord, to think more fully of him and less of myself.

"The next reason," I told them, "is to convince you that you are ungodly. For you say we can speak what we have a mind to, without the Lord as well as with him. But you cannot say so now, for you heard how I was speaking. But when the dear Lord took away his Spirit I could not say another word. Without my Lord I can do nothing.

"And the third reason," I said "is that some of you young men who are standing here may be called to stand in the pulpit some day, as I am. The Lord may take his Spirit from you as he has from me, and then you might say, 'It is no good for me to try to preach or exhort, for I was stopped the last time I tried to preach, and I shall preach no more.'

"But now you can say, 'I saw poor old Billy Bray stopped once like me. He did not mind it, and he told the people that he was glad his dear Lord had stopped him. And Billy Bray's dear Lord is my Lord, and I am glad he stopped me too. For, if I can benefit the people and glorify God, that is what I want.'"

I then spoke a great while, and told the people what the dear Lord gave me to say.

CG Honor[142] makes the following contribution in *The King's Son:*

> At a love feast in their chapel at St Blazey, when Billy was present, several people spoke of their trials, but said that their blessings more than counterbalanced them.
>
> At length, Billy rose. Clapping his hands and smiling, he said, "Well, friends, I have been taking vinegar and honey but, praise the Lord, I've had the vinegar with a spoon, and the honey with a ladle."
>
> Billy had the same trials as others, but said, "It was not worth while to speak or write anything about them. I would rather walk to heaven over the roughest road with bleeding feet, than ride to hell even in a fine carriage."

Bourne writes:

> Whenever Billy visited the sick and dying, he always expressed a wish that he might, "See them in heaven, dressed in robes of glorious brightness. For if I saw them there, I must be there myself too!"
>
> One night, before going up to bed, Billy said to a young friend, "If you find me dead in the morning, mind you shout Hallelujah!"
>
> She told him that she did not think it likely she would be able to do such a thing.
>
> "Why not?" asked Billy. "It would be all right."

Bourne continues:

> It seemed strange to Billy that the duty of visiting the sick should be neglected so much. Billy was surprised and dismayed to find

---

142 Identified only as a Primitive Methodist minister by Bourne. CG Honor wrote *Fish, Tin and Copper.*

someone whom his class leader had only visited once in the past year.

Billy visited an elderly Christian woman who was eighty years old. Billy said she knew as much about the dear Lord as he could tell her. She loved the Lord so much that she did not know a name *good enough* by which to call him.

"Every word she spoke was sweet to my soul," Billy said later. "And why? Because Satan can do nothing by those who are filled with the Holy Ghost."

When Billy heard of an old man who been seeking the Lord for a long time, he said he hoped he had been. Then Billy added, "It is dangerous to put off the salvation of our soul until we are on our death-bed. Where there is one who gets the prize, there are ten who lose it. The same old devil that got at them downstairs will get at them when they are in their beds."

Cornish mining scene
redrawn from an engraving in *The Treasures of the Earth*

CHAPTER 14

THE MINE AT BOTALLACK

[Some readers of this book will understandably have little interest in what life was like in a Cornish mine in the time of Billy Bray. If this is you, you may want to skip this chapter, or return to it later. If, on the other hand, you feel like taking an intriguing trip underground, read on.]

VISITORS TO CORNWALL today can have little idea of working conditions inside a Cornish mine in the time of Billy Bray. Although Billy makes several references to his work underground, the only one with any detail is a description he gives near the start of his *Journal*. This is what he writes:

> Because this book may be read with more people than miners, I am more particular in stating our rules. We were eight men worked together, four in our core, driving two ends — one east and another west — two men in each end. We worked in the western one, my partner and me. Our comrades went at six in the morning, and worked again two in the afternoon, and we went down in the mine, to come up at ten at night.

Researchers of mining history may find that bit fascinating (I omitted it in Chapter 1, in order to use it here) but it hardly brings underground conditions to life. For this we need to turn to *Rambles Beyond Railways,* a book by Wilkie Collins, the Victorian author of *The Lady in White, The Moonstone,* and other stories. First published by Richard Bentley in London in 1851, *Rambles Beyond Railways* is an account of a journey that Wilkie Collins and a companion made through Cornwall in 1850, when the steam railway finished at Plymouth on the border between Devon and Cornwall – hence the title.

The extract used here is from a "New Edition" dated 1861, but the expedition underground took place in 1850. Botallack Mine was extremely deep and mined mostly for copper and only a little tin, but the mining procedures were identical.

Botallack is by the coast close to Land's End, and much of the workings ran under the sea. Billy was preaching at St Just before going to St Ives to raise money for Great Deliverance Chapel, and Botallack Mine is only a short distance to the north.

Billy also worked deep underground in some mines. An excellent book on mining is *The Cornish Miner* by AK Hamilton Jenkin (George Allen & Unwin 1927). On pages 281-282 the author makes a reference to *Fish, Tin and Copper* by CG Honor, where Honor tells of a Methodist preacher who is speaking at a miners' camp. He says to his listeners, "The joys of religion are not all confined to heaven. Many of them may be realised down here." Billy, who is present, immediately calls out, "Praise the Lord, I've felt them at 250!" These are fathoms, 1500 feet, nearly 500m below ground level. Miners called this 'below grass', and in Billy's time involved climbing the whole distance down ladders to reach the place of work, and back up them at the end of the shift.

RAMBLES BEYOND RAILWAYS (Chapter 9):

We left the Land's End feeling that our homeward journey had now begun from that point. Walking northward, about five miles (8km) along the coast, we arrived at Botallack. Having heard that there was some disinclination in Cornwall to allow strangers to go down the mines, we had provided ourselves – through the kindness of a friend – with a proper letter of introduction in case of emergency.

We were told to go to the counting house to present our credentials, and on our road thither we beheld the buildings and machinery of the mine, literally stretching down the precipitous face of the cliff, from the land at the top to the sea at the bottom.

Here we beheld scaffolding perched on a rock that rose out of the waves. A steam pump was at work raising gallons of water from the mine every minute, on a mere ledge of land halfway down the steep cliff side. Chains, pipes and conduits protruded in all directions from the precipice. Rotten looking wooden platforms ran over deep chasms, supporting great beams of timber and heavy coils of cable.

Crazy little boarded houses were built where gulls' nests might have been found in other places. There did not appear to be a foot of level space anywhere, for any part of the works of the mine to stand on. And yet there they were, fulfilling all the purposes for which they had been constructed, as safely and completely on rocks in the sea, and down precipices in the land, as if they had been cautiously founded on the tracts of smooth solid ground above.

The counting house was built on a projection of earth about midway between the top of the cliff and the sea. When we got there the agent to whom our letter was addressed was absent, but two miners came out to receive us in his place. To one of them we mentioned our recommendation, and modestly hinted a wish to go down the mine forthwith.

But our new friend was not a person who did anything in a hurry. Did we know, he urged, that it was dangerous work?

Yes, we told him, but we didn't mind danger.

Perhaps, he said, we were not aware that we would perspire profusely, and be dead tired getting up and down the ladders.

Very likely, but we didn't mind that either.

Surely we shouldn't want to strip and put on miners' clothes.

Yes, we should, of all things. And pulling off coat and waistcoat on the spot, we stood half undressed already, just as the big miner was proposing another objection, which under existing circumstances he good-naturedly changed into a speech of acquiescence.

"Very well, gentlemen," he said, taking up two suits of miners' clothes, "I see you are determined to go down, and so you shall. You'll be wet through with the heat and the work before you come up again, so just put on these things and keep your own clothes dry."

The clothing consisted of a flannel shirt, flannel drawers, canvas trousers, and a canvas jacket – all stained of a tawny copper colour, but all quite clean. A white nightcap and a round hat, composed of some iron-hard substance, well calculated to protect the head from any loose stones that might fall on it, completed the equipment. Three tallow candles were afterwards added, two to hang at the buttonhole, one to carry in the hand.

My friend was dressed first. He had been given a suit that fitted him tolerably, and which as far as appearances went made a miner of him at once. Far different was my case.

The big miner stood six feet two inches; I stand five feet six inches. I put on his flannel shirt and it fell down to my toes like a bed gown. The drawers flowed in Turkish luxuriance over my feet. At the trousers I helplessly stopped short, lost in the voluminous recesses of each leg. The big miner, like a Good Samaritan as he was, came to my assistance. He put the pocket button through the waist button-hole to keep the trousers up in the first instance.

He pulled steadily at the braces until my waistband was under my armpits, and then pronounced that I and my trousers fitted each other in great perfection. The cuffs of the jacket were next turned up to my elbows, the white nightcap was dragged over my ears and the round hat was jammed down over my eyes.

We left the counting house and ascended the face of the cliff, then walked a short distance along the edge, descended a little again, and stopped at a wooden platform built across a deep gully. Here the miner pulled up a trapdoor and disclosed a vertical ladder leading down to a black hole, like the opening of a chimney.

"This is the shaft. I will go down first, to catch you in case you tumble. Follow me and hold tight." Saying this, our friend squeezed himself through the trapdoor, and we went after him as we had been bidden.

Cornish miner's hat
redrawn from an engraving in
Half Hours Undeground

The black hole, when we entered it, proved to be not quite so dark as it had appeared from above. Rays of light occasionally penetrated through chinks in the outer rock, but by the time we had got some little way farther down, these rays began to fade. Then just as we seemed to be lowering ourselves into total darkness, we were desired to stand on a narrow landing-place opposite the ladder and wait there while the miner went below for a light.

He soon re-ascended to us, bringing not only the light he had promised, but also a large lump of damp clay with it. Having lighted our candles he stuck them against the front of our hats with the clay in order, as he said, to leave both our hands free to use as we liked. Thus we resumed the descent of the shaft, and now at last began to penetrate beneath the surface of the earth in good earnest

The process of getting down the ladders was not very pleasant. They were all vertical. The rungs were placed at irregular distances, and many of them were much worn away and slippery with water and copper-ooze. Add to this the narrowness of the shaft, and the dripping wet rock shutting you in all round your back and sides.

Imagine yourself against the ladder with the fathomless darkness beneath, and the light flaring immediately above you as if your head was on fire, with the voice of the miner below tumbling away in dull echoes lower and lower into the bowels of the earth, with the consciousness that if the rungs of the ladder broke you might fall down a thousand feet (300m) or so of narrow shaft in a moment. Imagine all this, and you may easily realize what are the first impressions produced by a descent into a Cornish mine.

By the time we had got down seventy fathoms, or four hundred and twenty feet (nearly 130m) of vertical ladders, we stopped at another landing place that was just broad enough to afford standing room for us three. Here, the miner, pointing to an opening yawning horizontally in the rock at one side of us, said that this was the first gallery from the surface. We had done with the ladders for the present, and a little climbing and crawling were now to begin.

Our path was a strange one as we advanced through the rift. Rough stones of all sizes, holes here, and eminences there, impeded us at every yard. Sometimes we could walk on in a stooping position, sometimes we were obliged to crawl on our hands and knees. Occasionally greater difficulties than these presented themselves. Certain parts of the gallery dipped into black ugly-looking pits crossed by thin planks, over which we walked dizzily, a little bewildered by the violent contrast between the flaring light that we carried above us, and the pitch darkness beneath and before us.

One of these places terminated in a sudden rising in the rock, hollowed away below, but surmounted by a narrow projecting wooden platform to which it was necessary to climb by crossbeams arranged at wide distances. My companion ascended to this awkward elevation without hesitating, but I came to an awful pause before it. Fettered as I was by my oversize jacket and trousers, I felt that any extraordinary gymnastic exertion was altogether out of my power.

Our friend the miner saw my difficulty and extricated me from it at once, with a promptitude and skill that deserve record. Descending halfway by the beams he clutched with one hand that hinder part of my too-voluminous nether garments, which presented the broadest breadth of canvas to his grasp. I hope the delicate reader appreciates my ingenious indirectness of expression when I touch on the unmentionable subject of trousers!

Grappling me thus and supporting himself by his free hand, he lifted me up as easily as if I had been a small parcel, finally depositing me safely upon my legs again on the firm rock pathway beyond.

"You are but a light and a little man, my son," said this excellent fellow, snuffing my candle for me before we went on. "Let me lift you about as I like, and you shan't come to any harm while I am with you."

Speaking thus, the miner leads us forward again. After we have walked a little farther in a crouching position he calls a halt, makes a seat for us by sticking a piece of old board between the rocky walls of the gallery, and then proceeds to explain the exact subterranean position which we actually occupy.

We are now four hundred yards out (nearly 400m) under the bottom of the sea, and twenty fathoms or a hundred and twenty feet (nearly 40m) below the sea level. Coastal trade vessels are sailing over our heads. Two hundred and forty feet (nearly 75m) beneath us men are at work, and there are galleries deeper yet below that. The extraordinary position down the face of the cliff, of the engines and other works on the surface at Botallack, is now explained. The mine is not excavated like other mines under the land, but under the sea.

Having communicated these particulars, the miner next tells us to keep strict silence and listen. We obey him, sitting speechless and motionless. If the reader could only have beheld us now, dressed in our copper coloured garments, huddled close together in a mere cleft of subterranean rock, with flame burning on our heads and darkness enveloping our limbs – he must certainly have imagined, without any violent stretch of fancy, that he was looking down upon a conclave of gnomes.

After listening for a few moments, a distant, unearthly noise becomes faintly audible. A long, low, mysterious moaning that never changes, that is felt on the ear as well as heard by it; a sound so unlike anything that is heard on the upper ground, in the free air of heaven; so sublimely mournful and still, so ghostly and impressive when listened to in the subterranean recesses of the earth.

At last the miner speaks again, and tells us that what we hear is the sound of the surf lashing the rocks a hundred and twenty feet (nearly 40m) above us, and the waves breaking on the beach beyond. The tide is now at the flow and the sea is in no extraordinary state of agitation, so the sound is low and distant at this time. But when storms are at their height, when the ocean hurls mountain after mountain of water on the cliffs, then the noise is terrific.

The roaring heard down here in the mine is so inexpressibly fierce and awful that the boldest men at work are afraid to continue their labour. All ascend to the surface to breathe the upper air and stand on the firm earth, dreading, though no such catastrophe has ever happened yet, that the sea will break in on them if they remain in the caverns below.

Hearing this we get up to look at the rock above us. We are able to stand upright in the position we now occupy. Flaring our candles hither and thither in the darkness we can see the bright pure copper streaking the dark ceiling of the gallery in every direction. Lumps of ooze, of the most lustrous green colour, traversed by a natural network of thin red veins of iron, appear here and there in large irregular patches, over which water is dripping slowly and incessantly in certain places. This is the salt water percolating through invisible crannies in the rock. On stormy days it spurts out furiously in thin, continuous streams. Just over our heads we observe a wooden plug the thickness of a man's leg. There is a hole here, and the plug is all that we have to keep out the sea.

Immense wealth of metal is contained in the roof of this gallery, throughout its whole length. But it remains, and will always remain, untouched. The miners dare not take it, for it is part, and a great part, of the rock that forms their only protection against the sea. It has been so much worked away here that its thickness is limited to an average of three feet (one metre) only between the water and the gallery in which we now stand. No one knows what might be the consequence of another day's labour with the pickaxe on any part of it.

This information is rather startling when communicated at a depth of four hundred and twenty feet (c. 130m) underground. We would decidedly have preferred to receive it in the counting house! It makes us pause for an instant, to the miner's infinite amusement, in the very act of knocking away a tiny morsel of ore from the rock as a memento of Botallack.

Having, however, ventured on reflection to assume the responsibility of weakening our defence against the sea by the length and breadth of an inch (25mm), we secure our piece of copper and proceed to discuss the wisdom of descending two hundred and forty

Cornish miners at work underground
redrawn from an engraving in *Half Hours Underground*

feet more of ladders for the sake of visiting that part of the mine where the men are at work.

Two or three causes concur to make us doubt the wisdom of going lower. There is a hot, moist, sickly vapour floating about us, which becomes more oppressive every moment. We are already perspiring at every pore as we were told we should, and our hands, faces, jackets, and trousers are all more or less covered with a mixture of mud, tallow, and iron drippings, which we can feel and smell much more acutely than is exactly desirable.

We ask the miner what there is to see lower down. He replies that there is nothing but men breaking ore with pickaxes. The galleries of the mine are alike, however deep they may go.

The answer decides us. We determine to get back to the surface and return along the gallery, just as we had advanced, with the same large allowance of scrambling, creeping, and stumbling on our way. I was charitably carried along and down the platform over the pit by my trousers, as before.

Our order of procession only changed when we gained the ladders again. Our friend the miner went last instead of first, upon the same principle of being ready to catch us if we fell. One of the rungs cracked under his weight as we went up, but otherwise we ascended without casualties of any kind.

As we neared the mouth of the shaft the daylight looked dazzlingly white after the darkness in which we had been groping so long. When we once more stood out on the cliff we felt a cold, health-giving purity in the sea breeze.

On re-entering the counting house we were greeted by the welcome appearance of two large tubs of water, with soap and flannel placed invitingly by their sides. Copious ablutions and clean clothes are potent restorers of muscular energy. These, and a half hour of repose, enabled us to resume our knapsacks as briskly as ever and walk on fifteen miles (24km) to the town of St Ives, our resting place for the night.

Botallack mine is a copper mine, but tin and occasionally iron are found in it. The mine is situated at the western extremity of the great strata of copper, tin and lead, running eastward through Cornwall as far as the Dartmoor Hills. According to the statement of my informant in the counting house, Botallack mine has been worked for more than a century. In former times it produced enormous profits to the speculators, but now the case is altered. The price of copper has fallen of late years. The lodes have proved neither so rich nor so extensive as at past periods, and the mine when we visited Cornwall in 1850 had failed to pay the expenses of working it.

The organization of labour at Botallack, and in all other mines throughout the county, is managed in the following manner. The men work eight hours underground out of the twenty-four, taking their turn of night duty – for labour proceeds in the mines by night as well as by day – in regular rotation. It will be found that ordinary wages for mine labour are stated as ranging from forty to fifty shillings a month. Mention must be made at the same time of the larger remuneration which may be obtained by working on tribute, in other words by agreeing to excavate the lodes of metal for a percentage that varies with the varying value of the mineral raised.

It is however necessary to add here that although men who labour on this latter plan occasionally make as much as six or ten pounds each in a month, they are on the other hand liable to heavy losses from the speculative character of the work in which they engage.

The lode may for instance be poor when they begin to work it, and may continue poor as they proceed farther and farther. Under these circumstances the low value of the mineral they have raised realises a correspondingly low rate of percentage. When this happens even the best workmen cannot make more than twenty shillings[143] a month.

Another system on which the men are employed is the system of contract. A certain quantity of ore in the rock is mapped out by the captain of the mine and put up to auction among the miners. One man makes an offer of a sum for which he is willing to undertake excavating the ore, upon the understanding that he is himself to pay for the assistance, candles, etc, out of the price he asks.

Another man, who is also anxious to get the contract, then offers to accept it on lower terms. The third man's demand is smaller still, and so they proceed until the piece of work is knocked down to the lowest bidder. By this sort of labour the contracting workman, after he has paid his expenses for assistance, seldom clears more than twelve shillings a week.

143 One pound sterling.

Upon the whole, setting his successful and his disastrous speculations fairly against each other, the Cornish miner's average gains, year by year, may be fairly estimated at about ten shillings a week.

"It's hard work we have to do, sir," one miner told me when we parted, summing up the proportions of good and evil in the social positions of his brethren and himself. "Harder work than people think, down in the heat and darkness underground. We may get a good deal at one time, but we get little enough at another. Sometimes mines are shut up and then we are thrown out altogether. But good work or bad work, or no work at all, what with our bits of ground for potatoes and greens, and what with cheap living, somehow we and our families make do.

"We contrive to keep our good cloth coat for Sundays, and go to chapel in the morning, for we're most of us Wesleyans. Then we go to church in the afternoon, so as to give 'em both their turn. We never go near the mine on Sundays, except to look after the steam pump. Our rest, and our walk in the evening once a week, is a good deal to us. That's how we live, sir. Whatever happens we manage to work through, and don't complain."

Although the occupation of smelting the copper above ground is, as may well be imagined, unhealthy enough, the labour of getting it from the mine by blasting the subterranean rock in the first place, then hewing and breaking the ore out of the fragments, seems to be attended with no bad effect on the constitution. The miners are a fine-looking race of men, strong and well proportioned. The fact appears to be that they gain more physically by the pure air of the cliffs and moors on which their cottages are built, and the temperance of their lives – for many of them are teetotallers – than they lose by their hardest exertions in the underground atmosphere in which they work.

CHAPTER 15

SINGING GLORY AND CLOTHING THE POOR

BILLY IS STILL finding his Christian faith exciting. Later in the chapter we see that Billy is remarkably content with life, never using a lack of money and good clothing as an excuse to stay home and not preach the Gospel.

Billy writes:

> At Hicks Mill Chapel our people had a great many happy members, and many of them was sanctified. The dear Lord would make them so happy that they would shout and dance for joy. Because they was so happy, some of the professors did not like them. One man that I heard a man tell of, left the society at Hicks Mill, [144] and he ought to know better, for he was the father of children.
>
> He went with the Methodists to meet and, in the chapel where he went to meet, the dear Lord poured out his Spirit. They had a revival and there was many converted. That man's two sons was converted at that time, but I think not in the chapel, they was converted at home. Their father, while praying for the sons, he got happy himself and he could make a noise then as much as the people that he left at Hicks Mill. I heard a man say, that meet him in the morning after he had been praying with his sons in the night, that he was very happy. He could shout and praise God then, for he had the Spirit of the Lord.

---

144 Hicks Mill Chapel belonged to the Bible Christians

In *The King's Son* Bourne writes:

> When in the Penzance preaching circuit on special
> work, Billy slept at the house of TA, a friend. Very
> early in the morning Billy was out of bed, jumping,
> dancing, and singing the praises of God as usual.
>
> His friend said, "Billy, why are you up so early? You
> will disturb the family, and perhaps give offence."
>
> The next moment Billy was again leaping and
> praising the Lord. Then naming the members of the
> household, including TA, he said that they might lie
> and sleep and let their wheels get rusty if they liked,
> but he would see to it that his wheels were kept oiled
> and ready for work.
>
> Then he fell on his knees and prayed out loud for the
> members of the family, while his prayer for TA was
> that the Lord would have mercy on him, and "make
> him a better man than he appears to be."
>
> One morning Billy asked a friend how she was. She
> said she was tolerably well.
>
> Billy replied, with a face lit up with holy joy, "I was
> just thinking, my dear, of going a thousand miles the
> first flip, right into the heart of the City."
>
> Heaven was so attractive to Billy because it is the
> home of Jesus. In a small prayer group Billy once
> shouted with deep feeling, "The blood, the blood, the
> precious blood! The precious, precious blood!"
>
> The effect of this on Billy and the others was truly
> extraordinary. Christ was in his heart, and his faith
> was always so real. He said that while some were still
> opening the heavenly larder door, he took out the
> loaf and ate it.
>
> At a friend's house in Falmouth, Billy encouraged
> those present to praise the Lord. Speaking of himself,
> Billy said, "I can't help praising the Lord. As I go
> along the street I lift up one foot and it seems to say
> *Glory;* and I lift up the other and it seems to say *Amen.*

And so they keep on like that all the time I am walking."

Billy was leaving the house of a woman called Mrs Dinnick, in Devonport, to fulfil a preaching appointment three or four miles out in the country. He said to her, "Mary, shall us pray a bit?"

Instantly getting on his knees, Billy said, "We've nothing particular to ask thee for, Lord, but go with thy servant to K, and stay with these dear women and bless them, and keep them right."

This brought a great blessing on the house, which was remembered for a long time.

Bourne says that the Rev William Haslam of Baldhu once asked Billy for the secret of his constant happiness, comparing Billy's experience with his own, as he was not always "on the Mount". Haslam admitted that his prospects were sometimes clouded, and his fears rather than his faith prevailed at times. He therefore wanted to know how it was that Billy got on so much better than he did.

Billy answered that we must become fools for Christ's sake. He said Christians like Mr Haslam, who had so much book learning, were placed at a disadvantage when compared with some others, having so much to unlearn. "Some of us, you know," Billy added, "are fools to begin with."

Bourne tells us:

On most occasions Billy's wit sparkled and flashed without apparent effort on his part. But he knew how to hold it in reserve when people only wanted to satisfy their curiosity, or wished him to display his powers for their entertainment. Some got more than they bargained for.

To a lady who once interviewed him, Billy was very silent and reserved. She, hoping to draw him out, said, "You know we must be willing to be fools for Christ's sake."

"Must we, ma'am?" was his ready answer.

"Then there is a pair of us!"

Bourne also tells us:

There was much excitement and what seemed like confusion in some of Billy's meetings, more than enough to shock the highly sensitive. Billy could not tolerate "deadness" as he called it, either in a professing Christian or in a meeting. He had a deep sympathy with people singing or shouting or leaping for joy. He used to tell people, "I can *say* glory, glory; I can *sing* glory, glory; I can *dance* glory, glory." Then he usually acted out the words.

In *The King's Son*, Mr Gilbert[145] tells how he spent an hour or two with Billy one evening:

I told him that I had seen his mother at Twelveheads and found her in a very blessed frame of mind. I said that whilst I was praying with her she became so happy that, although quite blind, she jumped and danced about the house, shouting the praises of God.

Billy at once became much excited, and rising from his chair began to dance also. He said, "Dear old soul, dance, did she? I am glad to hear that. Bless the Lord. Well, I dance sometimes. Why shouldn't I dance as well as David? David was a king. Well, bless the Lord, I am a King's son. I have as good a right to dance as David had.

"Bless the Lord, I get very happy at times. My soul gets full of the glory, and then I dance too. I was home in my room the other day and I got so

145 This may be William Gilbert (1821-1885) of the Gwennap Circuit that included Hicks Mill Chapel. He started preaching in 1846.

happy that I danced, and the glory came
streaming down upon my soul. It made me
dance so lustily that my heels went down
through the planching."[146]

Billy has already told us how a Quaker gave him a new
coat, probably a jacket to replace his old fustian one. There
are many stories about Billy getting new clothes that fit him
perfectly, told by various writers, and repeated as folklore
today. Like Billy's old clothes, they seem to contain more
than a few holes.

Billy's memory is so good about the details in his own
accounts of being given clothes, that they seem reliable,
and are perhaps the only correct ones. The other stories
may fit in somewhere, but not obviously. What could be
important is everyone's definition of overcoats, coats,
waistcoats, suits and jackets.

Bourne recounts the following, undated:

Coming home one Sunday evening from his
appointment through a dirty road, Billy stuck in
the mud. In extricating one foot, he tore off the
sole of his shoe. Holding it up, now almost
useless, he said, "Here, Father, thou knowest I
have worn out these shoes in thy cause, and I
have no money to buy new ones. Help me."

The Lord heard him in this time of need, and
sent speedy relief. A friend the next week said
he wanted Billy to accompany him to Truro. On
their arrival he took him first to a shoe shop, and
bought for him a pair of shoes, and then to other
shops to get some needed articles of clothing.

In the next chapter the Rev William Haslam of Baldhu will
tell us that Billy is wearing a 'Quaker-cut coat' when Billy
calls to see him in 1852, and it looks too large – see p. 200.
This is almost certainly the one he is about to be given now,

146 Floorboards.

even though in Billy's eyes it fits him perfectly. Billy is writing about the Quakers:

When I go to some of their houses they ask me, do I want anything? And I should have it. I told one of the Friends that one pound would do me good, and I had it, for his good wife gave it to me.

She said to me, "What can my husband do for thee? He will feel it a pleasure to do it."

So I may say that the dear Lord opened their hearts to be my friends. In the winter I wanted an overcoat, and I went to a Friend's house. When I came there the master was not home, but the mistress was. I never saw her before, nor her husband that I know of. When I told her who I was, she very kindly asked me in. I sat down and then told her that I wanted an overcoat.

She said to me, "Thee sit down until my husband come home, and then I will tell him."

I was very kindly entertained, for she gave me tea. While I was to tea this good Friend's husband came and she went downstairs to meet him, for I was in an upstairs room. She told her husband that I was upstairs and that I wanted an overcoat. She came up in the room where I was to tea, with a coat on her arm.

She said, "I have coat here for thee, but whether he will suit thee or no I do not know."

Then I said, "If the Lord have put it in your dear heart to give me, it will suit me exactly."

After I had done my tea, I put on my coat and he suit me. And she said, "So it will suit thee."

I thank that Friend, that the dear woman's husband took his coat off his back for me, and that is some years ago since that Friend gave me that overcoat, and it is my overcoat still.[147]

That good Friend made a new shawl for me, for I wanted one, and the Lord knew it and put in her heart to make one for me. I have

147 in 1864

nothing to support me and my sick wife but what the dear people give me. As Elijah was fed by the ravens, so am I supported by what the people give me. Thanks be to God, I do not want, for the dear Lord have all hearts in his hand. My bread is given and my water is sure.

There is another Friend that have been very good to me and to mine, and I hope I shall meet all the dear Friends in heaven. And I shall, if they and me is faithful and love the dear Lord with all our hearts.

I have not done with the Friends yet, for I have more to say for the good they have done. When our people went out as (local) missionaries, the society was very poor, and they had to get meat and clothes where they could. The Lord called one of our preachers to preach to a very wicked people, and made him great blessing to the people in that place.

It is many years since I heard my brother tell this tale at a missionary meeting, but I will tell the tale that he told, as near as I can. If I miss, I do not mean to. Sometimes, he said, after he had done preaching he had no place to lodge for the night, and nothing to eat, poor dear man. I think he said that he have been out in a cold frosty night, and when he have awaked in the morning, after being out all night, he have been so cold that he have been forced to blow his breath and keep his hands by his mouth for a great while before he could get any heat into himself.

The devil would tempt him that his state was a bad one when his meat was short and his clothes was poor, and he had professors of religion for his enemies. He had no society there, and they that was converted went to meet with another society.

One man of another society said to him one day, "You are fine fellows for beating the bushes, but we have the birds."

Then the preacher said to him, "The day of judgement is coming, and every bird's cage door will be thrown open. Then every bird will fly to his own cage, and then thee wast look very foolish with an old empty cage in thy hand."

So that man said no more about the birds, nor the cage. I think it was well for the preacher to have missionary converts, and he went through so much poverty to get them, for he suffered hunger and thirst to do the will of his dear Lord. He suffered so much danger and thirst, and even nakedness. The devil is all busy to tell us, if he can, that the dear Lord is a hard master, and to try to put us out of the way. But he could not put my dear brother out of heart, for he was like St Paul. He could say, "None of these things moves me."[148]

When this brother's clothes got poor the devil tempted him, and said, "Now see how the Lord hath served thee, for thy clothes is just done. And what wast thee do then?"

But he trusted his dear Lord, and the Lord opened the heart of a friend. I believe it was a Quaker Friend that asked him one day, "Is that all the clothes thee hast got?"

And he said, "Yes."

Then the good Friend said, "Thee come to my house and I will give thee some clothes." He told him where he lived and when to come.

The brother went to the good Friend's house as he promised, and the good Friend told him to strip off his old clothes and to put up his new. So our brother did, and he was glad to do so.

After he had his clothes, my dear brother said, "Now, devil, see how the Lord have opened my way, and how I am dressed now."

Then said the devil, "Now thee hast no meat."

In a small span of time the dear Lord opened another heart, and that person sent him money. Then the brother said, "Now, devil, I chase thee all over this mission with penny loaves and water!"

You can see by what our brother said that he loved souls, and he did not look for a high life. He would live on bread and water to be instrumental in the hand of the dear Lord of saving blood washed souls. He was made a great blessing in the hand of the Lord in that

148 Acts 20:24

place, and to that neighbourhood. Many will have to praise God in heaven that ever that dear brother went to that place, for it was a wicked place before he went there. They carried on all sorts of wickedness, but he was an old man and cared for no man. He preached Christ and salvation, and hell and damnation, and the word was with power, for many heard and turned to the Lord.

Now who can tell the value of that suit of clothes that Quaker Friend gave to that preacher? No doubt but this was the best suit of clothes that he ever gave in all his life, and his dear Lord will reward him for that great kindness, if that Quaker Friend is on the right ground. But we must be born again, or there is no reward for us.

If we give our goods to feed the poor and our bodies to be burnt, if we have not charity it will not avail nothing.[149] That charity that the Apostle speak of is the love of God in the heart. If we have his love in our heart, then bless and praise his holy name, every promise is sure. The Lord's word is true, "Heaven and the earth shall pass away, but my word shall never pass away."[150]

That preacher, and the Quaker Friend that gave the clothes, and the other that gave the money, if they are born again and made new creatures, they shall all three have their reward in heaven.

May the dear Lord bless them, is the prayer of William Bray. I know this preacher well, and I have been to missionary meetings with him and to other meetings too. We have had many good meetings together, and have been very happy, bless and praise the dear Lord for he is good, and he is very kind to all them that love him. And I am glad that I do love him.

149 1 Corinthians 13:3

150   Matthew 24:35, Mark 13:31, Luke 21:33

CHAPTER 16

THE PARSON IS CONVERTED!

THIS WAS A TIME of much ill feeling between the established Church of England and the independent chapel members who were known as Dissenters because they disagreed with some of the teachings of the Church of England – they dissented. This meant that many Anglicans and Dissenters subsequently refused to join together in worship. Many Dissenters were also labelled as Nonconformists, because they refused to conform to the Act of Uniformity of 1662. This caused around 2,000 Puritan ministers (a fifth of the English clergy) to be ejected from their livings, because they were not prepared to adopt the 1662 Book of Common Prayer. It was not until 1812 that full freedom of worship was allowed in England.

Billy was praying for the Rev. William Haslam, Anglican vicar of Baldhu, who was also the designer of that church, now closed and semi-derelict, as well as of St George's in Truro. In his 1880 autobiography *From Death Into Life*, Haslam tells us that he was so determined to stamp out the Nonconformist influence in his parish that he thrashed one of the older boys in front of the whole school. The boy's crime? He had attended a Methodist service and said he was converted. Haslam thrashed the boy until he promised never to go to a Methodist chapel again.

Both Haslam in *From Death Into Life* and Bourne in *The King's Son* give similar accounts of the following. In the early editions of *The King's Son* Bourne says that he got his account directly from Ashworth and Haslam, although Ashworth does not appear to have put this information into print. The implication is that this account came in the form of personal letters, as Haslam was not to publish *From Death Into Life* until eight years later. Although Haslam uses the same memories when writing his autobiography, he does not always use the same words as those he must have written to Ashworth.

John Ashworth, who died in January 1875, wrote a chapter of 14 pages about Billy Bray in a booklet, *Strange Tales Volume 5*. My copy is dated 1879, but the account was published earlier in tract form. Ashworth was a Christian writer and philanthropist from Rochdale in the north of England. He visited Cornwall shortly after Billy's death to collect stories about various places and people.

Ashworth makes at least one major mistake about Billy, crediting him incorrectly with building four chapels, of which Gwennap is the odd one out. Great Deliverance Chapel is close to Gwennap, and may have caused the confusion. The chapter is short, and the few stories in it are generally in agreement with Bourne, Haslam and Pearse. It must be borne in mind that Ashworth got his material second-hand, and he adds very little that is new about Billy's life.

We will shortly read of the extraordinary events at Baldhu. I am quoting Haslam's story at some length, as his parishioners are Billy's neighbours and contemporaries. I have blended Haslam and Bourne's writing, and condensed parts of it considerably.

Pearse also wrote about Haslam in *The Ship Where Christ Was Captain*, published in 1926. Pearse says he, "Heard it from the clergyman himself." Pearse, of course, was one of the preachers who worked with Billy but he adds nothing new. There is no mention of Haslam and Baldhu in Billy's *Journal*. Even so, Baldhu and William Haslam are very much part of Billy's life.

The story involving Billy begins well before Haslam is appointed in 1846 to oversee the building of an Anglican church at Baldhu. Baldhu church is less than a mile

Baldhu church exterior
redrawn from an engraving in *The King's Son*

(1.5km) from Twelveheads, and the same distance from Kerley Downs. Haslam starts to build what he believes will be the perfect church with the perfect form of service that would nowadays be called High Church, or Anglo Catholic.

The church is opened in 1848 with a consecration service attended by the Bishop Phillpotts of Exeter, with the ritualistic proceedings and formalities that Haslam intends to introduce to the people of Baldhu. Billy also attends, and Haslam says he came out "checkfallen", and quite disappointed. He told "Father" that there was nothing but an "old Pusey preaching there", and that he was no good.

William Haslam, to whom Billy is referring, was greatly influenced by Edward Pusey, a leader of the Tractarian or Oxford Movement. Pusey's supporters helped build churches in deprived areas; their style of worship with all the ceremony would have been totally unacceptable to Billy. Although many in both groups got the balance right, some Evangelicals thought the Tractarians cared more for the body than the soul, and the Tractarians responded by accusing the Evangelicals of not caring enough about people's welfare in this life.

Once the church is finished, Haslam writes in *From Death Into Life* that he goes to see Parson Hawker at the parish church of Morwenstow, and spends a Sunday there. Hawker dresses in ornate clerical robes to take the service at Morwenstow, and preaches wearing a chasuble over his alb, amber on one side and green on the other. He is also wearing crimson gloves, which he says are the proper sacrificial colour for a priest. Haslam takes note.

Hawker obviously has a keen eye for fashion. He ridicules Haslam's top hat and tails, and persuades him to obtain a cassock and a square cap called a biretta. Haslam proudly wears these in his parish at Baldhu, but it seems the people are more amused than impressed. Haslam admits he is, "frequently laughed at and often pursued by boys."

Haslam realises he is getting nowhere with his preaching. He continues:

> I was beginning to see that I ought to care for the souls of my people – at least as much as I did for the services of the Church. I used to spend hours and hours in my church alone in meditation and prayer; and while thinking, employed my hands in writing texts over the windows and on the walls, and in painting ornamental borders above the arches. I remember writing over the chancel arch, with much interest and exultation, the words from Revelation 12: 10, *Now is come salvation, and strength, and the kingdom of our God, and the power of his Christ.*

> One day I saw a picture in a friend's house that attracted me. It was nothing artistic, nor was it well drawn, but it engaged my attention in a way for which I could not account. That night I

lay awake thinking about it – so much so that I rose early the next morning and went to a bookseller's shop. There I bought a large sheet of tracing paper and pencil, and sent them with a note to my friend, begging him to give me a tracing of the picture in question.

I had to wait for more than a fortnight before it arrived. I remember spreading a white cloth on my table and opening out the tracing paper on it. There was the picture of the Good Shepherd. His countenance was loving and kind. With one hand he was pushing aside the branch of a tree, though a great thorn went right through his hand, and with the other hand he was extricating a sheep that was entangled in the thorns. The poor thing was looking up in helplessness, spotted over with marks of its own blood, for it was wounded in struggling to escape. Another thing which struck me in this picture was that the tree was growing on the edge of a precipice, and had it not been for the tree, with all the cruel wounds it inflicted, the sheep would have gone over and perished.

After considering this picture for a long time I painted it in a larger size on the wall of my church, just opposite the entrance door, so that everyone who came in might see it. I cannot describe the interest with which I employed myself about this work. When it was done, finding that it wanted a good bold foreground, I selected a short text. *He came to seek and to save that which was lost.*[151]

God was speaking to me all this time about the Good Shepherd who gave his life for me, but I did not hear him, or suspect that I was lost, or

151 Luke 19:10

caught in any thorns, or hanging over a precipice. Therefore, I did not apply the subject to myself.

A woman in the parish, whenever I went to see her, made me read the story of her conversion that was written out in a copybook. Several others, men and women, talked to me continually about what they called their conversion. I often wondered what that was.

I made it a rule to visit every house in my parish once a week, visiting between twelve to twenty each day. I sought to enlighten the people by leaving Church tracts,[152] and even wrote some myself, but they would not do. I found that the Religious Tract Society's publications were more acceptable. To my great disappointment I discovered that Evangelical sermons drew the people, while sacramental topics did not interest them. So, in my ardent desire to reach and do them good, I procured several volumes of Evangelical sermons and copied them, putting in sometimes a negative to their statements, to make them, as I thought, right.

One day I went in my cassock and cap to the shop of a man whom I regarded as a dreadful schismatic.[153] He sold the publications of the Religious Tract Society. On entering, he appeared greatly pleased to see me, and took unusual interest and pains in selecting tracts, giving me a double portion for my money. His kindness was very embarrassing; and when, on leaving, he followed me to the door, and said,

---

152 Tracts at this time were extensive booklets rather than the small folded sheet we see today.

153 Someone who has broken away from the established Church.

"God bless you," it gave me a great turn. A schismatic blessing a priest! This, indeed, was an anomaly.

I was ashamed to be seen coming out of the shop, the more so because I had this large Evangelical parcel in my hand. I felt as though everybody was looking at me. However, the tracts were very acceptable at home and in the parish. I even began to think there was something good in them. So I sent for more.

Three men, one after another, told me that they had been converted through reading them. One said that the tract I had given him ought to be written in letters of gold; and a few months after, this same man died most happily, rejoicing in the Lord, and leaving a bright testimony behind. I mentioned the conversion of these three men to many of my friends, and asked them for some explanation, but got none. Still, the thought continually haunted me – what can this so-called conversion be?

I thought the Church was the Ark of Noah[154] and no salvation could be had outside it except by some unconvenanted mercy. My gardener was John Gill, a good Churchman who was duly despised by his neighbours for attaching himself to me and my teaching. He was a strong adherent who, with many others, upheld me and encouraged me in a place abounding with "Gospel men", against Dissenters of various kinds.

John fell seriously ill at this time (1851), and I sent him at once to the doctor who pronounced

154 See 1 Peter 3:20-21

him to be in a miner's consumption,[155] and gave no hope of his recovery. No sooner did John realise his position and see eternity before him, than all the Church teaching I had given him failed to console or satisfy.

John's views and religious practices did not comfort him in the hour of need, or give him assurance. He heard of others who could say their sins were pardoned, whereas with his, as he thought, superior teaching he was afraid to die. In his distress of mind he did not send for me to go and pray with him, but actually sent for a converted Dissenter who lived in the next row of cottages.

This man, instead of building John up as I had done, went to work in the opposite direction – to show my servant that he was a lost sinner and needed to come to Jesus, just as he was, for pardon and salvation.

The visitor was confident. "You must pray for yourself," he told my gardener, and explained the finished work of Christ as the sinner's substitute. The gardener was brought under deep conviction, and eventually found pardon and peace through the blood of Jesus.

Immediately the word spread all over the parish that the parson's servant was converted. The news soon reached me, but instead of giving joy, it brought the most bitter disappointment and sorrow to my heart, such was the profound ignorance I was in. Instead of rejoicing with Christ over a lost sheep that he had found, I was angry at the sheep for being found, and

155 A lung disease.

deeply mourned over what I considered a fall into schism.[156]

The poor man sent for me several times, but I could not make up my mind to go near him. I felt far too much hurt to think that after all I had taught him against schism he should fall into so great an error. However, he sent again and again, until at last his entreaties prevailed and I went. Instead of lying on his bed a dying man, as I expected to find him, he was walking about the room in a most joyful and ecstatic state.

"Oh, dear master," he exclaimed, "I am glad you are come. I am so happy. My soul is saved. Glory be to God!"

"Ah, John," I said, "you are excited. You have been taking wine."

"No, master," said the man, "I have not touched a drop of it. No, dear no, that is not it, dear master.

"Come, John," I said, "sit down and be quiet, and I will have a talk with you and tell you what I think."

But John knew my thoughts well enough, so he burst out, "Oh, master, I am sure you do not know about this or you would have told me. I am quite sure you love me, and I love you, that I do. But, dear master, you do not know this: I am praying for the Lord to show it to you. I mean to pray until I die, and after that if I can, until you are converted."

He looked at me so lovingly, and seemed so truly happy that it was more than I could stand. Almost involuntarily I made for the door, and escaped before he could stop me.

---

156 The reference to the lost sheep is only in Bourne's account.

I was as hopeless and miserable as I could be. I felt that my superior teaching and practice had failed, and that the inferior and, as I believed, unscriptural dogmas had prevailed. My favourite and most promising Churchman had fallen, and was happy in his fall. More than that, he was actually praying that I might fall too!

I was very jealous for the Church, and therefore felt deeply the conversion of my gardener. Like the elder brother of the Prodigal Son I was grieved and even angry, because he was restored to favour and joy. I thought I would give up my parish and church, and go and work in some more congenial soil; or else that I would preach a set of sermons on the subject of schism, for perhaps I had not sufficiently taught my people the danger of this great sin.

Every parishioner I passed seemed to look at me as if to say, "So much for your teaching. You will never convince us!"

I had promised to visit Mr Aitken,[157] the vicar of Pendeen, to advise him about his church which was then being built. So now, in order to divert my thoughts, I made up my mind to go to him at once.

Soon after my arrival, as we were seated comfortably by the fire, he asked me how my parish prospered. "I often take shame to myself when I think of all your work," he said. "But, my brother, are you satisfied?"

I said, "No, I am not satisfied."

---

157 In 1844 Robert Aitken was appointed the first vicar of the new Cornish parish of Pendeen. There he and the parishioners built their own church. A website gives the full biography of Robert Aitken: do a search on "aitken + manx" or follow the hyperlink on www.billybray.com.

"Why not?"

"Because I am making a rope of sand which looks very well until I pull, and then when I expect it to hold, it gives way."

"What do you mean?" he asked.

"Why," I replied, "these Cornish people are ingrained schismatics." I then told him of my gardener's conversion and my great disappointment

"Well," he said, "if I were taken ill, I certainly would not send for you. I am sure you could not do me any good, for you are not converted yourself."

"Not converted?" I exclaimed. "How can you tell?"

He said quietly, "I am sure of it, or you would not have come here to complain of your gardener. If you had been converted you would have remained at home to rejoice with him. It is very clear you are not converted."

[Aitken now asks Haslam if he would like to spend some time in prayer about the situation. Haslam agrees, but finds the whole experience too much]

I was completely overcome. I sat down on the ground sobbing, while he shouted aloud praising God. As soon as I could I took my departure. I was really afraid to stay any longer. I walked and ran all the seven miles (11km) to Penzance. My mind was in a revolution.

I reached home greatly disturbed in my mind – altogether disappointed and disgusted with my work among these Cornish people. I thought, "It is no use, they never will be Churchmen."

[Haslam now becomes aware that however much good he may have done for the Church, it will never be enough to get him into heaven]

The next Sunday I felt so ill that I was quite unfit to take the service at Baldhu. Mr Aitken had said to me, "If I were you I would shut the church and say to the congregation, 'I will not preach again until I am converted. Pray for me.'" I was now wondering if I should do this.

The sun was shining brightly, and before I could make up my mind to put off the service the bells sent their summons far away over the hills. Now the thought came to me that I would go to church and read the morning prayers, and after that dismiss the people. While I was reading the Gospel I thought, well, I will just say a few words in explanation of this and then I will dismiss them. So I went up into the pulpit and gave out my text. I took it from the Gospel of the day, Matthew 22 verse 42: What think ye of Christ?

As I went on to explain the passage, I saw that the Pharisees and scribes did not know that Jesus Christ was the Son of God, or that he was come to save them. They were looking for a king, the son of David, to reign over them as they were. Something was telling me, all the time, "You are no better than the Pharisees yourself. You do not believe that Jesus is the Son of God, and that he is come to save you, any more than they did."

I do not remember all I said, but I felt a wonderful light and joy coming into my soul, and I was beginning to see what the Pharisees did not see. Whether it was something in my words, or my manner, or my look, I know not; but all of a sudden a local preacher, who happened to be in the congregation, stood up, and putting up his arms, shouted out in Cornish manner, "The parson is converted! The parson is converted! Hallelujah!"

Baldhu church: "The parson is converted!"
Redrawn from an engraving in *From Death into Life"*

In another moment his voice was lost in the shouts and praises of three or four hundred of the congregation. Instead of rebuking this extraordinary 'brawling' as I should have done in a former time, I joined in the outburst of praise. Then, to make it more orderly, I gave out the Doxology, *Praise God, from whom all blessings flow.* The people sang it with heart and voice, over and over again. My Churchmen were dismayed, and many of them fled hastily from the place. Still the voice of praise went on, and was swelled by numbers of passers-by who came into the church, greatly surprised to hear and see what was going on.

When this subsided I found at least twenty people crying for mercy, whose voices had not been heard in the excitement and noise of thanksgiving. They all professed to find peace and joy in believing. Amongst this number there were three from my own house, and we returned home praising God.

The news spread in all directions that, "The parson is converted", and that by his own sermon, in his own pulpit! The church would not hold the crowds who came in the evening. I cannot exactly remember what I preached about on that occasion, but one thing I said was, "If I had died last week I should have been lost for ever."

Haslam invites Robert Aitken from Pendeen to preach at Baldhu, where a revival is taking place. He continues:

What tremendous scenes we witnessed whenever Mr Aitken came to preach. The church, which was built to hold six hundred, used to have as many as fifteen hundred packed into it. Not only were the wide passages crowded, and the chancel filled even up to the communion table, but there were two rows of occupants in every pew.

The great man was king over their souls, for at times he seemed as if he was endued with power whereby he could make them shout for joy, or howl for misery, or cry aloud for mercy. He was by far the most effective preacher I ever heard, or ever expect to hear. Souls were awakened by scores whenever he preached. Sometimes the meetings continued far into the night, and occasionally even to the daylight of the next morning.

To the cool, dispassionate outside observers and the newspaper reporters, all this vehement stir was very extravagant and incomprehensible, and no doubt they thought that it was done for excitement. Certainly they gave us credit for that, and a great deal more. Consequently we had the full benefit of their sarcasm and invective.

Cornish revivals were things by themselves. I have read of such stirring movements occurring occasionally in different places elsewhere, but in

Cornwall they were frequent. Every year, in one part or another, a revival would spring up, during which believers were refreshed and sinners awakened.

It is sometimes suggested that there is a great deal of the flesh in these things – more of this than of the Spirit. I am sure this is a mistake, for I am quite satisfied that neither Cornish nor any other people could produce revivals without the power of the Holy Spirit, for they would never be without them if they could raise them at pleasure. But, as a fact, it is well known that revivals begin and continue for a time, and that they cease as mysteriously as they began.

In 1852, when all the people who dwelt on the hill on which the church was built were converted, there came upon the scene a very remarkable person who had evidently been kept back for a purpose. This was none other than the veritable and well-known Billy Bray. One morning, while we were sitting at breakfast, I heard someone walking about in the hall with a heavy step, saying, "Praise the Lord! Praise the Lord!"

On opening the door I beheld a happy-looking little man, in a black Quaker-cut coat, which it was very evident had not been made for him but for some much larger body. "Well, my friend," I said, "who are you?"

"I am Billy Bray," he replied, looking steadily at me with his twinkling eyes, "and be you the parson?"

"Yes, I am."

"Thank the Lord. Converted, are ye?"

"Yes, thank God."

"And the missus inside," he said, pointing to the dining room. "Be she converted?"

"Yes, she is."

"Thank the dear Lord," he repeated, moving forward.

I made way for him, and he came stepping into the room. Then making a profound bow to the said missus, he asked, "Be there any maids?"

"Yes, there are three in the kitchen."

"Be they converted too?"

I was able to answer in the affirmative, and as I pointed towards the kitchen door when I mentioned it, he made off in that direction. Soon we heard them all shouting and praising God together in a loud Cornish style. When we went in, there was Billy Bray, very joyful, singing, "Canaan is a happy place, I am bound for the land of Canaan."

We then returned to the dining room with our strange guest, when he suddenly caught me up in his arms and carried me round the room. I was so taken by surprise that it was as much as I could do to keep myself in an upright position, till he had accomplished the circuit. Then he set me in my chair, and rolling on the ground for joy, said that he was "as happy as he could live." When this performance was at an end, he rose up with a face that was beaming all over.

I invited him to take some breakfast with us, to which he assented with thanks. He chose bread and milk, for he said, "I am only a child."[158]

I asked him to be seated and gave him a chair, but he preferred walking about, and went on talking all the time. He told us that twenty years ago as he was walking over this very hill on which my church and house were built – it was a barren old place then – the

---

158 This puzzling response appears only in the account by Haslam, who had presumably understood it. Billy is fifty-seven, and if he is having trouble with his teeth (see page 38) he might be unwilling to eat anything hard. Or perhaps Billy is making some obscure spiritual point.

Lord said to him, "I will give thee all that dwell in this mountain."[159]

Immediately Billy fell down on his knees and thanked the Lord, and then ran to the nearest cottage. There he talked and prayed with the people, and was enabled to bring them to Christ. Then he went to the next cottage and got the same blessing, and then to a third where he was equally successful. Then he told "Father" that there were only three "housen" in this mountain, and prayed that more might be built. That prayer remained with him and he never ceased to make it for years. The neighbours, who heard his prayer from time to time, apparently wondered why he should ask for what he called "housen" to be built in such an "ungain" place.

After sixteen years Billy received a letter from his brother James to say that they were hacking up the croft to plant trees, and that they were going to build a church on the hill. He was "fine and glad", and praised the Lord. Again he did so when his brother wrote to say there was a vicarage to be built on the same hill, and a schoolroom also. He was almost beside himself with joy and thankfulness for all this.

In the year 1848, when the church was completed and opened, Billy came on a visit to Baldhu, and was greatly surprised to see what a change had taken place. There was a beautiful church, a parsonage

159 This must have been about 1832, shortly before Billy started building Kerley Downs Chapel a few minutes' walk away. Readers who do not know Cornwall should understand that there are no mountains, although other writers of the period use this word to describe the Cornish hills. The counties of Devon and Cornwall are for the most part hilly with high moor land, most famously Dartmoor and Bodmin Moor, but Baldhu is in an area of sharp dips and rises of no great magnitude.

Illustration of Baldhu vicarage
redrawn from an engraving in *The King's Son*

with a flourishing garden, and a schoolroom, with a large plantation and fields round them.

This is when Haslam says that Billy came out "checkfallen" and quite disappointed, telling "Father" that that was nothing but an "old Pusey" (a Tractarian) there. The "old Pusey", of course, was Haslam himself.

While Billy was praying that afternoon, "Father" gave him to understand that he had no business there yet, and that he had come too soon, and without permission. So he went back to his place at once, near Bodmin, and continued to pray for the hill.

After three years his brother James wrote again, and this time it was to tell him that the parson and all his family were converted, and that there was a great revival at the church. Now Billy was most eager to come and see this for himself, but he obtained no permission, though he asked and looked for it every day for more than three months.

At last, one wintry and frosty night in January, about half-past eleven, just as he was getting into bed, "Father" told him that he might go to Baldhu. He was so overjoyed that he did not wait until the morning, but told me, "I put up my clothes again and hitched in the donkey, and comed singing all along the road." After a journey of nearly thirty miles (48km), Billy arrived early in the morning.[160] Having put up his donkey in my stable, he came into the house and presented himself as I have already stated, in the hall, praising God.

We were a long time over breakfast that morning, for the happy man went on from one thing to another, "telling of the Lord," as he called it, assuring us again and again that he was, "fine and glad, and very happy." Indeed, he looked so. He said there was one thing more he must tell us. It was this – that he had a "preaching-house", or mission-hall, he had built years ago.[161] He had often prayed there for "this old mountain", and now he should dearly love to see me in the pulpit of that place, and said that he would let me have it for my work.

Then Billy said to me, "I want to see thee in it. When will you come?"

160 This is early 1852. Bourne says Billy has come to Baldhu from Bodmin, which is in keeping with Haslam's distance. In the 1851 census, Billy and Joey are shown as living at 36 Blowing House, Bodmin.

161 Bourne writes that this is Three Eyes Chapel at Kerley Downs, but a careful reading of Haslam's account raises problems with both the identity of this chapel and the story of the pulpit told by five different writers, including Billy Bray. My theory is that this is the original Bethel, in use as a schoolroom and meeting room at this time. See Appendix 2 where the five versions are told in full and the possibilities are explored in detail.

I could not fix for that day or the next, but made arrangements to conduct a series of services the next week and promised to have them in that place.

Before he left us, Billy asked about the two other houses that had been built, who lived in them, and especially if all the, "dwellers was converted." Then he declared his intention to go and see the parties and rejoice with them, and testify how fully the Lord had accomplished the promise he gave him upon that very hill, twenty years before.

According to promise I went to Billy Bray's preaching-house. It was the first time that I had preached anywhere outside my church and schoolroom since my conversion. There it pleased the Lord to give me much help, and a great work followed, such as Billy had never seen in that place before. Several times we were detained there all night through, with penitents crying aloud for mercy and believers rejoicing.

As a rule Cornish people would remain at a meeting for hours, and come again the next day, and the day after if needful, until they felt that they could cry for mercy. And then they would begin and continue crying until they felt they could believe. At the conclusion of these services we returned to the schoolroom where our meetings were continued.

Our friend Billy remained with us at Baldhu, and was very useful. He spoke in the schoolroom with much acceptance and power in the simplicity of his faith, and souls were added to the Lord continually.

[A year later Haslam is holding a meeting with many visiting clergy present. He wants everything to go quietly. Then Billy turns up]

Many of the proceedings in our parish were, I confess, more tumultuous than I could justify, more noisy and exciting than I thought needful; but I could not control the people. To hinder their rejoicings would have been to withstand the Spirit of God.

One day, by way of change, I had a meeting for the Bible Society, and invited some of the clergy who sympathized with its object. They attended, and others came out of curiosity "to see these revival people". We had a large gathering and everything began smoothly.

My Scripture-reader, who was a most excitable and noisy man, tried to do his best before the clergy. He spoke of the sweet words which they had heard from the reverend speakers. It was charming, he said, to hear of a good cause supported in such "mellifluous accents", and so forth. He got a little wild towards the end, but on the whole he was to be praised for his kind efforts to give a quiet tone to the meeting.

By this time, our friend Billy Bray had appeared on the scene. He gave us chapter and verse, from one end of the Bible to the other, on the subject of 'dancing for joy'. He propounded his theory that if a man did not praise God he would not rise in the resurrection.

He said if he only praised God with his mouth, he would rise like those things carved on the tombstones, with swelling cheeks and wings. If he clapped his hands – suiting his actions to the words – he would have a pair of hands as well at the resurrection. And if he danced with his feet he would rise complete. He hoped to rise like that: to sing, to clap his hands, dance and jump too. The worst of jumping in this world, he said, was that he had to come down again. In heaven he supposed the higher he danced and jumped, the higher he would be. Walking in heaven, to his mind, was praising God, where one foot said "Glory," and the other "Hallelujah."

Under Billy's original theories the people were warming up, and becoming a little responsive, and Billy himself was getting excited. In reference to some remarks which had been made by a previous speaker about Samson, Billy said that he felt as happy and strong as Samson. Then suddenly he put his arms round me, as I was standing gesticulating and making signs to the people to be still. Taking me up as he had done once before, he carried me down the schoolroom, crying out, " Here go the posts! Glory! Hallelujah!"

It was useless to resist, for he held me with an iron grasp. So I remained still, hoping at every step that he would put me down. I suppose he imagined himself to be Samson carrying off the gates of Gaza. The people got what they called "happy", and shouted and praised God most vociferously. I gave out a hymn, but the joy of the Cornish people could not be restrained within the bounds of a tune, or form of words. Some of them became very excited and unmanageable. Only those who have witnessed such scenes can understand what I mean.

The power of God was great, though the demonstrations were very human. My visitors trembled with fear, and made their escape as precipitately as they possibly could. To those who are not in the power of the Spirit such rejoicings are unintelligible. Lookers-on are offended because they only see and feel the human manifestation and not the Divine power. They are like people who get all the smoke, and none of the warmth of the fire.

I made up my mind for the worst, for we had a reporter there, and some others who were only too ready to make the most of such a scene. Nevertheless I would rather have the same thing over and over again, than have the most stately and orderly ceremonials conjoined with spiritual death.

CHAPTER 17

PRAISE THE LORD, JOEY!

THIS CHAPTER IS a collection of stories told by Bourne and others. Billy and his family are not immune to the various illnesses and financial troubles that befall the mining families in his community. Billy's crops fail, his children become dangerously ill, and soon he will be faced with the predicament of fostering two orphan children.

The first account comes from MG Pearse's *Daniel Quorm and His Religious Notions, First Series.* Although the Daniel Quorm stories are fiction, they are based on real life incidents. Pearse gives an eyewitness account of Billy telling how he *"beat the devil"* when his crop of potatoes failed. Although there was a major potato famine in Cornwall in 1840 this seems to be a later event, around 1853, when Billy was nearly sixty. We know this because Billy was converted in 1823, and here he says he has been a poor servant of his heavenly Father *"for thirty years"*:

> Friends, last week I was a-diggin' up my 'taters. It was a wisht poor yield, sure 'nough. There was hardly a sound one in the whole lot. An' while I was a-diggin', the devil come to me, and he says,
>
> "Billy, do you think your Father do love you?"
>
> "I should reckon he do," I says.
>
> "Well, I don't," says the old tempter in a minute.
>
> If I'd thought about it I shouldn't ha' listened to 'en, for his opinions ben't worth the leastest bit o' notice.
>
> "I don't," says he, "and I tell 'e what for. If your Father loved you, Billy Bray, he'd give you a pretty yield o' 'taters – so much as ever you do want, and

ever so many of 'em, and every one of 'em as big as
your fist. For it ben't no trouble to your Father to do
anything; and he could just as easy give you plenty
as not, an' if he loved you, he would, too."

Of course, I wasn't goin' to let he talk o' my Father
like that, so I turned round 'pon 'en. "Pray, sir," says
I, "who may you happen to be, comin' to me a-talkin'
like this here? If I ben't mistaken, I know you, sir, and
my Father too. And to think o' you comin' a-sayin' he
don't love me! Why, I've got your written character
home to my house; and it do say, sir, that you be a
liar from the beginnin'. An' I'm sorry to add that I
used to have a personal acquaintance with you some
years since, and I served you faithful as ever any
poor wretch could. And you gave me was nothing
but rags to my back, and a wretched home, and an
achin' head, an' no 'taters, and the fear o' hell-fire to
finish up with. And here's my dear Father in heaven.
I have been a poor servant of his for thirty years. An'
he's given me a clean heart, an' a soul full o' joy, an' a
lovely suit o' white as'll never wear out. And he says
that he'll make a king o' me before he've done, an'
that he'll take me home to his palace to reign with
him for ever and ever. An' now you come up here
a-talkin' like that."

Bless 'e, my dear friends, he went off in a minute, like
as if he'd been shot – I do wish he had – and he never
had the manners to say good mornin'.

Bourne tells of a time when Joey is afraid one of their
children will die. We do not know if this is a boy or a girl.
Joey asks Billy to go to the doctor and get some medicine.
He takes eighteen pence in his pocket, all the money there
is in the house. On the road he meets a man who has lost a
cow and is out begging for money to buy another. His story
touches Billy's heart and he gives him the money. Bourne
writes that Billy says afterwards:

"I felt after I had given away the money, it was no
use to go on to the doctor for I could not have

medicine without money. So I thought I would tell my Heavenly Father about it. I jumped over a hedge, and while telling the Lord all about it I felt sure the child would live.

"I then went home, and as I entered the door I said to my wife, 'Joey, the child is better, isn't it?'

"Yes," she said.

"The child will live, the Lord has told me so."

At a chapel anniversary Bourne writes that Billy told the people:

I went in to Truro to buy a frock for my little maid. Coming home I felt very happy and got catching up my heels a little bit, and I danced the frock out of the basket.

When I came home, my wife Joey said, "William, where's the frock?"

I said, "I don't know. Isn't it in the basket?"

"No," said Joey.

"Glory be to God," I said, "I danced the frock out of the basket."

The next morning I went to the class meeting, and one was speaking of his trials, and another was speaking of his trials, and I said, "I've got trials too, for yesterday I went into Truro and bought a frock for my little maid. Coming home I got catching up my heels a little bit, and I danced the frock out of the basket."

So they gave me the money I had paid for the frock. Two or three days afterwards someone picked up the frock and brought it to me. So I had two frocks for one. Glory!"

Billy finished his story with one of his favourite sayings when anyone opposed and persecuted him for singing and shouting so much. "If they was to put me into a barrel, I would shout glory out through the bunghole. Praise the Lord!"

It seems strange to hear Billy boasting that he ends up better off, yet he apparently makes no attempt to repay the money to the class members when the dress is found. I am surprised Bourne has not made one of his many comments here in which he explains Billy's conduct, so Bourne seems to have been comfortable with the story. Bourne says it came from someone called Mr Robbins, and there must have been more to it at one time, even though Bourne only quotes this fragment.

A preacher, unidentified by Bourne, who met Billy says:

> I was holding special services in one of Billy's chapels, making his humble house my temporary home. One morning, after breakfast and prayer, Billy went out. He soon returned with two little children, a boy and a girl, one in each arm.
>
> His wife said, "Billy, where are you going with the children?"
>
> He replied, "The mother's dead and the father's run away and left them on the stream, and I thought I'd bring them in and rear them up with ours."
>
> His wife remonstrated, saying, "We have four of our own that you can only just maintain, and these must go to the workhouse."
>
> Billy answered, "The Lord can as well feed them here as he can in the union." The same instant he put them with his own children, saying to them, "Here, my dears, this is your home now."
>
> His wife was very downhearted at these two little strangers being thrust upon her, and she having such a small income. I thought Billy had a much bigger heart than me, as I had a competency[162] and no family, but would have shrunk from the responsibility of bringing up two children.

I thought I would give Billy something, and found I had two pounds fifteen shillings and tenpence in my pocket. Seeing Billy's wife Joey in so much distress I decided to give Billy five shillings[163] towards this maintenance.

When Billy received it, he said, "There, Joey, the Lord has sent five shillings already, although the children have not eaten a penny loaf;" while I felt as if I had stolen the five shillings.

We know the names of four of Billy and Joey's children: James, Mary, Anne and Grace. While building Three Eyes Chapel at Kerley Downs (p. 81), Billy refers to *a little son* who is helping him, and having *five small children* at home. This makes a total of at least six, unless the son is still living at home, and Billy thinks of him as *little*. Billy calls 12-year-old John Hicks, who was converted after the whirlwind, a *little boy*. If James has left home, then these two may be part of the *five small children*.

Surprisingly little is known about Billy's children. See Appendix 3. Many people called Bray believe they are descended from Billy's family, but don't have the proof. Bray was a widespread name in Cornwall at the time. Anyone with a cast-iron family tree should contact the Billy Bray Memorial Trust, where the members would like to hear about it. See Appendix 5 for contact details.

It was impressed on my mind I had not given enough, and I said, "Here, Billy, give me that five shillings, and take ten shillings for the children."

Billy replied, "Praise the Lord, Joey. Didn't I tell you the Lord could feed them here as well as in the union?"

---

162 A private income large enough to live on.

163 See box on page 71 for the value of money.

But I became more miserable, and felt I ought to give Billy more. At last I said, "Here, Billy, the Lord is displeased with me. Give me that half sovereign back and take a sovereign."

He began to praise the Lord, and told his wife to shout "Hallelujah", for the Lord would provide.

I tried to read, but a feeling of wretchedness quite overcame me, and I said, "Lord, what am I to do?"

And the answer was, "Give Billy more."

So I told Billy I had not given him enough yet. "Take another sovereign."

Billy again shouted, "Glory be to God. Cheer up, Joey, the money is coming."

I then asked the Lord to make me happy, as I had only fifteen shillings and tenpence left. But the impression still was that I ought to give Billy more. I then gave him ten shillings, but could not rest until I had given him all I had.

But Billy refused to take the odd tenpence, saying, "No, brother, keep that to pay the turnpike gates when you go home."

Billy then said, "Let's have a little prayer."

While Billy was praying, such a divine power rested on us as I cannot describe, and I never expect such a blessing again this side of heaven. I have been reliably informed that these children were brought up by Billy until they were able to earn their own living.

In the Shaw Collection, in the Courtney Library at the Royal Institution of Cornwall in Truro, is a handwritten family tree made, "From the notes of the Reverend Tom Shore (sic)." At first sight this seems to throw light on this episode. However, although much of Shaw's work is reliable, some collected records are of dubious value, and some are definitely incorrect. Unfortunately, Shaw gives no indication as to the reliability or otherwise of the material in his collection.

The family tree says Billy's brother James Trewartha Bray married a widow Sarah Hooper (née Cornish) in late 1841. They had two children, although it is not clear if the children were theirs, or Sarah's from her previous marriage. When she died, James "ran off", according to the note. This sounds like a perfect fit for the above story, for Billy would have felt under an obligation to look after his brother's children, even if they were stepchildren.

In keeping with the sensitivities of the time, neither the preacher nor Bourne would have wanted to identify the man who "ran off" as Billy's brother. However, a recent examination of the marriage certificate indicates that this James' father was alive at the time of the wedding in 1841, and was a carpenter. Billy's father died in 1802 when Billy was seven and his mother seems to have remained a widow. James has no middle name on the marriage certificate, which is suspicious. Where did the late Tom Shaw get the information that enabled someone to draw up the family tree? More research is needed.

CHAPTER 18

JOHN OATES' DIARIES

IT IS TIME to look inside the diaries kept by John Oates (1853-1939) the master of the Boards School at Blackwater in Cornwall, a village only 3 miles (5km) north of Twelveheads. The diaries run from 1878 to 1939, and include details of the weather as well as local and national events. There are a few entries about Billy in the form of abbreviated notes, a reminder for the stories Oates collects from local people. Billy has been dead fourteen years by 1882, the time he gets his first mention in Oates' diary.

Oates shortens many words and often uses dialect spelling, as well as deliberately bad grammar, when recounting stories he has been told. I have removed most of the dialect spelling but kept much of the original grammar, as this is in keeping with Billy's own writing. On several occasions Oates writes *Willy* and overwrites the W with a B. On two occasions he fails to make the correction, so obviously he was not very familiar with the name. The original diaries, still in copyright, are available for inspection in the County Record Office in Truro, with the reference X629/1-18.

November 30th 1882, Thursday

Rather nice day but cold. At Library Room for a short time. Arrangements for Billy Bray Entertainment on Saturday.

December 2nd 1882, Saturday

Came home about 5.30 pm. Had bath, and then up to school to take money for Entertainment. Only about 80 present in consequence of miserable weather. Not bad singing with the Green Bottom Choir. Mr Messa at the Harmonium. Mrs Treseder read the literary part of the Service, Billy Bray, very well indeed. Billy born at Twelveheads 1794. Little wiry man.

One tale of young woman bad and Billy praying and telling them to boil some fish and 'tateys. She recovered, ate some "fish and 'tateys", and lived to be the mother of ten children.[164]

Mr Jon Rowden in chair told two tales of Billy. (1) About Billy and his wife and faith and the Burrow. (2) Billy with comrade working in bottom of shaft. "Now," says Billy, "thee goes into the hole there in the side out of danger. For if the chain should break and kibble[165] come down upon me I should go straight to heaven. But if he was to come 'pon thee, thee's go straight to hell." Noise of kibble overhead. Billy pulled man out and got in himself. After Entertainment, coffee and cake at the Reading Room.

Jonathan Rowden's two stories are puzzling. Oates has an entry a few days earlier of a walk to Two Burrows, a place still called that today. So the first story may refer to what was a well-known local incident. Rowden's second story seems to be a joke told at Billy's expense, but this explanation does not fit comfortably with a meeting that had a reading from *The King's Son*. However, the evening was scheduled as entertainment!

October 25th 1884, Saturday

Miss S one day walking to Scorrier[166] passed a small, meanly dressed man. The man called after her, "How'n 'e walking so fast! If you knowed who I was you would'n walk so fast. Don't 'e know who I am?"

"No," said Miss S.

---

164 See page 73.

165 bucket

166 Scorrier is 3 miles – 5km north west of Twelveheads.

"I'm the King's Son. Are you the King's daughter?"

Miss S said it was hard to tell who were King's sons and daughters. He chatted away and left her at the Spread Eagle, he going up to Mrs Crage's.[167]

Miss S heard Billy preach at Wheal Busy[168] in meadow before chapel on an old wagon. Crowds of people, especially young people, and at Billy's sallies and rustic wit there were roars of laughter. Billy had been upward and gave a short history of where he'd been. "I went into one house and danced their kitchen all over. Each have spreaded a fruit table in the wilderness, and on the table is a laughing dish, a dancing dish, and when me (or thee) and the old Dan Pat (these words are unclear) was converted over to Twelveheads Chapel, it am said to me, 'Billy, 'tis like eating honey out of a mug with a spoon.' But I said, 'So I am just eating it with a ladle.'

"God's sheep do know each other. 'Tis like a lot of sheep in a field and some more do jump over the hedge to them, and they do smile to one another. And then a great dog – what is the old devil – do jump up upon the hedge and do say, 'Yap, yap.' But, bless 'e, the sheep isn't feared. They do turn round and say, 'What are thee doing up there, yap, yap, you great ?maased ?thing?'"

These final two words are not clear. Probably the first is *maased*, a dialect spelling of the Cornish word *mazed* meaning variously *crazy*, *stupid* or *mad*. The last word could be *thing*. I am reproducing this section here, with acknowledgment of the copyright held by the Trustees of the Estate of John Oates, so readers can make their own

---

167 On 29th November 1882, a Mr Crage finished some work in John Oates' bedroom.

168 Near Carharrack.

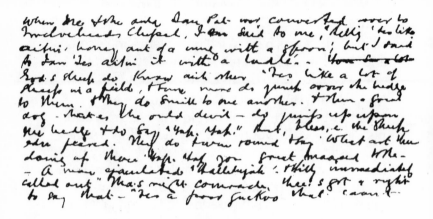

A few lines from Oates' diary

deductions. In the original, the mark below the centre of the word *maased* is clearly the dot of the letter *i* from the word immediately below.

A man articulated, "Hallelujah," and Willy (Billy) immediately called out, "That's right, comrade, thee's got a right to say that. It's a poor cuckoo that can't say cuckoo in the summer. When I do get to heaven I'm going to have a new pair of hob boots, and I'll dance with they boots in the golden streets till I do make them ring. As for the lukewarm professor he only just fit inside the gates of heaven. He won't have a crown no bigger than a little glow-worm."

Billy had hats, coats etc given to him. One day a man said, "Now, Billy, I've a coat home I've altered for you, but I don't know whether he'll fit you."

"Oh," says Billy, "yes he will. Father lent 'un and Father do know my size nicely."

Everything with Billy came from "Father".

March 22nd 1885, Sunday

Cold in morning with heavy hail. Showers from NE in morning but bright afternoon. As I JA to tea and stopped the evening. Mr WA Rowe at tea. Billy (was once) asked how he had been serving the Lord. "Well," says Billy, "'tis 42 years ago since I ?mit the old ?linit sometime secretly ?face up here upon the Downs and had a rasole (?wrestle) with 'n and (illegible word) 'n too."

Lukewarm professors: Billy preaching outside a chapel to large crowd, and pitching into lukewarm professor. Drew illustration. A hundred sheep feeding in a field all so comfortable. Turn in a hundred more and they all smile to see one another and go in all comfortable together. Up jumps a little dog, "Yap, yap," and away the sheep all run, and so with the lukewarm professor. Put a hundred Methodists in the chapel and they will be happy and comfortable, saying "Hallelujah." Put a hundred Bryanites in and they all shake hands and say, "Praise the Lord." But in will walk Mister Lukewarm Professor and say, "Hello, what's all this noise and excitement about?" 'Tis like a dish of cold water. He'll measure their bushel (8 gallons) by his peck (2 gallons) and that couldn't (be) much bigger than half a noggin (1/8 pint)."

3rd November 1889

(Someone known to John Oates as SK tells him): "Years ago I was working in the Caradon district near Liskeard, and we was out four or five of us young men sleuthing.[169] We was up round Brown Willy and Rowtor[170] where Matthey Wicks murdered Charlotte Diamond. As we was creeping round the front of one of the tors[171] we spied an old donkey

---

169 Presumably hunting.

170 Now called Rough Tor.

171 Tall rocky outcrops. The story of the murder is still known locally.

jogging along with an old pack like a flour bag across his back, but we couldn't see a living soul with him or near him.

All to once we heard a sound coming from a pit, but what 'twas we couldn't tell. In a few minutes we seed a man coming and dancing as if he was 'lectrified. If he was jumping one foot from the ground he was jumping two every step or two, and singing out, "Hallelujah, glory be to God!" and so on. 'Twasn't long before I could see who 'twas. 'Twas Billy Bray himself. Well, when he spied us, up he comes, and says he, "I can see you's out sporting a bit. I've been over here from the down[172] and had a good time with Father, and I hope you'll have a good time of it." He didn't find no fault with us, but was so merry as a cricket. He said, "Mind that all these things will come to an end. And mind you prepare for the time when it do come."

One night Billy was coming home from preaching, and he was a long way from home and 'twas pitch dark, the wind howling and rain coming down in torrents. "Just as I was out from the downs," says Billy, "old Black Face comed up and laughed at me, and said, 'What a fool thou art. Here thee art, aren't 'a. There thee's out walking miles in this bitter weather to tell the little thee'st know to a few people!'

"I know I'm fool bad enough," retorted Willie (Billy), "but I aren't such a fool as thee wast now: for thee doesn't know how to keep a good place when thee's had 'en, for thee'st got kicked out of heaven because thee wasn't pleased."

Oates follows this with another story told to him by SK, which provides an intriguing look into Cornish chapel life.

---

172 Maybe the downs, a local term for the open hillside.

(For another instance of giving out a hymn before praying, see the story about 'Grandfather' on p. 233):

> "I knowed at M two men especially who were so ignorant they couldn't tell a letter in the book, and when they was called upon in a prayer meeting to give out a hymn they used to tremble like leafs, and their jackets would fairly shake from their shoulders. They would take a book, but of course they had learnt up a little hymn or two before. Well, they would begin to pray, stuttering and stammering like. But in five minutes, my son, t'would come out in a perfect stream. If they had a steam pipe pouring of it into them, and a boiler back making more, it couldn't come out of them faster."

CHAPTER 19

BITTER MIXED WITH SWEET

BILLY SEEMS TO be retired now, and living at Twelveheads. He is free to travel surprisingly long distances to take up his preaching engagements. This often involves a stay with friends. Joey has become seriously ill, and Billy too suffers from ill health from time to time. But he has no fear of the death. He intends to carry on telling people the good news of Jesus Christ while he still has the strength.

In *The King's Son* Bourne tells us about a conversation Joey has with Billy:

"William," she tells him, "I do not see anything from heaven."

"Neither do I," he replies. "What need has the Lord to show us sights, when we can believe without it? If I saw the Saviour a babe in the manger, I should not believe it more than I do now. If I saw him raise Lazarus out of the grave, I should not believe it more than I do now. If I saw the Lord Jesus raise the ruler's daughter or the widow's son to life, I should not believe it more than I do now. And if I saw the dear Lord nailed to the cross, and heard him cry *It is finished*, and saw him give up the ghost and rise from the tomb the third day, I should not believe these things more than I do now."

Then Joey exclaims, "And so do I believe it." And they greatly rejoice together.

Bourne writes:

The devil tempted him Billy these words. "Well, I'll have thee down to hell after all."

Billy retorted, "I'd as soon go to hell with thee as not. For I'd bring Jesus Christ with me, and shout and sing and praise the Lord, and I know thee wast'en like that."

If Billy was tempted with the thought that he was a fool to go and preach, as he would never get anything for it, his answer to the devil was, "Not so big a fool as thee art. For once thee was in a good situation, and did not know how to keep it!"

One of Billy's three sisters (probably Anne) suffers from an unspecified mental disability. She is very difficult, and sometimes so irritable that she tries Billy's faith and patience. Referring to this, Bourne says:

Billy tells us he had one unfailing resort in trouble. "I cried to the Lord and he heard me, for he made me so happy that I could not hold it in. I had a joy unspeakable and full of glory. I had good measure, pressed down, and running over. Now what was that trial compared with the blessing I received? I was so happy that I felt none of these things could move me. I could say, 'I long to be with Christ now. My dear Lord, let me die, and take me to heaven.' I felt so much of the Divine glory that I longed to be there. I cannot tell what I felt."

Billy is writing his *Journal* in 1864, at the age of 70. By September he is using his entries more as a diary, although sometimes he is two or three weeks in arrears:

September 1864. Breage Friends asked me down on Sunday the 11 to speak in their chapel, and I had to go through Helston to go to Breage. When I came to Helston there was a man and his wife that sold clothes, and they was very kind friends. They asked me to sit down by their stoning[173] and I did, and I think I caught a cold. I had hard work to get to Breage. My breath was so short that I had hard

173 A market stall.

work to breathe. This was the Saturday, and that night I was bad. On the Sunday I had to speak twice, but I was very unwell.

On the Monday evening we had a meeting, but I was still unwell. The Breage Friends was very kind to me, and on Tuesday morning I left Breage for home. I walked as far as Helston, and they say that is three miles and a half, but it was a hard job for me to do. I was so bad in Helston that I got into the bus[174] and rode to Penryn station, and while I was in Penryn I went to see a friend of mine and wait till the train did go to Perranwell.

I was so bad when I was at my friend's house in Penryn that I thought I could not get to the station, but the dear Lord helped me. I rode in the train to Perranwell station, and I got home to my house that night, but it was a hard job. What a great blessing health is. Before the dear Lord afflicted me, I could walk eighteen or twenty miles in a day and feel nothing from it.

I was bad for three weeks nearly. Bless and praise his dear and holy name, he that tear down can build up. There was a friend that lived a mile from where I lived. He was unwell, and I went to see him. While we was together the Lord was with us, and when I came out of his house I was so light that I thought I was no weight at all, for I was as well as ever I was in all my life.

I said, "What is this then, that I am so well in one minute?" Then it came to my mind, "Mount up as on as the wings of eagles. Run and be not weary, walk and not faint."[175]

All this last week I was never better than I have been, for the dear Lord hath blessed me with health and strength. My wish is to honour the dear Lord in all I do, and all I say, and all I write, for it is from him we have every good thing, bless and praise his holy name. You that read this must remember that I am more than

174 A horse-drawn carriage for public transport.

175 Isaiah 40:31

seventy years old, and if I make a little blunder, no wonder, for it is once a man and twice a child.

I remember being at a meeting in this friend's house more than thirty years agone, when his father and his mother was living. The power of God came down then and ten women danced for joy, and I could dance with them. I was very happy at that time, and I am very happy now, for in the dear Lord there is everlasting strength. He is my Lord, and now he has given me this strength I can work for him again.

If I have been suffering the will of the dear Lord in some way for weeks, that is past, but not like some of my dear brothers and sisters who suffer much in body. The dear Lord said, "They that suffer with me shall reign with me."[176] And Mister Wesley say, "He that suffer with his master here, shall before his face appear, and by his side sit down."[177] So that is a rich place to sit, by the Saviour's side in joy. And now I have new strength given me, thanks be to the dear Lord for his goodness to we his children.

The next Sunday I had to go to Leedstown. I went from home on Saturday and travelled to Camborne. I slept at a friend's house that night and walked to Leedstown on Sunday morning without breakfast. That, they told me, was five miles. I had to speak in the morning at half past ten to a large congregation, and the Lord was with us. At half past two I had to speak again to a chapel full of people, and the dear Lord was with us, for we had a blessed meeting.

I went into a friend's house and had my breakfast,[178] and in the evening we expected Miss D, but she did not come. So I had to speak again in the evening to a chapel full of people, and our great Captain was with us. I had strength according to my day, and the

---

176 Billy is probably referring to 2 Timothy 2:12.

177 This is part of verse 3 of *Come on, my partners in distress*, Hymn 316 in Wesley's Methodist Hymnbook, 366 in the Bible Christian Hymnbook.

Friends was very kind to me.

One kind woman that was at the chapel Sunday night begged me very much to see her on the next day, so I promised her that I would. When I came to her house I was kindly received with her husband and she. They was very kind friends[179], and the good woman said to me, "We will go over and see aunt[180] after dinner, for she can afford to give you something if she will."

I had not anything to live on but what the friends gave me, and my poor wife was bad in bed, and all we had was what the dear Lord put in the hearts of the dear people to give us. But our bread is given and our water is sure, for he that sent the ravens to feed Elijah, bless and praise his holy name, he does not forget we.

Then the good woman's husband said to her, "There is the horse and the trap out there, and if you are going over to aunt's, take the old mare. Go in the trap, and you and he ride over after dinner."

Then we prayed and asked our Heavenly Father to go with us. The trap was got for us, and the mistress drove the horse and I rode on like a gentleman. When we came to aunt's we was kindly received, for aunt was glad to see Beley Bray.[181]

We had a happy time telling about the dear Lord, for aunt did meet with our people the Bible Christians. So we had tea and she gave me a shilling to carry home to my sick wife. Then we got the trap and rode away for Leedstown.

That night we had a class meeting in the chapel. The class leader was a good man and the Lord was with him. He had a good class

---

178 Literally breaking the fast, in the late afternoon in Billy's case.

179 From the wording it seems that these may be Quakers, although I am not putting a capital F. If they are Quakers, I find it interesting that this woman was at the chapel service

180 It is not clear if this is the woman's aunt, or Billy's.

181 Billy's spelling

and the Lord was with them, for the women as well as the men was shouting and was praising of God, and some was dancing for joy. There was one very old man leaping and praising God, and who can we praise better? So we had a blessed meeting.

On Tuesday I went around to see Leedstown friends, and they was very kind friends. That evening we had a meeting again, and the dear Lord was with us. The chapel was full of people, and the dear Lord was with us and we had good meetings together.

On Wednesday morning I left Leedstown friends for home, and I walked to our house on that day. Our house from Leedstown is thirteen or fourteen miles, and I walked it. I found my dear wife in bed ill.

October 16 1864: I agreed with the friends near Connor Downs to go there on that day, for they owed some money on their chapel and they wanted some special service to pay it off. I left my house Saturday the fifteenth to get to Connor Downs as I promised. And see here what a mighty deliverance my dear Lord worked out for me.

The Saturday I was walking on my way about two miles and half from our house, and a cart with two boys overtook me and there was some iron in the cart. Some was long bars and some was short bars. The boys stopped the cart and asked me to ride. At first I thought I would, and then it came into my mind, "You are better not."

Then I said, "No, I shall not ride."

I went on, and they had not gone far before the pony came out of the forepart of the cart and off went the cart from the wheels. The iron was down in the road, and one of the boys was going very lame.

If I had got up in that cart I might have had a broken leg or arms. So when I saw the cart down in the road, and the iron strewed in the road, I could not help praising of the dear Lord for the deliverance he had wrought out for me. Had not the Lord put it in my heart not to ride in that cart I might have been groaning with broken limbs. But I went to Camborne with a thankful heart.

I slept at Camborne that night and went to Connor Downs the Sunday morning. There the friends was waiting for me at the new Camborne chapel.[182]I had to speak twice to a chapel full of people and we had a good meeting, for the Lord was with us. Some of our friends came up from Hayle Copperhouse, and they was good men and was much alive to god.

The Sunday and Monday night we had a teetotal meeting. Copperhouse friends came up to help me, and we had twelve that signed the pledge, and a good meeting we had. The King of kings and the Lord of lords was with us; and where he is his people never want a friend, bless and praise his holy name for he is very good.

Sunday the 23 (October): I was appointed at Penhallow and at Goonhavern, and in the week friend Hicks told me that he would go with me on the Sunday if all was well. So I went to his house, but he said that he was unwell and that he could not go with me, so I left him and walked away for Penhallow without breakfast. It was my plan to speak at Penhallow half past two and a good meeting we had, and our dear Lord was with us. I spoke and we had a teetotal meeting on the Monday night and friend Jankin (sic) helped me to carry on the meeting.

We had some to sign the pledge but not many, for the people is more fond of gratifying than they be of mortifying. We can get many to go to the ale house, but we cannot get many to go to the house of prayer. There is many that will do the work of the devil, but not many that love the work of the dear Lord. Many that call themselves Christians would rather go and have a pint of beer or a pale ale or the pipe than they would go and see their poor sick brother. Yes, they would rather spend their money in that good-for-worse-than-nothing than they would help their poor brothers. But may the dear Lord have mercy on them.

182 Probably Troon Bible Christian Chapel, which had opened a year earlier.

November 6 1864. I was appointed to the Deliverance Chapel the forenoon, and I had a great many people to speak to. There was some young converts there and they was very happy, and so was I, for the dear Lord was with us. We had a good meeting, bless and praise his holy name for ever.

My dear wife was in the bed very ill. I went home that evening to pray with her, and one of my happy sisters came[183] into our house to see my sick wife. After I had rosed up from praying, our dear happy sister sung a little light tune, and the power of the dear Lord came down among us and made us all very happy. My dear sick wife was very happy, thank the dear Lord for great goodness to we.

Monday the 7 (November). We had at Quenchwell our missionary meeting, with Brother Coles and Kenner and Reed and me, and Brother Martin [184] was chairman. We all had a good time while we was speaking, and had a good collection. Our meeting went off well and all the people seemed to be pleased, and I ought to be well pleased. While I was in the chapel I was very happy, and when I was going home the power of the dear Lord came down in that way that I could not stand on my feet.

I was so filled with the love of God that I fell down by the hedge, and then I rose on my feet, and then I fell down again. Thanks be to the dear Lord, he gave me good measure, pressed down, shaked together and running over. For his brightness shines full on all,

---

183 Probably Frances, born in 1798.

184 We can only guess who these men are, but the following were all Bible Christian preachers at this time, and are therefore possibilities.
James Coles (1822-1909) entered the Bible Christian ministry in 1850.
Henry, John and William Kenner were brothers. John and William were both in Cornwall in 1864, but Henry was probably in Canada by this time.
William Bryan Reed (1836-1936) was the son of William Reed (1800-58) who was one of the early leaders of the Bible Christian Connexion.

which makes us to the pavement fall.[185] He filled me so with love that I could not contain it. How sweet is the precious love of Christ to them that have it. It is sweeter than life and stronger than death.

This is the last entry in the *Journal*. Joey dies five weeks later, on December 13 1864, and is buried in Baldhu churchyard. Her death certificate records:

> Johanna Bray, Female, 72 years of age, wife of William Bray, Copper Miner, Debility, No medical attendant. Informant Wm Bray in attendance, Twelveheads, Kea, Fourteenth December 1864.

Wm Bray in attendance means Billy was looking after Joey, but was not present at the time of her death. This is in agreement with the following account by Bourne of Joey's death. Compare the wording with Billy's death certificate on page 238, where Anne Mary, his granddaughter, was present at his death.

Bourne tells us:

> During Joey's long illness, which ended in her death, Billy said, "I had many blessed seasons while praying with her, and promises from the dear Lord."

> The words, "She is mine for ever," were so deeply impressed on his mind that tears came into his eyes. He was so overpowered with the thought of his Joey having escaped from earth's toils and sufferings, to the rest and bliss of heaven, that he began to jump and dance about the room, exclaiming, "Bless the Lord, my dear Joey is gone up with the bright ones. My dear Joey is gone up with the shining angels. Glory! Glory! Glory!"

> Billy said, "I had no reason to doubt of my wife's going to heaven. Nevertheless, the devil often tempted me that because I was not home with her

---

185 This sounds like part of a hymn, but one I am unable to identify.

when she died, it was not well with her. But the devil could not make me believe it. Since the dear Lord has settled the matter, the devil does not tempt me that she is not in heaven. When the dear Lord speaks to his children's hearts, he speaks the truth. He is a God of truth, and all who love him are children of the truth."

"Here," Billy would say, "we have a little bitter, but it is mixed with a great deal of sweet. The sinner (mistakenly) thinks he has to give up something very good in exchange for what is not so good, when he comes to Christ."

CHAPTER 20

STILL TOO MUCH NOISE

FRUSTRATINGLY, BILLY'S *JOURNAL* is not complete. The pages of the original *Journal* in the John Ryland's archives (and on the microfilm in the Truro Record Office) finish on the page numbered 269, with the entry for 7 November 1864. Bourne quotes from Billy's writing from 1865 onwards, and possibly from written records made before this date. The stories that Bourne says are written by Billy, as readers will now appreciate, sound exactly like the style of entries in the *Journal.*

Billy seems to have travelled extensively after Joey's death, so he may have handed his *Journal* to Martha Bowden before leaving, and carried on with another book that is now missing. Three of the last four pages of Billy's *Journal* have *No 1* written at the top, implying he planned to continue his life story in book *No 2.*

Bourne says Billy wrote the following in February 1865, telling about the area around Newlyn, and it certainly reads like an excerpt from the *Journal*. If this is the town of Newlyn near Penzance on the south coast, it is hardly surprising that Billy's companion nicknamed 'Grandfather' is about to come to a halt. The distance from Newlyn to Kestle Mill is about 35 miles by road! Newlyn here is obviously Newlyn East, a village about three miles from Kestle Mill on the north coast, close to Newquay. This is in keeping with Billy's description of a journey of *some miles*.

A few days later Billy is speaking at "Newlyn", and says that after the meeting "we travelled home", so it seems Billy is now living in the Crantock area, rather than staying at Twelveheads.

Here is Billy's account as told in *The King's Son:*

I went to Kestle Mill to a Wesleyan Chapel to hold a teetotal meeting, a place some miles from Newlyn. A man who lived in Newlyn was known locally as 'Grandfather'. He was very lame but wished to go with me. When we had gone a little way he said he was so lame that he would not be able to go on.

I said to him, "You must go. Father must heal you."

Grandfather was going very lame when I said this, and it was a great pain for him to walk. So I looked up to heaven, and prayed, "My dear Father, heal him." And the dear Lord made him a sound man.

The man said, "All my pain is gone," and he went on to Kestle Mill as fast as I could go.

When we came to the place, Grandfather gave out a hymn and prayed. Then he told the people what a bad drunkard he had been, but he was a teetotaller now. He said that the Lord had converted his soul, and he was a happy man.

When Grandfather had done speaking, I spoke. Twenty signed the pledge. Then we travelled home, but I heard no more about Grandfather's pain. On the Tuesday we had a teetotal meeting at our chapel in Newlyn, and several Wesleyans were on the platform.

On Thursday the 16th February after I had spoken in the Wesleyan Chapel at Newlyn, Grandfather rose from his seat and told all the people in the chapel how he was almost a cripple last week. He told how the dear Lord had healed him on Monday while going to Kestle Mill, and that he had not felt any pain since.[186]

At a district meeting held at Hicks Mill Chapel in 1866, Bourne says that Mr Oliver describes the death of a woman who died shouting, "Victory!"

This touches Billy's heart, and he shouts "Glory! If a dying woman praised the Lord, I should think a living man might!"

Bourne writes:

Billy tells a woman friend in Liskeard, "I shan't see you many times more, ma'am."

"Why not, Billy?"

"My Heavenly Father will want me home – will be sending for me soon."

She then asks him, "Do you think we shall know each other in heaven?"

Billy replies, "Why, missus, do you think we shall be more ignorant in heaven than we are down here? We are not going to spend our time there saying, 'Who's that over there?' We shall spend our time in singing the song of Moses, the servant of God and of the Lamb. I shall know Adam as soon as I see him, as if I had been reared with him all my life."

In January 1867 Billy goes to Plymouth and Devonport to hold some meetings for the Primitive Methodists. As always, the meetings are noisy. Bourne writes that a man in the street reproves Billy for making so much noise. Billy tells him he does not mind who hears him, and those who love the Lord ought not to be ashamed to praise him in the chapel.

Billy says, "I told the man that I did not fear him nor his master the devil, and if I had hearkened to such as he I would have lost my best Friend long ago."

Three or four months later the writer Frank Vosper meets Billy in the same area. In *Real Life Sketches*, published in 1903 by Jennings and Pye, London, Vosper shares his memories of Devon and Cornwall in the second half of the nineteenth century. In a foreword he assures his readers that every account is accurate,

---

186 Bourne gives no other identification, but presumably he was someone well known to Bourne's readers at the time.

including the dates. I realise Billy's words in the following account may cause offence to some readers, but I think he is using a deliberate distortion of Roman Catholic doctrine simply to emphasise the simplicity of his own faith.

Vosper comes across Billy near Beeralston in south Devon, on the border with Cornwall, in the spring of 1867. Although this is only a year before Billy dies, he seems surprisingly spry. Bourne mentions Billy visiting his children in Liskeard shortly before his death, so it seems he has enough energy to travel until the end of his life. Vosper is attending an open-air meeting to discuss the problems left by earlier laws intended to stop Christian worship outside the Anglican authority.

I have left the original dialect spelling on this occasion, as Vosper gives us a perceptive picture not only of Billy's appearance in later life, but also of the way he spoke. There are photographs of Billy wearing a top hat and long coat taken around this time, and these may be the clothes he is wearing here.

Vosper writes:

The Rev W Hill opened the meeting with an eloquent and stirring address. As Mr Hill concluded his address there was a slight movement on the outskirts of the crowd, with encouraging and cheery shouts as though an unusually hearty welcome was being extended to someone. The crowd parted, and in response to, "Come on, Billy," there advanced to the wagon a little man of something over seventy. He was attired in a black, rather rusty frock coat, which reached nearly to his heels. He wore an extremely high silk hat, which was rather shaggy and weather-stained, while his neck was encased in a white cotton neck handkerchief of the kind worn at that time. His dress, though somewhat the worse for wear, was spotlessly clean, and his whole appearance was the embodiment of neatness.

He had a peculiarly happy expression of countenance, which conveyed the impression that it required a constant effort to keep the intensity of his feelings from bursting their bounds. Passing close to where I was standing, he placed himself between the shafts of the wagon, exclaiming, "My dear friends, I've got something I want tu say tu 'ee."

"Up here, Billy, up here," and the speaker was at once assisted on to the wagon in full view of the people, who awaited the resumption of his address with an interest which showed how intensely popular the speaker was.

Pausing a moment to gain his breath, Billy went on, "My friends, we are not like the Rumman Catholacks, 'cause when they want ennything they've got tu go tu a priest, an' then the priest he 'ave tu go tu the bushup, an' the bushup 'e 'ave tu go tu the caardinal, an' the caardinal 'ave got tu go tu tha poap; an' tha poap 'e 'ave got tu go tu Saint Pittur; an' Saint Pittur 'ave tu go tu the Virgin Maary, an' the Virgin Maary she 'ave to go tu Christ en pray tu he vor 'ee. Naow, my dear friends, be the time Saint Pittur 'ave bin tu tha Virgin Maary an' 'ad a bit of crib,[187] tha poap 'ave bin tu Saint Pittur, tha caardinal 'ave bin tu tha poap, tha bushup 'ave bin tu tha caardinal, an' tha priest 'ave bin tu tha bushup, et's a turmenjus long time avore yu git what you're axin' vor.

"But, Glory to God!" shouted the little man. "it's our privileege tu go direct tu God through Jesus Christ an' git the blessin' vor ourselves!"

With that the speaker clapped his hands in an ecstasy of joy, and danced around on the wagon in a way that indicated that getting the "blessin'" was a

187 A snack.

daily and hourly occurrence with him. And such indeed was the case. Billy died a little over a year from the time I saw and heard him at Beeralston.

Billy's visits to the sick are becoming even more frequent than before, and his spiritual enthusiasm is the same as always. Bourne gives us one of Billy's last written records, for February 10 1868:

In the morning after I had breakfast, bad as I was, I thought I would go to see some friends. After calling on some of them I went home, but I had hard work to get home I was so ill, and my breath was short.

Bourne continues with the following:

"I think I shall be home to my Father's house soon," Billy says one day when he returns home pale and exhausted.

He leaves his house only once more after this, when he goes to Liskeard to see his children. He gets much worse and appears to be in the last stages of consumption.

Billy sends for a medical man. When he arrives, Billy says to him, "Now, doctor, I have sent for you because people say you are an honest man, and will tell them the truth about their state."

After the doctor has examined him, Billy asks, "Well, doctor, how is it?"

"You are going to die."

Billy shouts "Glory, glory be to God! I shall soon be in heaven!" Then he adds, "When I get up there, shall I give them your compliments, doctor, and tell them you will be coming too?"

The doctor says later, "This made a wonderful impression upon me."

Bourne adds:

It need scarcely be said that Billy retained all his old love for shouting. He even said if he had his time over again he would shout ten times as much.

In his final illness Bourne relates that Christians of all denominations visit Billy, and they contribute generously to his support:

On Friday May 22 1868 Billy comes downstairs for the last time. One of Billy's friends asks him if he has any fear of death, or of being lost.

Billy responds, "What, me fear death? Me, lost? Why, my Saviour conquered death. If I was to go down to hell, I would shout glory, glory, to my blessed Jesus, until I made the bottomless pit ring again. And then miserable old Satan would say, 'Billy, Billy, this is no place for thee. Get thee back!' Then up to heaven I would go, shouting, 'Glory, glory, praise the Lord!'"

A little later Billy says, "Glory!" which is his last word.

Billy dies on Monday May 25 1868, just a few days short of his seventy-fourth birthday. His death certificate records:

William Trewartha Bray, Male, 74 years, Copper Miner, Dropsy,[188] *Not certified, Informant Mary Ann Bray*[189] *present at the death, Twelveheads, Kea, Twenty-seventh June 1868.*[190]

On the Friday Bourne tells us that a large number of Billy's friends and neighbours assemble at his house. The coffin is brought out into the yard and two great friends speak to the people. One is Billy's pastor, JD Balkwill,[191] and the

---

188 Dropsy is a lung disease.

189 Mary Ann Bray is probably Billy's granddaughter who was then 19.

190 If the date on the certificate is correct, Billy's death was not registered until over a month after his death.

191 James Damrel Balkwill (1828-1905) was born at Shebbear to Bible Christian parents and was converted at school. He entered the Bible Christian ministry in 1850 and spent over fifty years in local circuit work.

other is Thomas Hicks, an old friend. In the early editions of *The King's Son* Bourne adds:

> Funeral sermons were preached by Mr Johns, Mr Braund[192] and others, persons of all classes being present.

Billy Bray's remains are then interred in Baldhu churchyard, where his wife Joey was buried four years earlier. This is where Billy first saw the Rev William Haslam, although Haslam has long moved on by this time. Ten years later a tall granite obelisk is erected over the grave. It is not known if Billy and Joey are buried together. There is no mention of her name on the obelisk. The obelisk can be seen today and has the following inscription:

In memory of William, better known as "Billy" Bray who died at Twelveheads, May 25th 1868, aged seventy-three years. He was a local preacher with the Bible Christians forty-three years. By his sanctified wit, Christian simplicity, fervid faith, and many self-denying labours, he commended himself to a wide circle of friends while living, and the published record since his death of his memorable sayings and doings has made his name familiar as a household word in our own and other lands.

The story of Billy Bray has left me breathless, challenged in my own faith, and often in tears. I would love to have been at Billy's funeral, but would I have felt completely at ease meeting this man of God in person?

Pearse says, "If you gave Billy half a chance there would certainly be a straighforward question about your soul, in wise pithy words. And if the answer was what it should be, the lanes would ring with his happy thanksgiving."

---

192 These two names are only in early editions of *The King's Son*. This is probably Thomas Braund (1842-1914), born in Devon who trained for the Bible Christian ministry at Shebbear College, commencing circuit work in 1863.

All that remains is for me to write the Epilogue and ask myself this question. If I had met Billy, how loudly would those lanes have rung?

EPILOGUE

MY QUEST BEGAN with one of several visits to Billy's chapel at Kerley Downs. I set out to explore the 'mine of words' and bring everything of value to the surface. Have I found a different Billy to the one portrayed in *The King's Son*? Most certainly not. Bourne seems to have given us a fair, but much condensed picture. I must take issue with Bourne when he says, "If his (Billy's) chief characteristic as a speaker was liveliness, as a writer it was certainly dullness."

Of course, I have never heard Billy preaching, but to me his writing sparkles with enough energy to make me feel I have met the man – and enjoyed and been challenged by the encounter. Billy is still held with fondness in the hearts of the Cornish people, and now that his complete *Journal* is available for everyone to read, that fondness can only increase.

The *Journal* and *The King's Son* provide most of the recorded accounts of Billy and his life. *The King's Son* contains stories collected by Bourne from Christian leaders who knew Billy. Since they were collected within a few years of Billy's death, and Bourne was careful with his sources, the majority of these will be reliable. I have used a selection in this book, and apologise to anyone whose favourite has been left out. Other people such as John Oates recorded incidents from eyewitnesses, and I have included these. There are stories about Billy that were told to me by people in Cornwall. They have been passed down the generations through word of mouth, and may have become corrupted in constant retelling. These I have omitted.

We can see from his *Journal* that Billy felt he was always right, but his confidence was more in God than in himself. Without this confidence he would never have undertaken the incredible task of building three chapels, with no money in the bank. And we would never have heard the name of Billy Bray. It is interesting to see that by the time Billy was building his third chapel, people were more inclined to give money and other help towards it. Clearly his work was being seen of value – and the community was accepting him, in spite of his often unconventional behaviour.

On his own admission Billy got under the skin of a few preachers. Some undoubtedly deserved his scathing criticism, while others seem to have been judged rather harshly. With hindsight we can see that the noisy services for which Billy craved were not the only valid form of worship in Cornwall. Many chapels and churches with quieter services flourished at the time, and continue to flourish today. Yet numerous Christians around the world will identify with jumping and clapping and shouting, and some would probably say that Billy showed too much restraint.

I know that people have wondered exactly what form the noisy services took. For example, did the people, as in the charismatic churches today, speak and sing in tongues? Billy refers to singing and praying in the Spirit, but we must be careful not to put a modern interpretation on these words. Billy could easily mean doing this while filled with the Holy Spirit, but singing and praying in English. Bourne makes the following cryptic statement in *The King's Son*:

> Calling at a friend's house at a time when he had two or three visitors, Billy received a hearty welcome to remain and dine with them. He soon began to praise the Lord, which was as natural to him as for the birds to sing. He was asked if it was not possible for a man to get in the habit of praising the Lord without knowing what he was saying. He very coolly said that he did not think the Lord was much troubled with that class of persons.

Although this could be interpreted as a reference to speaking in tongues, it is more likely to refer to people standing up and praying aloud without giving any thought to what they were saying. The questioner referred to getting in the habit, which fits in better with the latter. When Billy writes about the congregation getting the "Victory", what does he mean? And is "shouting" a manifestation of tongues? Although this is possible, my own view is that if speaking and/or singing in tongues was practised within the local chapels, Billy would surely have mentioned it – in some detail. Instead, Billy says that when he prayed with the miners, *I should pray in what the people call simple words, and in the way that I hope the Lord would have me.*

What should be a lesson to all Christians, however we choose to worship, is the way Billy and William Haslam were eventually able to praise God together at a time of much bitter division between denominations, just as there was in the earlier time of John Wesley, and there is between some churches today.

Two stories of love and reconciliation told by Billy strike me as particularly remarkable. The first is his account of the impoverished preacher who, unable to be supported by his own people due to lack of money, is mocked by a member of another society and forced to sleep outside in the frost. It is the Quakers, representing a very different group of Christians, who provide the love and care he so desperately needs.

The second memorable story of reconciliation is Billy's account of the woman who wants to beat her daughter who has just been converted, and Billy has to hold her back. He writes: "That old woman, the night after she was going to beat her daughter, she was converted. She went around the chapel praising the Lord for what he had done for her soul. And then she loved her daughter well enough to take her in her arms and hug and kiss her."

Without doubt the Cornish people can be proud of Billy Bray – a giant whose life still brings a thrill of pleasure today. He gave his time, his energy, and what little money he had to meet the spiritual and physical needs of the local people. Many of Cornwall's mining towns and villages were places where fighting, prostitution and heavy drinking were everyday occurrences, but during the early nineteenth century these settlements were encouraged by the Methodists and Bible Christians, among other groups, to keep themselves and their homes clean, keep their children well fed and clothed, and live decent, honest and sober lives, looking after each other as well as themselves.

Billy planted 'churches' in what were thriving areas with no gathering place other than the local alehouse. He badgered and bullied those with money into helping with his building work. No doubt some will see him as no more than a historical curiosity, or a religious fanatic. But having considered all the evidence, I believe he was an awe-inspiring man of God who is even now, as he so definitely believed he would be, dancing in heaven with hundreds, perhaps thousands, of people who put their trust in Christ through the words that he spoke and wrote.

APPENDIX 1

THE JOURNAL OF BILLY BRAY

I HAVE UNCOVERED very few inconsistencies when comparing the various third party accounts with Billy's *Journal*, and have tried to deal with the small number I have found, rather than pretend they don't exist. I think most difficulties are caused either by carelessness by those who contributed to *The King's Son* or, and this is more likely, repeating stories that had already grown with the telling. Billy's 'new' clothes are a good example of this. Different writers have given Billy more clothing than he could ever have worn – and everything fits him perfectly! The cupboard bought for a pulpit is another where not all the accounts can possibly be accurate (See Appendix 2). But none of these problems is serious.

As we have seen, not all branches of the Christian faith were in harmony at this time. Haslam, in *From Death Into Life*, shows just how much animosity existed between the Anglo-Catholic wing of the Anglican Church and the Nonconformists. If any major fault had been found with the published stories, someone hostile to Billy or the Christian faith would surely have made it known at the time, thereby discrediting *The King's Son*.

The most convincing testimony of Billy's experiences comes from his own writing – what has become known as the *Journal of Billy Bray*. In the front of *The King's Son* Bourne says his book is *A Memoir of Billy Bray, Compiled Chiefly from his Own Memoranda*. The *Memoranda* here refer to entries in Billy's written *Journal*, a fact that could have been stated more clearly. When I first read *The King's Son* I thought this referred to spoken memories that Bourne had written down when talking to Billy, and never dreamt there was such a thing as Billy's own *Journal*. By the

1880s Bourne has collected so many eyewitness accounts that *The King's Son* grows by almost fifty percent. He changes the word *Chiefly* to *Largely*.

A book with the title *Memorials Of Frederick William Bourne* by WB Luke was published by WH Gregory, London in 1906. In it Luke, a Bible Christian at that time, tells us that: "Mr Bourne met this extraordinary man (Billy Bray) shortly after coming to Devonport, and said that if ever he spent a day of joy and blessedness in his life, it was that day."

Luke quotes Bourne's account of how the *Journal of Billy Bray* and *The King's Son* came to be written. This is my condensed copy of Bourne's own words:

Not to waste any words, let me say at once that I wrote it of necessity. Billy Bray himself, at the earnest request of a lady named Bowden, who belonged to the Society of Friends, had written a kind of autobiography. It was far easier for Billy to tell the story a thousand times than to write a single page of it; but for no other reason probably than to gratify a friend who had shown him and his family much kindness, he slowly and laboriously set about the task. She, on the other hand, thought that Billy's life of faith, if it were made widely known, would be a blessing to multitudes.

She placed the manuscript in my hands at, I believe, Billy's request; but I did not think anything could be done with it. If his chief characteristic as a speaker was liveliness, as a writer it was certainly dullness. True, there was a vein of fine gold running through the manuscript, but it was almost hidden by the iron and the clay. It had hardly a trace of the wit and humour for which Billy was so justly famous. The calligraphy was difficult to decipher, the words were misspelt, and the repetitions frequent; the meaning in many places was obscure, and the simplest incidents were mixed up in a most confusing manner.

I promised Mrs Bowden, however, that I would, if possible, find a biographer. The manuscript was sent, in due course, to five or six persons who knew Billy well, but who one and all declined the task. When this fact was reported to Mrs Bowden, she at once said to me, 'You must do it yourself.'

As I was extremely busy at the time, my friend the Rev JH Batt[193] kindly undertook to make a fair copy of the manuscript, omitting the repetitions. I also endeavoured to recall the more remarkable of the many sayings I had heard from Billy's lips, and sought to lay all his friends that I knew under tribute. I then did the best I could with what I had collected, and was not at all surprised, when the book appeared (in 1871), that the judgment of his intimate friends was that though Billy Bray was fairly portrayed in its pages, the half had not been told.

The first edition of three thousand copies was sold out in a few weeks, almost wholly among our own people. More than one person said an edition of five thousand would have been enough to meet every demand. But the second edition, mainly in consequence of a generous and appreciative article by Mr Spurgeon in the *Sword and Trowel*, was more speedily disposed of than the first.

Some corrections and additions were made before the third edition was sent to press, and the book was then stereotyped. Since then, edition has followed edition – more than one of twenty thousand copies – until thirty-nine editions have been sold. A thousand copies were sold every month for nearly thirty years. It has also been reprinted in America, and it has appeared several times in serial form both here and there.

I have received scores of letters from all sorts and conditions of men – from ripe scholars, able ministers, valiant soldiers, great sufferers, paupers, prisoners in jail and after they have been released, all gladly testifying to the fact that they had been greatly blessed, or actually converted by reading the life of Billy Bray.

Before going any further, I want to look closely at five of Bourne's comments:

193 John Herridge Batt, 1845-1917, the son of Bible Christian
     minister George Batt.

The calligraphy was difficult to decipher. Yes, certainly, although it gets easier to read with practice.

The words were misspelt. True, but the misspelling, although bad, is generally consistent. For example, a word used frequently, like *bleved* for *believed*, presents no problem. A variation on this is *blevet* for *believe it. Meeting* is consistently spelt *metten*. Billy obviously sounded each letter or syllable aloud and wrote it down as it sounded. Being familiar with the Cornish dialect is a help, and of course the context in which words are used makes their reading easier. The names of people and places present some of the biggest challenges, and I may not always have interpreted them correctly.

The repetitions frequent. I am not sure what Bourne means. Occasionally Billy repeats a word or two, but he never repeats a story. Maybe Bourne is referring to the constant use of phrases like, *Bless and praise his holy name*, and the overuse of link words like *and, so, for, then* and *but*. However, these are easily dealt with in a transcription.

The meaning in many places was obscure. I am looking now at some of my early efforts at transcription. Misinterpreted words caused me much confusion, luring me into misreading other words associated with them as I tried to make sense of a difficult section. But everything fell into place eventually. This book, surely, is proof that the whole *Journal* is extremely readable and almost nothing is obscure. Maybe it is easier for us to engage with Billy's easygoing writing style than it was for a rather formal Victorian.

The simplest incidents were mixed up in a most confusing manner. Not so, although occasionally I have altered the placing of a sentence within a paragraph to make the account easier to understand. Billy tends to give away what is about to happen, and so looses the impact of the 'punch line', and I have omitted the occasional sentence for this reason. Also, the name of a featured man or woman is often not given until near the end of an account, and I have brought these names forward.

We must bear in mind that Billy wrote his thoughts and memories without any subsequent editing. Many writers, myself included, would be very pleased to come up with such a readable first draft. On page 7 of his *Journal* Billy talks about *the good brother that translate this Journal*. I don't suppose Billy meant *translate* literally, although it did seem that way at first. Once I had completed the transcription, the *Journal* needed very little editing to knock it into shape and I have erred very much on the side of caution. If I could go back in time and edit the *Journal* for Billy in 1864, I would congratulate him on his efforts and then diplomatically suggest we make a copy with correct spelling, and add some punctuation. Then I would ask if I could make more changes to the wording than the few I have made here. But would the end result be as engaging as Billy's distinctive style?

The original *Journal of Billy Bray* is held by the Methodist Archives and Research Centre, John Rylands University Library of Manchester, Oxford Road, Manchester M13 9PP, United Kingdom. The document is too fragile for examination, and at the time of writing there are no plans to make a copy. The good news is that a microfilm copy is available for viewing at the County Record Office in Truro, Cornwall, although the clarity of reproduction is variable and some pages are poor. The reference is FS 2/7a. Due to ownership copyright restrictions it is not possible for the County Record Office to make copies without permission from John Rylands, but the microfilm can be examined free of charge at the Record Office. It is advisable to book a viewing time a few days in advance. The address is: Cornwall Record Office, County Hall, Truro, TR1 3AY, United Kingdom.

The *Journal* has the handwritten title: *Original ms Journal of William Bray presented to AE Bray January 1899.* The first thing that struck me was the unexpectedly large number of pages. The pages are numbered by hand, and the last page number is 269. Only the first 114 pages have been numbered by Billy. The others are done in a much more modern style. The numbers 162 to 173 have accidentally been used twice, and there is an unnumbered page between 150 and 151. This makes 282 pages, with an average of 175 words a page, producing a total of 49,000 words. Of these I calculate Bourne has used a mere 12,000.

It is strange that Bourne makes no mention of John Batt's mammoth work of transcription in his preface to *The King's Son*. Nor does he directly acknowledge the *Journal* as being the source of Billy's words, but calls it simply *from his own memoranda.* Why Bourne gives no credit to John Batt I cannot say, although he subsequently gave him five pounds of the twenty he received from the book. If twenty pounds sounds so little for such a best-selling title, Luke has an explanation in *Memorials Of Frederick William Bourne:*

> It ought to be stated, to avoid misunderstanding, that
> the book was of slight pecuniary advantage to Bourne.
> On its publication he registered the copyright in the
> name of the Connexion,[194] and the Book-Room enjoyed
> the full benefit of the sales. Once the Conference voted
> him an honorarium of twenty pounds – of which he
> gave five pounds to the copyist – but the whole of the
> profits thereafter, amounting in the course of years to
> thousands of pounds, went to Connexional uses.

Some three-quarters of Billy's *Journal* that is omitted from *The King's Son* contains the previously unknown and fascinating accounts reproduced in this book, but the transcription has not been easy and there may be some very minor mistakes. Here are three examples of the difficulties involved, copied for me letter-by-letter by the Principal Archivist at the Cornwall Record Office, a charged task that took him nearly three hours. At this point Billy's writing came alive. It was as though I could hear him speaking, and I used the librarian's transcription as a *Rosetta Stone* to tackle the whole *Journal*, having a good understanding of the way Billy formed letters and words. I am reproducing it exactly as written by Billy. At first glance it looks like nonsense. But when read aloud, especially with a Cornish accent, it suddenly becomes clear.

Pages 22 to 24 of the *Journal* (see pages 28f in this book for the corrected version). My treatment of this section is typical of the way I have dealt with the whole *Journal:*

> at that time we had a Lettell pig and this was the Wednesday wile in
> Bed Room Lucking to heven with all the poures of my Sule and it
> apeard to me i had all most Had hold of the Blsen But the pig Came
> up to our Dore and i thought never hard a pig Cry So in all my Life i
> Shold have been verey glad if Some person had Drive him away if i
> never Sowe him no more So i Did not get it then tho it Seam So So
> nigh me by So the Devel and the pig i goat it not then the pig Down
> Stears Cryin and the Devil tempting for want of a Lettele more

---

194 The Bible Christian Connexion.

A few lines of Billy's handwriting in the Journal

feaith i goat not the Blessing and it was Come time for me to go work to mine askin the Lord for marcey all the way we Chenged our Close And went Down in the mine onderground as we miners Call it and my partner was in the end Breaking the Stofe and i was weting of a way from him out to place we Coal pleat or Shaft thire was at that Day a hores wem to Drawe up the Stofe to the Sarfes that we men Brook and as i was weling out the barow the Devil tempted me i Shal never find it

A section from page 25 of the *Journal*, following Billy's conversion (see page 30 in this book):

the Dear Lord made me So hapey that i Can not expres what i felt i Shouted for Joey and presed god for what he had Done for me a poor Sener for i Cold Say by hapey hart felt expearins that the Lord had pardoned all my Sins and it Semed to me that i was in a new world i think it was in november 1823 what Day of the month i Do not know but Every thing Looked new to me.

Bourne omits any reference to the pig and the mine in *The King's Son,* and condenses the three *Journal* pages to the following:

The Lord made me so happy that I cannot express what I felt. I shouted for joy. I praised God with my whole heart for what he had done for a poor sinner like me. I could say, "The Lord hath pardoned all my sins." I think this was in November 1823, but what day of the month I do not know. I remember this, that everything looked new to me.

Whether Billy shouted for Joey or shouted for joy is initially unclear. The word is spelt Joey in the *Journal*, with a capital letter, and both words sound the same if said with a Cornish accent. Almost certainly Bourne is right and Billy shouted for joy. I imagine he pronounced his wife's name as Joy, but he has never written it in his *Journal*, simply referring to her as my wife or my dear wife. Billy uses a capital letter for all words starting with J.

This next paragraph is one I picked at random when I first opened the *Journal*. I see from my early notes, made while struggling with the handwriting, that I thought at first this was a rather touching record of people shouting for Billy's wife Joey, and she and Billy being given shoes and then dancing for joy. The subsequent reading of this section by the Principal

Archivist at Truro helped open up the whole *Journal*. It is page 164a of the *Journal*. See page 125 in this book for corrected spelling and added punctuation:

> in another place we had a revival and there was maney Converted
> and the was made verey hapey when the Dear Lord Converted there
> souls some of them shouted for Joey and some of them Danced for
> Joey and we had a penteycost shoer and the seaid we was fools and
> mad men But we was wise and glad men so the poor men mest we
> have the right and the have the have the wronge But what had you
> had that you Dance so and shout so Davoed done it before the Lord
> so he told his wife.

John Batt would have been familiar with the style of handwriting of his contemporaries. Maybe he found the transcription of the *Journal* straightforward, but somehow I doubt it. Bourne and others felt unable to take on the task, and Bourne subsequently resorted to paraphrase. It took me several months to complete my copy, and after correcting the spelling it still needed sorting into sentences and paragraphs. This is a relatively uncomplicated task with a word processor, and I was surprised how the insertion of commas, full stops and correct capital letters could make sense of a previously confusing section.

After comparing Billy's *Journal* with Bourne's wording in *The King's Son*, it is obvious that Bourne often chooses to paraphrase extracts from the *Journal* rather than give a full and exact quote. Here is an example, with uncorrected spelling, straight from page 13 of the *Journal*, where Billy writes about reading Bunyan's *Visions of Heaven and Hell* before his conversion:

> while I was Seting Down to the end of the table reading the Book my
> wife was Seting By the fire She had Been Canverted when young
> But She went Back Before we went to gether So She was a
> Backslider So I asked har what it was to Be hapey and She Seaid
> No toung Can tel what the enjoy that Sarve the Lord then I Said wy
> doant you Begin again I may Begen to for I thought if She was to
> Begen it wold Be Better for me for I was a Shamed to go to my nees
> to prey Before har that very night I filt in my mind that I oft to foal
> on my nees and ask god for marcy But the Devil had C Such a hold
> in me that he made me a Shamed of my wife

Here is my transcription, with corrected spelling and added punctuation. The full text is on page 24 of this book:

> When I was sitting down to the end of the table reading the book, my wife was sitting by the fire. She had been converted when young but she went back before we went together, so she was a backslider. I asked her what it was to be happy.
>
> She said, "No tongue can tell what they enjoy that serve the Lord."
>
> Then I said, "Why don't you begin again? I may begin too."
>
> I thought if she was to begin it would be better for me, for I was ashamed to go to my knees to pray before her that very night. I felt in my mind that I ought to fall on my knees and ask God for mercy, but the devil had such a hold in me that he made me ashamed of my wife.

Some of the original words are extremely hard to read, and the last sentence requires a footnote in my transcription, whereas Bourne is able to clarify Billy's meaning in his paraphrase in *The King's Son:*

> His wife had been converted when young, but had gone back from the right way before marriage. The remembrance of what she had enjoyed was very sweet, and yet very bitter. She told her husband that "no tongue could tell what they enjoy who serve the Lord."
>
> "Why don't you begin again?" was his pertinent inquiry; adding, "for then I may begin too." He was ashamed to fall on his knees before his wife, "for the devil had such a hold of him;" but he knew it was his duty to pray for mercy.

I find Billy's wording in the *Journal* has more impact, especially the small detail of Joey sitting by the fire. But it does take a lot of deciphering!

When Bourne retells parts of the *Journal* in the third person it may be that Batt had difficulty in reading every word in the time available. Even where it is possible to read an episode perfectly, Bourne uses a paraphrase to condense the account, and in doing this he occasionally puts longer words into Billy's mouth than I believe Billy would have used. Having said that, Billy does use some unexpectedly long words.

Pearse in *The Story of Billy Bray*, which was probably published shortly after Bourne first published *The King's Son*, uses these words to describe Billy's conversation with Joey:

(His wife) had once enjoyed the favour of God, but had left her Saviour. She frequently would talk of the remembrance of her joy and peace. "Oh, Billy, no tongue can tell what they enjoy who serve the Lord!"

"Why don't 'e begin again, then?" asked Billy, "for then I might begin too. Get converted, and show me the way, for you bean't such a sinner as I be."

The last sentence in Pearse's book may come from his conversations with Billy, or from one of the many people who would have heard Billy's testimony in chapel, but it is certainly not in the *Journal*. When quoting Billy's writing, Pearse uses Bourne's words from *The King's Son*, or a variation of them. It is possible Pearse never saw the *Journal*, and used Bourne's first edition as his main source.

I have been told by two people in Cornwall that a large box of papers relating to Billy, collected by Bourne, ended up in the hands of a man who had a great interest in Billy's life. The box supposedly contained letters sent to Bourne by people who knew Billy, and Bourne used some of their memories in later editions of *The King's Son*. The box also seems to have contained letters, photographs and other unspecified items. When the man died, so the story goes, his wife had no idea of their value and burnt them. It is reasonable to assume that John Batt's transcription was in the box, and maybe the missing sections of the *Journal*.

In the archives at the John Rylands University Library of Manchester, England, is the *Lewis Court Bible Christian Collection*. John Rylands have an unpublished detailed catalogue of the collection, which I have examined. I can find nothing significant relating to Billy Bray. However, I have been told by one of my sources that it was Lewis Court who had the box of Bourne's papers, although this was not told with any certainty. I find this unlikely, since so much material that came from *Lewis Court* is of relatively minor significance. Something as historic as Billy Bray's writing would surely have been included in the catalogue.

A more likely explanation comes from the *Shaw Collection* in an extract of an undated interview, by an unidentified person talking to the Rev JH Messa, the Superintendent of St Columb in Cornwall:

> Rev Messa born at Greenbottom, nr Threemilestone. Mr M knows many stories of Billy. He made enquiries and says that Billy was certainly sincere and genuine and no whit a charlatan. Mr M told how his mother remembered Billy coming into the house, catching her up – he was then quite an old man and she a girl of 15 – and waltzing round with her – she not much in favour if it. Mr M said that FW Bourne's papers might have gone to his daughter, who married WB Luke, a Bible Christian civil servant, who later became a RC. WB Luke is dead and Mr M doesn't know of Mrs Luke.

Luke, who had earlier written the biography of Bourne in *Memorials of FW Bourne*, became a Roman Catholic in 1912. He then wrote several letters to his Bible Christian friends, asking them to try to understand his reasons for changing his faith, and pointing out that the Protestant teaching he had received about Roman Catholic doctrine was full of biased errors. The Catholic Truth Society subsequently published three of these letters in 1921 in a 32 page booklet entitled *Letters to a Bible Christian*.

This makes it easier to understand why a wife would destroy her husband's papers, especially if the Lukes and the Bible Christians were never reconciled. It might not have been done in resentment, but simply because Mrs Luke had lost all contact with the Bible Christians and did not know where to go with the collection.

It is, of course, frustrating not to have more records, but we should be grateful for the large quantity still in existence. Special thanks must go to Frederick Bourne, Martha Bowden, and of course Billy Bray for having the foresight to give us so much in writing. Maybe there is still a box somewhere?

APPENDIX 2

THE GREAT PULPIT MYSTERY

ONE OF THE best-known stories about Billy Bray is Bourne's account of Billy trying to buy a cupboard at an auction sale, for use as a pulpit in Three Eyes Chapel at Kerley Downs. Imagine my dismay at finding a very different version in Billy's *Journal*. Not only does Billy write that the cupboard was for Bethel Chapel at Cross Lanes, but he also says a friend bought it for him!

The 'famous' account occurs in the writings of four of Billy's contemporaries – Pearse, Bourne, Haslam and Ashworth. After considering the evidence, my own feelings are that the story was going around towards the end of Billy's life. It was based on a real event, but had been changed (probably deliberately) to become one designed to raise a smile. Maybe unaware of its dubious origins, the four writers repeat it as fact.

Let's start by trying to identify the chapel. Haslam, Pearse and Bourne say the cupboard was taken *down* to it. Ashworth's slightly different version of the story does not mention in which direction the cupboard was taken. On this word alone, Three Eyes at Kerley Downs is extremely unlikely, as it is at the top of a hill. Haslam, living locally, preached there. Unfortunately, he does not name the chapel. It is only Billy who identifies it as Bethel at Cross Lanes, which is much lower down the hill.

We start with Billy's account on page 128 of his *Journal*. The last part of the page has been deliberately crossed out, with some words obliterated completely. My reading of a few crossed out words is sometimes little more than a guess. Obliterated words are indicated as such. Billy, it must be stressed, is clearly writing here about the original Bethel Chapel, for he has just bought timber for the chapel from a mine that has already closed.

JOURNAL OF BILLY BRAY

1864

In the count house of that same mine there was a very large cupboard. It was very large and high, and there was an old friend of mine that said, "I will buy that cupboard, for he will do for a pulpit for Wm Bray chapel."

And there was another man that was a landlord, that said "And I will buy that cupboard."

Then said my old friend, "That cupboard is for a pulpit in Wm Bray's chapel. For," said my old friend, "if you buy the cupboard (the crossing out and deleting starts here) it will not go in (deleted word) ?rather (3 deleted words) you get the landlord said that I ?t——- (2 deleted words) so ?they bought the cupboard and he ?carried the cupboard home and ?said ?and ?in (deleted word) and the cupboard wouldn't ?fit in the (deleted word) my old friend said (deleted word) came to pass first (deleted word) pulpit ?for (2 deleted words – but definitely not Billy Bray, Kerley Downs or Bethel) chapel ?thing and when they brought (deleted word) cupboard or pulpit my old friend paid for it and it cost him ?ten (deleted word) shillings so the Lord helped me and I had many ?enemies ?or (deleted word) missed.

The *Journal* page overleaf (page 129) starts with: *Some said I ought to put chembels in my chapel, and some said, "When the chapel is built you shall not have it planned." So I went on and finished my chapel.* (Page 76 in this book.) This, and the following *Journal* page are definitely still about Bethel. The word after what looks like *ten* and before *shillings* starts with a high slender letter that can only be an F, H, L or T in Billy's writing, possibly followed by an I. The word – if it is a single word – has five or six letters, and could end in an R. Of course, Billy may have intended to write *shillings*, made a mistake after writing *ten*, then crossed out the wrong word before writing *shillings* correctly.

It is worth noting that Billy's initial Bs and Ks are particularly high, and would rise well clear of the crossing out. There is no unidentified word starting with these letters anywhere in this excerpt, so we can be sure that neither Bethel nor Kerley Downs is mentioned.

FROM DEATH INTO LIFE
William Haslam (1880)

(Billy) said there was one thing more he must tell us; it was this – that he had a "preaching-house" – what we should now call a mission-room – which he had built years ago. In answer to prayer he also obtained reed for thatching the roof, and by the same means timber for the forms and seats.[195]

It was all done in a humble manner, so that he did not dream of buying any pulpit; but one day, as he was passing along the road, he saw that they were going to have a sale at the "count-house" of an old mine. He went in, and the first thing which met his eye was a strong oak cupboard, with a cornice round the top. It struck him that it would make a grand pulpit, if only it was strong enough: on examination, he found it all he could desire in this respect. He thought if he could take off the top and make a "plat" to stand upon, it would do "first-rate".

He "told Father" so, and wondered how he could get it. He asked a stranger who was there, walking about, what he thought that old cupboard would go for?

195 These words may be crucial in identifying the chapel, for in his *Journal* Billy tells at some length how he got reeds for the roof of Bethel, and timber for the forms, through prayer. The engraving of Kerley Downs Chapel in *The King's Son* dating around the mid 1870s shows slates, although a thatched roof could have been replaced when the chapel was lengthened. The engraving shows the lengthened chapel. Billy writes about slates when building Great Deliverance. For Kerley Downs he simply says, *The chapel was built and the roof put on*. There is no mention of obtaining reeds or timber by prayer, or by any other means. This makes Bethel a likely contender, as all the details fit.

"Oh, for about five or six shillings," was the reply.

And while Billy was pondering how to "rise" six shillings, the same man came up and said, "What do you want that cupboard for, Billy ?"

He did not care to tell him, for he was thinking and praying about it. The man said, "There are six shillings for you; buy it, if you will."

Billy took the money, thanking the Lord, and impatiently waited for the sale. No sooner was the cupboard put up, than he called out, "Here, maister, here's six shillin's for un," and he put the money down on the table.

"Six shillings bid," said the auctioneer- "six shillings-thank you; seven shillings; any more for that good old cupboard? Seven shillings. Going-going-gone!" And it was knocked down to another man.

Poor Billy was much disappointed and perplexed at this, and could not understand it at all. He looked about for the man who had given him the six shillings, but in vain - he was not there. The auctioneer told him to take up his money out of the way. He complied, but did not know what to do with it. He went over a hedge into a field by himself, and told "Father" about it; but it was all clear- "Father" was not angry about anything. He remained there an hour, and then went homewards.

As he was going along, much troubled in his mind as to this experience – for he still felt so sure he was to have that cupboard for a pulpit – he came upon a cart standing outside a public house, with the very cupboard upon it, and some men were measuring it with a foot rule.

As he came up, he heard them say, "It is too large to go in at the door, or the window either." The publican who had bought it said, "I wish I had not bid for the old thing at all; it is too good to 'scat' up for firewood."

At that instant it came to Billy's mind to say, "Here, I'll give you six shillings for un."

"Very well," said the man, taking the money; "you can have him."

Then Billy began to praise the Lord, and went on to say, "'Father' as good as told me that I was to have that cupboard, and He knew I could not carry him home on my back, so He has found a horse and cart for me. Bless the Lord!"

Promising to bring it back very soon, he led the horse down the hill, and put the old cupboard into the preaching-house. "There it is!" he exclaimed, "and a fine pulpit he does make, sure enough! Now," said Billy, "I want to see thee in it. When will you come?" I could not fix for that day, or the next, but made arrangements to conduct a series of services the next week, and promised to have them in that place.

Before he left us, he made a particular inquiry about the two other houses which had been built, who lived in them, and especially if all the "dwellers were converted." Then he declared his intention to go and see the parties, and rejoice with them, and testify how fully the Lord had accomplished the promise He gave him upon that very hill, twenty years before.

According to promise, I went to Billy Bray's preaching-house, or mission-hall. It was the first time that I had preached anywhere outside my church and schoolroom since my conversion. There it pleased the Lord to give me much help, and a great work followed, such as Billy had never seen in that place before. Several times we were detained there all night through, with penitents crying aloud for mercy, and believers rejoicing.

SHORT STORIES AND OTHER PAPERS
MG Pearse 1886[196]

The little place at Kerley Downs was up, but it wanted a pulpit. Billy began to think within himself where that could come from. At last, as he looked about among

---

196 The chapter on Billy Bray was first published in the early 1870s as a tract.

some furniture at an auction sale, his eye fell upon an old three-cornered cupboard.

"The very thing," cried Billy, "the very thing. I can cut a slit down the back of un, and strengthen the middle of un, and put a board up in front of un, and clap a pair o' steers behind un, and then the preacher can preach out of un pretty."

With much glee he turned to some one near him, and asked, "What do 'e think they'll want for that there cupboard ?"

The man looked, and gave it as his opinion that it would go for six shillings. Billy told him what he meant to do with it, and the man said, "Why, you're Billy Bray! Here, I'll give 'e the six shillings to buy it."

After a while the cupboard was put up. Billy knew nothing of auctions. All eager to have his pulpit, he cried, holding out his hand, "Here, Mister Auctioneer, here's six shillin' for un, I do want un for a pulpit."

Of course there was a great laugh at Billy's expense. As it passed away the auctioneer cried, "Six shillings, going for six."

A nod from behind Billy was quickly caught.

"Seven," said the auctioneer, "seven shillings."

"No," cried Billy, "'tis on'y six, there's the money."

Of course, down went the hammer, and much to Billy's astonishment the cupboard was not his.

"Well, Father do know best," said he, in a rather disappointed tone; "but anyhow I must give the man back his six shillin'."

The man was gone, nor was Billy likely to see him again. This was a new and even greater trouble.

"I'll be gone down an' tell Father about it," said Billy, as he started off for his little chapel.

With faith renewed, and a comfortable assurance that it would be all right, he was coming from the chapel, when he saw the cupboard going up the hill in a cart.

"I'll follow un, anyhow," he whispered, "an' see the end."

They carried it to a house, and tried to take it inside, but it was just too big to get in. They twisted and turned, they pulled and pushed, but it was no use.

"Here's a mess," said the purchaser, angrily; "I've given seven shilling for en, an' shall have to skat en up for firewood."

Then as his eyes twinkled, Billy stepped over and put his hand on the man's shoulder as he stood, hat in hand, wiping his forehead.

"I'll give 'e six shillin' for un, if you'll carry un down to my little chapel."

"That I will," said the man, pleased at being so well out of it.

"Bless the Lord," cried Billy, "'tes just like him. He knew I couldn' carry en myself, so He got this man to carry en for me."

STRANGE TALES, VOLUME 5
John Ashworth 1879

(Ashworth is writing about Billy and Kerley Downs.) The place was finished, except the pulpit. Passing through a neighbouring town, he stopped at an auction sale. A large square cupboard was put up. Billy said, so that all could hear, "That would just do for our pulpit, but I have no money. Will anybody lend me some, and I will bid? Bless the Lord, the pulpit is for him."

A man who knew Billy lent him seven and sixpence, the price he thought it might fetch, but the cupboard was knocked down for ten shillings. This rather shook Billy's faith. He handed back the money, and walked away; but before he got home he saw several men trying to get the same cupboard into a house, but it was too large. Billy rubbed his hands, and exclaimed, "It will not go in, bless the Lord: the door is too small, bless the Lord."

The owner asked him what he meant; and when he heard what it was wanted for, he put it on his own cart, and sent it to the chapel. Billy walked behind it, singing and dancing, saying to all he met, "I have got it for nothing. I see now why the Lord would not let me give the seven and sixpence for it; bless him, bless him. The Gospel trumpet shall sound out of that old cupboard, and sinners shall hear it; glory, glory."

Two other chapels were soon after built through the same unspoken faith in God – one at Gwennap, the other at Carharrack. The latter is still known as the 'Great Deliverance;' and all four are yet frequently called 'Billy Bray's chapels.' [197]

THE KING'S SON
FW *Bourne*

Bourne uses Ashworth's account word-for-word from the third edition of *The King's Son* (1872) onwards, but replaces it with Pearse's account from the eleventh edition (1875) onwards. In the 1875 edition Bourne says, "This graphic description is from the pen of the Rev MG Pearse." Bourne must have felt, for some reason, that Pearse's version was preferable. The first and second editions of *The King's Son* make no reference to this story.

All very confusing, especially Ashworth's *ten shillings*, although this seems to be in agreement with the sum mentioned by Billy. One possible solution is that Billy's friend bought a cupboard to use as the pulpit in Bethel, as Billy writes in his *Journal*. Subsequently the idea of adapting a cupboard appealed to Billy, so he personally bought another one for Kerley Downs. The part about the landlord wanting it may have been a mix-up with the later event, and Billy crossed out just that part.

This brings us to another possibility, in which Billy does indeed get his pulpit for Bethel from the mine sale, and as he says in his *Journal* it is his friend who buys it. This would be around 1830. The folk at Bethel may want something better as time goes on, or it may be in the way when the building is no longer used as a chapel. Perhaps they give the converted

---

197 Ashworth is wrong. Great Deliverance Chapel is in the *parish* of Gwennap, but there is only one of Billy's chapels in the area - at Carharrack.

cupboard to Billy for Kerley Downs, hence the confusion of the location by Bourne, Pearse and Ashworth.

In 1852, when he visits Haslam, Billy is living in Bodmin. Haslam writes:

> He (Billy) said there was one thing more he must tell us. It was this – that he had a "preaching-house", or mission-hall, he had built years ago. He had often prayed there for 'this old mountain', and now he should dearly love to see me in the pulpit of that place, and said that he would let me have it for my work."

Haslam also says:

> He (Billy) told us that twenty years ago as he was walking over this very hill on which my church and house were built – it was a barren old place then – the Lord said to him, "I will give thee all that dwell in this mountain."

This dates Billy's walk to 1832, after Bethel but before Kerley Downs was open. Referring to the time he was building Kerley Downs, in the early to mid 1830s, Billy writes, *You that read this must remember that this was not the place where I met, for my meeting house was Bethel Chapel.*

The account of the auction first appears eight years before Haslam published *From Death Into Life* in 1880. Haslam obviously thought the account worth repeating in his own book, even though Bourne, Pearse and Ashworth had already published it.

Ashworth seems to have got his account from a different source. There is a discrepancy in the price it sold for at auction, he says the cupboard was square, and Billy was given it for nothing. Ashworth also says Billy, "Put it on *his own* cart, and sent it to the chapel." Haslam certainly preached out of it and would have been familiar with the shape. Unfortunately he does not state the location. Note that Pearse and Bourne refer to the *little chapel*, which would certainly apply to Bethel.

A rumour that I have not been able to substantiate says that the pulpit went to a farmhouse in the district. Although finding it would be unlikely to prove anything, unless there was a provenance pinned to the back, it would be interesting to know if it is still in existence.

So who crossed out the lines in the *Journal*? Visually the ink appears to be the same as the handwriting, the standard colour of ink from this period. Some words are lightly crossed out while others seem to have been selected for total obliteration. I find myself wondering if some well-meaning person did it after publication of *The King's Son*, when Bourne's book had already sold in large numbers, to avoid the problem being addressed here.

I think the problem has arisen in this way. Billy tells Haslam in 1852 that the pulpit at Bethel is made from an old cupboard from a sale at a local mine, but doesn't know who bought it, or how it was bought. We can be sure that Haslam is not the only person Billy tells the story to. Over the years the story is passed around the chapels, and *sale* changes with the telling to *auction sale*, and with frequent repetition it becomes a humorous tale of Billy buying the cupboard at auction, and not knowing how to bid.

Ashworth and Pearse both pick up versions of this story, are amused by it, and maybe carry out a little creative embroidery. Pearse, especially, turned many local events into fiction in his two *Daniel Quorm* books. Standards of accuracy were not so demanding then, as long as the story was good. Bourne, on his own admission, copies it first from Ashworth and then from Pearse. Twenty years later, Haslam confuses what Billy told him with the myth. In any case, Haslam wouldn't want to contradict Bourne's best-selling account. He gets some bits right, such as the involvement of the landlord, but not everything. But crucially he does *not* say it was bought for Kerley Downs.

One vital ingredient in Haslam's account that cannot be sloppiness is when he says the cupboard was carried *down* to the chapel. Haslam lived on the doorstep of Kerley Downs, which is at the very top of the hill. So however good Haslam's memory may or may not have been of Billy's story, I cannot believe he would have inadvertently written *down* instead of *up* about a place he knew well. And, of course, Bourne and Pearse also say *down* in their shared account.

Billy writes in his *Journal* that the cupboard was bought for Bethel. This chapel was replaced ten years or so later by a larger Bethel on the opposite side of the lane, and the original building, using Billy's words in the *Journal*, *"Kept for a school and for class meetings."*

Haslam writes:

Then Billy said to me, "I want to see thee in it (the pulpit). When will you come?" I could not fix for that day or the next, but made arrangements to conduct a series of services the next week and promised to have them in that place.

Would an Anglo Catholic priest, even a converted one, be welcome in a Bible Christian Chapel, with no questions asked? There is some evidence that the Methodists were running Kerley Downs by this time, in which case Billy would have no say over who preached there.

Surely there would be less of a problem with Haslam speaking in a building no longer in use as a chapel. Billy has travelled nearly thirty miles (48km) from Bodmin to get to Baldhu, yet he manages to stay in the area and help Haslam. Maybe Billy decides on the spot, or has planned in advance, to hold a mission in the area. But why is he able to give an immediate invitation, even for that day, without the apparent need to consult with anybody? This would only apply if he knew the venue was vacant. The original Bethel would certainly be a more likely location than a chapel in regular use.

One further comment by Haslam could be important. He writes that after speaking in the preaching-house:

A great work followed, such as Billy had never seen in that place before. Several times we were detained there all night through, with penitents crying aloud for mercy and believers rejoicing.

Assuming the "preaching-house" is not Great Deliverance, which is extremely unlikely as it is some considerable distance from Baldhu, does this comment by Haslam apply best to the old Bethel, the new Bethel, or to Kerley Downs?

A possible answer comes from Billy's *Journal* when he is writing about Bethel. *I saw at one time fifteen down asking for mercy, and mercy they had. Some of them is now in heaven praising the dear Lord, and will praise him for ever.* Fifteen down on their knees would thrill many preachers in a large building, let alone a small chapel. Is Billy referring to Haslam's visit? Or were the numbers even greater in another chapel when Haslam went there? Or was Bourne right in changing *fifteen* to *fifty*?

Finally, from the evidence of the *Journal* as a whole, does Billy seem like a man who would behave in such a gullible way at an auction? I think not.

A theory I am warming to is this: the pulpit is bought for Bethel by Billy's friend and used there until some time after 1852, which is when Haslam says he preached out of it. It is subsequently moved up to Kerley Downs before Bourne and Pearse come on the scene. Maybe Pearse sees the pulpit there, hears a version of the story and assumes the cupboard was originally bought for Kerley Downs. Therefore he writes Kerley Downs. Bourne, who probably sees the pulpit there, copies Pearse's wording into The King's Son without asking questions. In that way, like some of the stories of Billy's new clothes, the legend becomes fact.

These are the five accounts. Readers must feel free to study the evidence and make up their own minds about this puzzle. In the end, unless new facts come to light, any conclusion will only be an opinion. The story is a famous one, but it has all the marks of fiction, loosely based on a real event, told for no other reason than to raise a smile.

APPENDIX 3

THE BRAY FAMILY HISTORY

THE INFORMATION IN THIS APPENDIX has been supplied by Peter Tremewen of the Billy Bray Memorial Trust, and is reproduced here with his permission. It is drawn from various records, including Billy Bray's *Journal*, parish records and the Census. There is much speculative available regarding the family, which cannot at present be supported from documentary sources. None of this is included.

William Trewartha Bray was born at Twelveheads in the parish of Kea on 1 June 1794. He was baptised at Gwennap Parish Church on 22 August 1794 (Parish Registers).

The farm cottage where Billy was born is on the road from Cross Lanes to Twelveheads village, situated on the right hand side opposite the lane that leads to both the old and 'new' Bethel chapels. The farmstead is now derelict and the 'new' Bethel Chapel is now a domestic property.

Billy's parents were William Bray and Ann, nee Trewartha. They were married at Kea Parish Church on 27 January 1794 (Parish Register). William Bray died when Billy was about 8 years old, c1802 (*Journal*). Billy was raised by his paternal grandparents at Twelveheads. His grandfather was a leading member of the Twelveheads Methodist Chapel having been converted at an open-air meeting (*Journal*).

At the age of about 17 Billy left the Baldhu area and went to Devon, where he worked for some time at Wheal Friendship mine, Tavistock. There, free from the constraints of a Methodist home, he led a wild drunken life. He returned to Cornwall seven years later (*Journal*).

On 16 July 1821 Billy married Joanna Bray at Kea Parish Church. Joanna was the daughter of Joseph and Jane Bray. Billy continued his drunken life until his conversion in November 1823, when his whole life underwent a complete change (*Journal*).

Details of Billy and Joanna's children are few. The names of 4: James aged 18, Mary aged 17, Ann aged 15, and Grace aged 13, are recorded at the 1841 Census living at Little Beside, Gwennap with their mother, although Billy's name is not included on the entry.

In his *Journal* Billy records that at the time of building Kerley Downs Chapel, (c832-1835), he received help from his 'little son' and also comments that at that time he had a wife and 5 children to support. It has not been possible to obtain information regarding the fifth child.

More is known of Billy's daughters. According to the 1841 Census, Mary was born in 1824. Ann was born 15 March 1825 in Kea Parish, and baptised at Hicks Mill Bible Christian Chapel on 23 April 1826 (Bible Christian Chapel Records). Ann married James Bray on 23 September 1841 at Kea Parish Church (Parish records).

Grace was born 27 December 1827 in Kea Parish, and baptised at Hicks Mill Bible Christian Chapel on 13 July 1828 (Bible Christian Chapel Records). She married William Davey of St Veep at St Neot Parish Church on 11 February 1846 (Parish records). Grace is possibly, but not certainly, the child mentioned in Billy's *Journal* as his sick child who recovered and became "*the mother of ten children, and she is well to this day*" (in 1864). From the 1861 and 1871 Census records it appears that William and Grace had at least 7 children, the youngest being 8 years old at the 1871 Census. However, there are gaps between the birth dates of the children, which would have allowed for the birth and early death of others.

In the 1851 Census, Billy and Joanna were living at 36 Blowing House, Bodmin, together with a grandson, Mark Davey aged 1 year. Living at 38 Blowing House,

Bodmin were his daughter Ann, son-in-law James and 3 children, Joanna, Joseph and Mary Ann.

By the 1861 Census, Billy and Joanna were resident at Highway Village, Tywardreath, together with 2 grandchildren, Joseph and Mary Ann, the children of Ann and James Bray. At the time of the birth of James and Ann's son Joseph, in March 1844, that family was living at Mount Pleasant, Menheniot (Birth Certificate).

Sometime between 1861 and 1864 Billy and Joanna returned to Twelveheads where Joanna died on 13 December 1864 (Death Certificate).

William Trewartha Bray died at Twelveheads, Kea on 25 May 1868 aged 73 years (Death Certificate). Mary Ann Bray (probably Billy's granddaughter) was the informant on the death certificate.

APPENDIX 4

KERLEY DOWNS INDENTURE

THE BILLY BRAY Memorial Trust in Cornwall hold the original indenture for the building of Kerley Downs Chapel. This is the opening section. The full transcription is available on the author's website www.billybray.com, with kind permission of the Billy Bray Memorial Trust. Some of the words are not clear, especially those along folded lines. The series of ellipses denote illegible words. There is an excellent colour photograph of the chapel on:
www.cornwall.gov.uk/history/ab-hi-p44.htm

This Indenture of two parts made the fourth day of July in the year of our Lord one thousand eight hundred and thirty six ?between Benjamin Paul of the parish of Kea in the County of Cornwall, Carpenter[198] of the first part, John Scoble, Blacksmith, ?Richard Northey, Miner and John Paul, Mason all of the ?parish of Kenwyn in the said County. Jesse Moyle and Thomas White of the parish of Gwennap in the said County, Miners and

198 Billy says a farmer offered the land, and writing in 1864 seems to claim that he still knows him well, although an alternative reading of Billy's words is that the 'friend' is not the farmer, but the leaseholder, who may also be a Quaker Friend. An expert in property conveyancing suggests that the most likely explanation is that Benjamin Paul, a carpenter, is the legal leaseholder of the land, but someone else, maybe a neighbour, farms it. As far as Billy is concerned it is the farmer's land, as he is the one who offers it for a chapel.

William Bray, Robert Burgan, Simon Jenkin, James Thomas, Richard Thomas, John Thomas and Francis Yourner, Miners and James Bullen, Labourer and Samuel Paul, Carpenter all of the said parish of Kea of the second part.

Whereas by Indenture of lease bearing date thirty first day December in the year of our Lord one thousand eight hundred and thirty one made between the Right Honourable Edward Earl of Falmouth of the one part and ?the said Benjamin Paul of the other part the said Earl of Falmouth for the consideration therein mentioned did grant demise and lease the said Benjamin Paul his executors Administrators and assigns amongst other things all that ?plot or parcel of ground on which a chapel for divine worship has been lately erected and built situate in the north west corner of a croft leading from Kerley to Wheal Sperris Mine being forty feet in length by forty feet in breadth and is part ?and parcel of a tenement called or known by the name Tregonings Tenement situate in the said parish of Kea TO HOLD to the said Benjamin Paul his Executors Administrators and Assigns for the term of ninety nine years if Samuel Moyle ? gentleman and Alice wife of the said Benjamin Paul and Mary Ann their daughter or either of them shall so ??? under and subject to the rents covenants conditions exceptions and agreement in the said lease contained AND WHEREAS ?a chapel as aforesaid hath been erected upon the said plot or parcel of ground But in regard that the same chapel not erected at the expense of the said Benjamin Paul but with monies whereof part was raised by public collection and the voluntary ?donations of the Society of Bible Christians at Kerley and its vicinity for whose use the said chapel was intended and the remainder hath been borrowed and taken up at interest on the personal security of the parties hereto of the second part or ?some of them.

APPENDIX 5

FURTHER INFORMATION

BILLY BRAY BUILT three chapels in Cornwall, although according to some local traditions he helped build others. The first of the three that can definitely be attributed to Billy is the original Bethel Chapel at Cross Lanes. The date it was built is unknown, but it has to be after Billy's conversion in 1823 and before the building by Billy Bray of Kerley Downs (Three Eyes) which was fully open by 1836. Finally, Billy built Great Deliverance at Carharrack, completing it in 1841/42. The replacement Bethel was probably built in 1842, but not by Billy.

At the end of the nineteenth century many mines were forced to shut for economic reasons, and the dramatic loss of population led to the eventual closure of two of these chapels. Only Three Eyes at Kerley Downs is still in use, though not on a regular basis. It was closed in 1982, but rededicated on June 1 1984 as a memorial to Billy Bray. A few special services are held there each year. Three Eyes Chapel is supported by the Billy Bray Memorial Trust, a group of Methodist trustees. The best way to get information on the Trust, and find out what is happening at Three Eyes, is to log on to their website www.billybray.org.co.uk. You can find a link on the author's website www.billybray.com where there are more links to other sites of interest.

A web search under "Billy Bray" + Cornwall can bring up several hundred sites. Be warned – not all sites are reliable. I have found Billy described as a Scottish tin miner, a Welsh coal miner, and a Cornish coal miner! He is sometimes pictured as a huge brute of man (he was small and wiry), a boxer, a wrestler and given other completely inaccurate descriptions.

Second-hand copies of FW Bourne's original book on Billy Bray, *The King's Son*, can be found at various internet shops. (www.abebooks.co.uk is my favourite.)

One area I have only explored briefly is the Shaw Collection in the Courtney Library in Cornwall. Details of access can be obtained from The Librarian, The Courtney Library, The Royal Institution of Cornwall, River Street, Truro TR1 2SJ, UK. The late Tom Shaw took a great interest in Billy Bray, and collected a large number of press cuttings and other literature, including handwritten notes from various sources. However, most of the material was written at the end of the nineteenth and early twentieth centuries, generally too late for eyewitness accounts. For this book I have tried to get first-hand reports. I am sure, however, that the collection would be worth examining in detail, but not all the records collected by Shaw are reliable. Some are totally wrong.

I have a collection of old books on mining. Two of them have what seem to be genuine first-hand accounts of trips down Cornish mines – *Half Hours Underground* and *Rambles Beyond Railways*. The books have provided the basis for some of the illustrations here. *Half Hours Underground* was first published in 1878 by Dalby, Isbister & Co, London. The author is unnamed. *Rambles Beyond Railways* by Wilkie Collins was first published by Richard Bentley, London in 1851. My copy is called a "New Edition", published in 1861.

Another book that has provided an illustration is *The Mine*, a children's book by the Rev Isaac Taylor. John Harris, London, first published *The Mine* in 1829. In it Isaac Taylor takes the young reader on visits to mines around the world with Mr Thompson and his son James. James seems to be there solely to be fed an overabundance of facts. These two characters are almost certainly imaginary, and the account of the descent in a bucket in a mine at Polgooth is seriously at odds with mining practice. Miners were never lowered in this way because of the danger of the rope or chain breaking. Such a risky descent would surely have merited more than a couple of lines! It is worth noting that *The Mine* coincides exactly with the working lifetime of Billy Bray, and the Cornish mining details are probably accurate even if the author did not actually venture down the mine.

A fourth book in my collection, *The Treasures of the Earth* by William Jones, is full of technical details. It was published by

Frederick Warne & Co, London and New York. My copy is undated, but has a presentation label for 1892. One chapter deals with the mechanics of mining, and Cornish tin mining in particular. Again, it has provided the basis for an excellent illustration.

The most important contribution in recent years to the life of Billy Bray is the play by Tony Jasper, a Cornishman from Penzance, entitled *Glory! Glory! Diolch Iddo!*. During 1995/1996 it played at 70 venues throughout much of Britain, and received high praise in theatre and newspaper reviews. Jasper brought together tin miner Billy with Evan Roberts, the young Welshman at the centre of the Revival in 1904. In 2005 Jasper launches a new production that will focus solely on Billy Bray, using much of the material from this book.

I want to thank Barrie S May for allowing me to print the following biographical contribution he made to the Journal of the Cornish Methodist Historical Association in 1994. It is entitled *Billy Bray, Some Sources of Information*. I am reproducing it in a slightly updated form. It will be invaluable to anyone wanting to research the life of Billy Bray and the beginnings of the Bible Christians in greater depth. However, with regards to Billy, the later writers mostly refer, sometimes inaccurately, to events already recounted by Bourne, Pearse, Ashworth and Haslam, and add very little that is new.

> Many will regard *The King's Son: A memoir of Billy Bray*, F W Bourne (London, Bible Christian Bookroom 1871) as the primary source of information. From its first publication it was popular to the extent that, by the time the Bible Christians became part of the United Methodist Church in 1907, no less than 38 editions (possibly 39) had been published, as well as special illustrated editions. The United Methodists carried on the publication and, after Methodist Union in 1932, the Epworth Press did so, issuing 14 editions by 1974. Most of these are catalogued in *A Bibliography of the Bible Christians*, Oliver A Beckerlegge (Westcliffe on Sea, Laurie Gage 1988) – number BB 37 et seq. There is an interesting edition not in Beckerlegge. In this *The King's Son* was bound together with Daniel Quorm: *First and Second Series* by MG Pearse. Each of the constituent books had its own title page (Pearse – London Charles H Kelly, no date (nd):

Bourne – London, WH Gregory-Simpkin, Marshall, nd.) Illustrated, Bourne's preface is dated 1890.

MG Pearse wrote a 16-page pamphlet *The Story of Billy Bray* (London Wesleyan Conference Office nd): Beckerlegge BP 7. This was probably during the 1870s; he ends by referring to Bourne for further information. The contents of this pamphlet were included in Pearse's *Short Stories and Other Papers,* T Woolmer (London 1886). Additional references to Billy Bray are in *The ship Where Christ was Captain* (London, Epworth 1926, chapters 2 and 3.)

In the third edition, *The King's Son* received a further boost to popularity from a good review by C H Spurgeon in his monthly magazine *Sword and Trowel.* Spurgeon later wrote *Eccentric Preachers* (London, Passmore and Alabaster, 1880). In this he devoted a chapter to Billy Bray – The Uneducated Soul Winner. At about the same time *The Story of Billy Bray* compiled as a Musically Illustrated Service by John Burnham (London Weekes & Co, nd) appeared. This is probably the one attributed to MG Pearse in Beckerlegge (BP6), the author acknowledges permission to reprint the tract.

Coming later was *Billy Bray, the Cornish Miner* S E Burrow (London Pickering and Inglis nd, Beckerlegge BP 112). A paper covered booklet, it was 52 in the Lily Library, apparently issued monthly. *The Lily Library* was commenced in 1921, so 52 would be 1925.

At this stage it might be well to consider the source of Bourne's information. Early editions of *The King's Son* carried the sub title 'compiled chiefly from his own memoranda'. In *The Bible Christians: their Origin and History,* FW Bourne (London, BC Bookroom 1905) Beckerlegge BB 32 the story of the writing of the *Memoir of Billy Bray* is related in detail. In the preface to the first edition of *The King's Son* Bourne hopes that personal friends of Billy "will furnish characteristic facts and incidents not included." In the second edition "but few have replied." However, he tenders thanks to several Ministers in the third edition for interesting incidents.

Bourne named some in thanks for assistance. Amongst them was the Rev W Haslam. His autobiography *From Death Into Life* (London, Morgan and Scott c1880) Beckerlegge BH 10 contained 2 chapters on Billy Bray, and a later reference. A paperback edition was published by Good News Crusade, St Austell (1976). Bourne also acknowledges permission to quote from a tract by Mr John Ashworth of Rochdale; reprinted in *Volume 5 of Strange Tales* (Manchester; J Brook & Co, and London; Simpkin, Marshall, preface dated 1879).

First-hand information also appears in *Real Life Sketches,* Frank L Vosper (Cincinnati, Jennings & Pye 1903). A recent biography is *The Glory Man,* Cyril Davey (London, Hodder & Stoughton 1979) Beckerlegge BD 5. The present author Christopher Wright's *I Can't Help Praising the Lord* (Bridge UK, 1987) is a reworded edition of the greater part of *The King's Son.*

From mainly biographical material we move to Methodist sources. The earliest references are found in the *Bible Christian Magazine.* Although he was highly thought of in the whole of Methodism, main references to Billy Bray begin with his obituary in 1868. From 1872 there are regular contributions and particularly in 1894, the centenary year of his birth, a series of articles covered 40 pages. After Bourne's *Bible Christians,* already mentioned, came *A New History of Methodism,* Townsend, Workman & Eayrs (London; Hodder & Stoughton, 2 vols. 1909) where there is a reference. Richard Pyke in *The Golden Chain* (London; Henry Hooks, nd.) gives more space to Billy. There is a long gap then to *The Methodist Story* CJ Davey (London; Epworth 1955). There is a short reference in *Methodism,* RE Davies (London; Epworth 1963).

We would expect to find reference in the books of the Rev Tom Shaw – *The Bible Christians* (London; Epworth 1965) and *History of Cornish Methodism* (Truro; Barton 1967). The late Kathleen Evans contributed a good summary of *Billy's life to Methodist Celebration. A Cornish Contribution* ed. Sarah Foot (Redruth; Truran 1988) *The United Methodist Conference Handbook* (Redruth 1931) contained an article by GP Dymond.

One important item is a summary of one of Billy's sermons in *The Worship and Devotion of Cornish Methodism*, JCC Probert (Redruth; by the author 1978). *Cob and Moorstone*, L Maker (London; Epworth 1935) dealing with Cornish chapels has references and there are references scattered amongst CMHA Journals.

In Cornish books the first is *A Compendium of the History and Geography of Cornwall 4th edn.* TC Peter (Truro; Netherton and Worth 1906). The most numerous references are found in the works of AK Hamilton Jenkin – *The Cornish Miner* (London; George Allen & Unwin 1927) *Cornwall and its People* (London, Dent 1945) and *The Story of Cornwall* (London, Nelson 1934) *Claude Berry's Cornwall* (London, Robert Hale 1949) has three pages but F E Halliday in *A History of Cornwall* (London, Duckworth 1959) only brief. Likewise Daphne du Maurier in *Vanishing Cornwall* (London, Gollancz 1967) has but one mention. Donald Rawe refers to Billy Bray in *Cornish Villages* (London, Robert Hale 1978) and *A Prospect for Cornwall* (London, Robert Hale 1986).

Cornish Men and True; David Mudd (Newcastle, Frank Graham 1971) devotes a short chapter to 'The Converted', linking Billy with Michael Verran. *Curious Cornwall*, B Trevail (Truro, Tor Mark 1969) has an article on Billy Bray's chapels and *A Cornish Bedside Book.* John Keast, (Redruth, Truran 1980) has passages quoted from *The King's Son. Cornwall Forty Years After*, J S Flynn (London, Truelove & Hanson 1917) has a chapter on The Local Preacher with references. *A History of Evangelical Christianity in Cornwall* by Peter Isaac (published by the author nd c2000, chapter 6, *The Forgotten Revival 1790-1840*, contains several pages on Billy Bray.

The Manuscript Diaries of John Oates of Blackwater are at the Cornwall Record Office (DDX629/1 18). These contain original reports of Billy Bray incidents in entries for 1883-5 and 1885-95.

Billy Bray has been sometimes given a saintly status. The Rev John Angus began this trend in 1899 with an article in the *Wesleyan Methodist Church Record* entitled In the Footsteps of the Saints – Billy Bray. William

James could be said to have continued the idea in his *Varieties of Religious Experience* (London, Collins Fontana Library 1960, first published 1902). He quotes with approval 'Billy Bray, an excellent little illiterate English evangelist' – his conversion, post conversion experience and purity of life.

Claude Berry contributed to the *West Country Magazine* in 1947 Cornwall's Last Saint, and Billy's position was confirmed by inclusion in *The Saints of Cornwall*; CR John (Redruth, Truran/Lodenek 1982). Two articles in the magazine *Cornwall Today* by the late Rev Tom Shaw were headed St Billy of Baldhu (issues 1 and 2, July and August 1994. There are other books with passing references, and most of these mentioned repeat well-known Billy Bray incidents However, there are occasional comments and judgements which are enlightening.

Finally, mention must be made of newspapers. The references are too many to give in detail. Someone once said 'There is no substitute for hard work', so consulting the *West Briton, Western Morning News* and *Royal Cornwall Gazette* files can be fruitful. A short comment or report might well spark off a series of letters.

Always we need to watch out for 'clangers'. Examples are John Betjeman (*Shell Guide*) saying Billy Bray was the founder of the Bible Christians, and a photograph in *The Pageantry of Methodist Union* (London Epworth 1936) shows a chapel at Gwennap "built by Billy Bray". It turns out to be Busveal!

Index

This index is divided into three sections: one that focuses on Billy Bray, one that focuses on Church matters and then a General index that has Proper Names and some topical entries especially about mining in Cornwall.

General Index

(*some Proper Name entries may cover more than one person*)